KT-157-927

The European Union:
How Democratic Is It?

Edited by
Svein S. Andersen and Kjell A. Eliassen

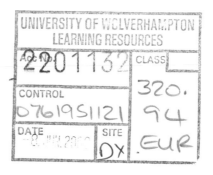

UNIVERSITY OF WOLVERHAMPTON
LEARNING RESOURCES

ACC No.	CLASS
2201132	320.
CONTROL	94
0761951121	
DATE 8 JUL 2000	SITE DX	EUR

SAGE Publications
London • Thousand Oaks • New Delhi

© Sage Publications 1996
First published 1996, Reprinted 1998

All rights reserved. No part of this publication may be reproduced, stored in a retrieval system, or utilized in any form or by any mean, electronic, mechanical, photocopying, recording or otherwise, without permission in writing from the publishers.

SAGE Publications Ltd
6 Bonhill Street
London EC2A 4PU

SAGE Publications Inc
2455 Teller Drive
Thousand Oaks, CA 91320

SAGE Publications India Pvt Ltd
32, M-Block Market
Greater Kailask - I
New Delhi 110 048

British Library Cataloguing in Publication data
A catalogue record for this book is available from the British Library.
ISBN 0 7619 5112 1
ISBN 0 7619 5113 X (pbk)

Printed in Great Britain by
The Cromwell Press Ltd, Trowbridge, Wiltshire

UNIVERSITY OF
WOLVERHAMPTON

THE EUROPEAN UNION: HOW DEMOCRATIC IS IT?

WITHDRAWN

WP 2201132 3

Contents

Preface

The process of making this book has in many ways had its democratic shortcomings. This has been necessary for reasons of efficiency. As always, it is a question of striking the right balance. However, this book is a collective effort and we hope that the result reflects adequately the views of the authors as well as of the editors. We also hope that this volume can stimulate the ongoing debate on European democracy.

The point of departure for the book is that the problems facing the EU are variations of those imperfections, contradictions and dilemmas that all political systems have to deal with. This perspective is developed in the Introduction and is further pursued in Part IV of the book. Part I deals with the two major challenges of interest articulation in the EU – political parties and lobbying – examines the question of what kind of political system the EU represents. Part II explores the tensions and the different types of relationships that exist between the EU and national political systems. In Part III the focus is on the democratic nature and efficiency of key institutions at the EU level. The final part discusses EU democracies in relation to the ongoing debates and changes in modern societies affecting more traditional concepts of democracy.

We would like to express our thanks to the Norwegian Research Council and the Norwegian School of Management for giving financial support to the project. The book is published as part of the project on EU/EEA, Institutions, Decision-making Process and National Implementation.

The contributors and other colleagues have provided valuable comments and ideas regarding the scope and organisation of the book and we thank them all. In particular we would like to thank our colleague and friend Jan Erik Lane for his insistent and energetic interest during the final completion of the manuscript. We would also like to thank our assistants and staff at the Centre for European Studies, in particular Gillian F. Kennedy, Katrin Einarsdottir, Marit Sjøvaag and Grethe Haug. Tore Rokstad has proved invaluable in producing lay-out, figures and final corrections.

Svein S. Andersen and Kjell A. Eliassen
Oslo, May 1995

1
Introduction:
Dilemmas, Contradictions and the Future of European Democracy

Svein S. Andersen and Kjell A. Eliassen

DEMOCRACY, EFFECTIVENESS AND SOVEREIGNTY

Democracy in the EU is closely linked to two critical aspects of governance, namely effectiveness and sovereignty. EU in this book refers to both the European Union after 1 November 1993 and the previous European Economic Community. Effectiveness is a key argument for increased supranational authority where the EU makes it possible to address problems which cross national boundaries. Along this dimension the problem is that the EU may not be international enough. Another aspect of governance concerns the locus of legitimate authority, or sovereignty. In the European nation states there are historically constructed polities, manifested in parliamentary institutions to which sovereignty has been entrusted. Even a strong European parliament does not recreate the kind of sovereignty associated with the nation state, because there is no encompassing European polity. At most, popular sovereignty could be based on the formal recognition of the rights and obligations of citizens independent of cultural differences.

The debate on democracy in the EU has not received much attention in academic research. In this book we focus primarily on how decisions are made at the national and supranational level. The key issue is how democratic requirements can be handled in a system which is neither federal nor intergovernmental. The EU represents a new type of political system within the tradition of parliamentary democracies. A major challenge for the EU is institutional design, that is, how to establish democratic institutions and procedures for supranational policy-making which take account of the roles of formal and informal actors, associations, citizens and societal interests in the decision-making process. The democratic challenges have to do with how authoritative decisions can be made, within a framework of effectiveness and sovereignty.

In the traditional nation state, democratic process and sovereignty were two sides of the same coin. However, the internationalisation of economics and politics gradually undermined efficient problem solving within the boundaries of the nation state. At the same time, the emergence of a supranational authority implies the partial decoupling of democratic process and sovereignty. In the EU sovereignty is transferred to institutions that are not controlled by democratic processes similar to those found in national systems. This development, which most actors have viewed as a sacrifice, has been regarded as necessary to achieve a supranational problem-solving capacity.

However, the EU may in this respect have reached a turning point. Concern for democracy is increasingly placed on an equal footing with effectiveness. This is reflected in the 1996 EU Intergovernmental Conference debate over the need for effectiveness as well as the preservation of member state autonomy within the framework of the EU. This raises two major sets of questions which call for more attention:

1. Western political systems have a common normative underpinning. What are these classical assumptions? And what refinements have been made during the last decades regarding the foundation and the challenges of modern democratic development? What is the relation between the EU institutional development and normative democratic theory?
2. From a strict normative position, all Western systems have democratic deficits. The nature of institutions, processes and the degree of transparency vary considerably across European states. What are the differences and similarities between the EU on the one hand and national political systems on the other?

CORE IDEAS OF DEMOCRACY

Concern with normative democratic issues has a long tradition in political science and sociology (Schumpeter 1942; Dahl 1963; Lindblom 1965; Pitkin 1967; Dahl 1971, 1989; Liphart 1977; Sartori 1987; Held 1991a). Compared to the 1960s and 1970s such issues have received relatively little attention in the last decade. Lately the development of the EU has put normative democratic issues back on the political agenda, but so far few social scientists have taken up the challenge.

The major themes in the post World War II debate have been power and influence (Dahl 1963), decision-making rules, participation and democracy, equality and democracy, liberty and democracy, elites and democracy and the question of representativity (Pitkin 1967; Held 1991a). A special case of the latter discussion has contrasted functional versus territorial representation (Anderson 1977). The EU represents one of the few attempts at creating a new form of political system within a liberal democratic framework. Despite this, the challenges and problems of the EU as a democratic political system have only been dealt with in a very limited way (although there are exceptions such as Dahl (1989) and Held (1991a), for instance).

An important reason for this is that the incremental development of EU has made it difficult to identify its true nature with regard to democracy at any point of time. The EU has been characterised by continuous change into new and more complex political constructions. The social scientists who have paid most attention to the EU are the integration theorists and in particular the functionalist school which has been more concerned with the possibility of a fully fledged democracy in a federal Europe than the bumpy road towards it. The same has been the case for the founding fathers and the main architects of recent institutional changes.

The core of every representative system is its parliamentary institution. The main challenge for the EU is the current impossibility of creating a true parliamentary basis for democracy because few, if any, member countries accept a federal solution. The paradox is that those who are least content with the present imperfections are also the most hostile to a federal state. In what ways does the EU today represent a challenge for democratic theory? The problem of democratic legitimacy in the EU has two closely linked aspects: the lack of a responsible EU parliament and the lack of a European polity. The problem of the EU parliament is closely linked to the member states' desire that the Council of Ministers should be the main decision-making body.

On the other hand, the lack of clarification when it comes to basic democratic principles in the EU may strangely enough contribute to its success (Moravcsik 1993). Flexibility may enhance effectiveness, and the EU's ability to deliver results is itself seen by the electorates as a major source of legitimacy.

In normative democratic theory effectiveness can, however, not replace representativity as an independent basis of legitimacy (Anderson

1977). On the contrary, democracy and effectiveness are often seen as contradictory concerns. However, the tendency to emphasise effectiveness at the expense of parliamentary control is common also in national political systems in Western Europe. This tendency has been paralleled by the diffusion of decision-making authority from parliamentary bodies to informal groups and networks in society. Thus, we arrive at what has been labelled post-parliamentary or organic democracy (Andersen and Burns 1992a).

Why, then, has the tendency towards organic democracy in national systems – of which corporatism and lobbying is an important part – not been interpreted as a radical deviation from democratic principles? The reason seems to be that national parliaments fulfil the basic requirements of democratic theory. They are formally free to overrule any informal political decision-making processes at any time, and the parliaments represent important symbolic centres of authority. The lack of all such factors in the EU leads to a more critical discussion of the democratic problem of the EU.

Until now the European Union has compensated for the lack of its own parliamentary legitimacy by relying upon the link to the electorate created by the national parliaments and their control of the national representatives in the Council of Ministers (Eliassen 1993). But the indirectness of the link between the individual citizens and the directives approved by the Council of Ministers troubles those who believe that the link between voter and policy-maker should be more direct and more robust (Sbragia 1992). The indirect link is not robust as the national assemblies are not always able to participate in the EU decision-making process prior to a final vote in the Council.

Denmark has established a special parliamentary committee responsible for EU matters. The important difference from other parliamentary committees in EU member countries is that on all major issues there has to be a vote in the 'Markedsutvalget' on the position of the Danish government before they give their vote in the EU Council (Andersen and Eliassen 1992). After the problems of ratifying the Maastricht treaty other states have discussed such an institutional solution. For instance, Germany and Britain have decided to introduce parliamentary scrutiny of EU affairs prior to Council voting, although there is not a binding vote.

The procedure is of particular importance in Germany because of public reactions to the Maastricht ratification and the vote of the Constitutional Court in Karlsruhe. As the Judges stated: The democracy principle does not prevent Germany joining a supranationally organised community of states. But a precondition of membership is a guarantee that legitimacy and influence by the people are secured within the association of states. If an association of democratic states takes on sovereign tasks and exercises sovereign powers, it is principally the people of the member states who must legitimate this through their national parliaments. Thus, democratic legitimisation ensues from the linking of the actions of European organs back to the parliaments of member states. (Cited in *The European*, 14th–17th October 1993. Their translation.)

There were plans for a more effective parliamentary EC committee in Germany, even before the verdict of the judges. All European countries will have to find workable solutions to this problem of democratic legitimacy in the EU. In the new member countries, as well as in non-member Norway, this issue has been important in the national membership debate.

Below we will discuss how the democratic challenges and problems have been dealt with in the national systems and how the EU creates new challenges.

PARLIAMENTARY DEMOCRACY VERSUS FUNCTIONAL REPRESENTATION

Traditionally, democracy is defined as government by the people through elected representatives with Parliament as the central political institution. Or, put in another way, 'democracy is a regime in which citizens elect their leaders in regular and competitive elections and in which basic civil rights are protected' (Steiner 1991:3). Two other sources of legitimacy have increasingly been of importance. One is the functional and direct articulation of societal interests into the political systems. The other is the increasing weight paid to the ability of political systems to deliver stability and welfare, i.e. effectiveness (Offe 1972). These three sources of legitimacy are partly competing, but also complementary. However, these three factors are all complex and there is considerable empirical variation in how they are expressed institutionally in various political systems (Steiner 1991; Lane and Ersson 1993).

The *parliamentary* dimension is related to several important aspects of democracy: a constitutional basis, parliament as the political centre of the system, the expression of voter preferences through electoral systems, a party system. These aspects form an ideal type referred to as the parliamentary chain of government. Unless a system has a high score on all these dimensions, there is by definition a democratic deficit. Real political systems typically have some deficit on one or more of these dimensions, and the influence and role of parliaments have always been questionable. The interesting question is the degree of deficit in each country at each point in time.

The backbone of all political systems in Europe with the exception of Britain, is a formal constitution defining the role of the institutions and the role of the citizens. There are, however, substantial differences between the different countries in how specific rules, mandates and rights are defined as well as discrepancies between the letter of the constitution and the institutional set-up in the daily operation of the system. For instance, the Fifth Republic in France gives specific rights to the presidency in relation to Parliament and the government in certain policy areas. And some countries have written parliamentarianism into the constitution (e.g. Sweden), while others have not (in the Norwegian constitution neither parties nor parliamentary government are mentioned).

The EU has no formal constitution, but the constitutional basis is defined in treaties between the member countries which have been subsequently revised. There is an international agreement giving the right of the EU to make supranational decisions. Institutions are well defined, but no formal single centre of power in the system is defined. In the national constitutions Parliaments are the legislative assembly of the state, but not so in EU. Another difference between national constitutions and the EU treaty is that citizenship rights were introduced only recently and remain weakly defined.

Electoral systems in Western Europe vary considerably from single member constituencies with majority voting (as in Britain) to proportional representation with the whole country as the electoral district. The main tendency since World War I until 1990 has been towards more and more mathematically just representation. Thus, in most countries, the concern for a high degree of representativity has been expressed by mechanisms which compensate for the lack of equal mathematical representation of the political parties. The emphasis on strict mathematical representation makes the system more sensitive to minor political changes and differences, which result in a reduced ability to create stable majorities decreasing the governing ability of the system. From the early 1990s, there has been an increased interest in reducing ungovernmentability, as reflected in proposals for a return to majority voting or more restrictions on the representation of small parties, for instance, as has happened Poland and Italy.

The EU does not have one electoral system for its Parliament. The EP is elected according to twelve different national laws. The same diversity is reflected by the lack of one unified EU polity and the absence of real European political parties. At the national level, party systems serve as the main aggregator of societal interests into the parliamentary system. There are, however, significant differences with respect to the effectiveness and legitimacy of party systems, both historically and at the present. In Britain, where there is in no constitution, the political system is based on parties and the party system. Even thought the state was created several hundred years before the parties. By contrast, the developments in Italy, where the parties created the modern state in 1945, imply an almost a total breakdown of the party system. The impact on the Italian political system reflects the constitutional function of parties in the state – a correspondence to which one can find only in new democracies in Eastern Europe (Hine 1993).

At the EU level the lack of a powerful Parliament and a unified polity makes it difficult to establish strong European political parties. Even the Social Democratic parties, which have a long history of close European co-operation and a strong European Parliament group, have not been able to create an effective transnational party organisation and platform. From a normative democratic point of view the lack of a unified polity is the most serious democratic deficit, since the legitimacy of the parliamentary institution as such is based upon voters having at least a common frame of political reference. The formation of such a common identity is at best a long-term project.

Historically, the formation of a polity is a lengthy process and closely linked to a generalised notion of citizenship. The growth of these ideas in Western Europe coincided with the development of the nation-state (Bendix 1969). The gradual codification of such rights corresponds to the formation of a dominant national political culture. Today the close interrelationship at the national level between rights and identity creates obstacles to the development of a European polity (Meehan 1993).

The parliamentary systems in Europe were developed in the late nineteenth century within a minimalist liberal state model. Political legitimacy was drawn from the individual as a citizen. Since the turn of the century, and particularly since World War II, Western political systems have witnessed the growth of supplementary forms of *functional interest representation*. In Europe most attention has been paid to various forms of corporatism, while in the US lobbying has dominated. There is a literature that studies such functional links as policy networks and comprehensive negotiation processes in Europe (Richardson 1982), while others examine these at the national level (Schmitter 1974, 1977, 1982; Rokkan 1966; Andersen 1989; Heisler 1974; Scandinavian Political Studies 1979); a third group of studies deal with the meso-level (Cawson 1985) and local politics (Hernes 1974).

Corporatism and lobbying constitute alternative channels of interest articulation. Small countries tend to develop strong corporatist structures, due to less sectoral diversity and cultural homogeneity (Katzenstein 1987). However, in recent years there has also been an increase in the use of lobbying strategies in corporatist regimes (Andersen and Eliassen 1993). There are now fewer limitations to the participation in public decision-making to companies and smaller groups that cannot claim representation as sectoral or territorial units. This development has been encouraged by the growth of lobbying within the EU system (Andersen and Eliassen 1991), but also reflects the insufficient influence given to special interests in corporatist systems.

The strengthening of direct functional interests can be regarded as part of a broader diffusion of decision-making authority from the parliamentary core to affected interests (Andersen and Burns 1992b). A special case is the formation of so-called Quangos where authority is formally transferred to quasi autonomous non-governmental agencies. However, Quangos apart, the diffusion of authority normally has an informal character where affected interests are allowed to provide important inputs and influence before formal parliamentary decisions are made. Interestingly, studies have shown that the more inclusion of interests in the pre-parliamentary phase, the less debate and conflict in parliament (Damgaard and Eliassen 1978). However, to the degree that such informal activities are directed towards Parliament in a lobbying fashion, it tends to increase parliamentary conflict.

Increasingly the players in the political system are not only individual citizens but corporate actors with functional interests. There has taken place over recent decades a diffusion of central decision-making authority to geographical sub-units of the national state, a development of decentralisation which has come under increased scrutiny in the 1990s. The dilemma is that in the national polity the national politicians are responsible, while at the same time they have given up their final authority in many matters. The ongoing debate on the degree of self-government in Scandinavian countries illustrates this as does the case of Belgium, an extreme case of formal decentralisation where a large part of formal parliamentary power is located in local parliaments; this includes the core of the national state's power, such as the ratification of treaties between foreign countries.

On the EU level functional interests have a different role from that in the national systems. Functional representation is the core of a system of interest articulation which is independent of the member states. The EU Parliament is weak while the system as a whole allows open access for all actors independently of their representational or sector adherence. One important exception is the social dialogue where corporatist patterns develop even on the EU level. Overall, the use of lobbying strategies has been adopted by all participants whether they come from countries with strong corporatist or lobbying traditions.

In member countries, direct interest representation developed as a supplement to strong parliaments and party systems. In the EU the lack of a strong parliament and weak party groups have to a considerable extent decoupled these two channels of influence. Thus, general citizenship rights as the basis for governance are only loosely coupled to the legitimacy of the EU's political institutions themselves. The major source of legitimacy is member state support. On the other hand, the need for lobbying to legitimise individual decisions is higher. This also points to the core reason for the continued development of the EU, namely the need to achieve more efficient solutions to those problems where the nation states fail.

The EU generally lacks the formal authority that the member countries possess. However, there are several examples of authority being passed down from EU institutions to the national level, such as the European Commission's procedure for the implementation of EU policy. Overall, however, the EU lacks formal political authority and legitimacy and has to rely on the national systems. The lack of a strong parliamentary centre, symbolically and in terms of institutional competence, makes the EU democratic deficit a more visible and a more fundamental shortcoming than any of the known democratic problems in national systems.

DEMOCRATIC PROCESS VERSUS EFFECTIVENESS

When viewed from the central EU level the system is characterised by a mix of legal-bureaucratic delegation and attempts to achieve centralisation of political authority in relation to member states. However, when seen from sub-national units both bureaucratic and political authority are transferred from the centre.

In a parliamentary democracy the most important features are representation through elected assemblies, and functionally, the democratic making of policies; also the ability to provide security, welfare and acceptable solutions to political problems are important. This is often discussed as the effectiveness dimension of democracy (Dahl 1963). Effectiveness is the perceived effects of the political decisions, the outcomes of the authoritative decisions (Easton 1965). The legitimacy of political systems is normally dependent upon an acceptable mixture between representativity and effectiveness. These two dimensions may be mutually supportive, but there are also elements of conflict. In some cases mathematically just representation may undermine the basis for effective government, for example in the Weimar republic in 1920s Germany. In other cases effectiveness may be threatened by too much openness in the public decision-making processes. The paradox is that too much democracy is dangerous for democracy exactly for the reason that it might threaten effectiveness (Huntington 1975).

Often effectiveness presupposes some elements of depolitisation. In the European tradition, technical competence and professional knowledge are key factors in the creation of a stable framework. Another key factor may be legal constructions. The latter play a more important role in the US than in Europe. Also, legal constructions play a more important role in the EU than in European nation states. Democratic control of technical and professional knowledge may lie in the periodic repoliticisation of the aspects of the national political/administrative system which in a given period may have been taken for granted.

In some cases effectiveness may be the core of democratic legitimacy. In extreme cases the legitimacy of a regime may rest primarily on effectiveness, for instance Mussolini's ability to get the trains to run on schedule. Often effectiveness may appeal to specific segments or sub-groups of the electorate, for example the clientella systems in Italy (Hine 1993).

Again, the EU is a special case. A driving force behind the development of the EU has been the promise of more effective solutions than the member states alone can deliver. Yet no other system has used so many political resources over such a long period trying to find solutions to the fundamental constitutional problems such as the role of member state sovereignty versus EC supranational authority, and the role of parliamentary government in the EU, and so on.

The particular challenge for the EU is that it has to improve both effectiveness and democracy at the same time. Whether both can be achieved simultaneously is problematic. In the national systems, which are both more democratic and more efficient at the outset, politicians are usually confronted with only one of these two problems at any moment. The solution can then allow for some sacrifices on the one dimension to achieve better results on other, at least for a period of time.

Finally, the problems of democracy, legitimacy and effectiveness in the EU can never be solved within the present set of constraints placed upon it by the member states. The only logical solution from a strict democratic point of view is to strengthen the EU Parliament at the expense of member states, which implies moving towards some form of federal system. The paradox is that those who are most concerned with the democratic deficit are also most strongly against such a development.

Part I
Numerical Democracy, Corporative Pluralism and Lobbying in European Politics

2
Euro-parties and European Parties: New Arenas, New Challenges and New Strategies

Mogens N. Pedersen

Although it is possible to think of political systems in which political parties do not operate at all – and although such political systems exist in real life – it is commonplace to say that politics cannot be conducted in a modern nation without the assistance of political parties. Parties are even considered functional pre-requisites for a democratic process. Why is this so?

Political parties have developed into organisations that dominate, sometimes even monopolise, an important part of political life, that nuclear part of democratic activities usually named the electoral process. Parties take care of the political mobilisation of the voters; they provide political recruits for the nomination processes, which they also control; they provide ideologies, programmes and platforms; and they attend to conflicting interests in society, trying to integrate these and provide compromises. These tasks are performed by parties that comprise a more or less volatile electorate, plus a national organisation with members, activists, bureaucrats, leaders and apparatus, plus a parliamentary group, which plays a more or less autonomous role vis-à-vis the national organisation. Although, there are differences across parties as well as across national borders within Europe, these are the basic facts about political parties at the national level.

Although it is hard to do without them, parties are not always looked upon with friendly eyes. Since the days of Jean-Jacques Rousseau political parties have also been considered parasites on the body politics, organisations that distort public opinion and make it impossible to find out what the Common Will of the People really is. In modern times, when political parties and their activities are increasingly becoming financed by the public purse, new forms of criticisms have been raised against these semi-public organisations.

On the supra-national level in Europe, it is also possible to identify party activities. First, and of only minor importance, there are transnational associations of like-minded national parties, which mainly bring together members for social and cultural purposes. Second, and much more important, Euro-parties exist in a loose and embryonic form within the European Union.

The Euro-parties of the European Parliament are, however, not genuine parties, if by this we mean organisations that span and control the electoral linkage. First, these new parties do not have an electorate. In elections for the European Parliament the voters within each nation vote for their own parties. Few, if any, voters care about 'The Rainbow Group', the 'European Democratic Alliance', or some of the other, more or less, stable groups within the Parliament in Strasbourg, when they go to the poll station. Second, these 'parties' do not have an internal organisation to carry out the policies of the leadership. There may be some kind of executive board that co-ordinates the work of the supra-national group, but the emphasis is just on co-ordination, advice, and on the administration of the considerable funds and other perks provided for the activity by the EU itself. Third, the cohesion of such groups is not comparable to the cohesion of most national parliamentary groups. Group-consciousness is not high, and the same goes for the stability of the group's structures. After each election to the European Parliament new groups have arisen, and older ones have disappeared. Splits and mergers take place now and then, and individual members frequently switch from one group to another.

Critics of the European project, and especially of the extension of the powers of the European Parliament, find this situation understandable and even welcome it. They prefer to see the European Common Will materialise in a process of continuous negotiation, in which only national governments participate – governments which are responsible to national parliaments and to national electorates. Seen from this perspective, present-day Euro-parties operating in the political vacuum of the European Parliament may not be dangerous – but neither are they useful. Rousseau would probably have looked upon these institutional refinements with double contempt, since they are so far removed from the proverbial 'band of peasants regulating the affairs of state under an oak tree, and always acting wisely'.

It may be, however, that this analysis is on its way to becoming obsolete. Proponents and advocates of European integration look toward a future in which the European Parliament will play an important role. When this change – eventually – takes place, there will also be an important role for the Euro-parties, and – even more important – a need to strike a new balance between the Euro-party system and the national party systems. Some of the problems arising from the present system and the possible future changes are discussed below.

Briefly we may start by stating that the the European Parliament is on its way to becoming a genuine institution of representation, i.e. a parliament. As an integral part of this transformation, a kind of party system is emerging at the European level. This new system of embryonic Euro-parties bears some superficial resemblance to the party systems in the individual parliaments in Western Europe. MEPs from the member states register and affiliate with these political groups, which bear names that give associations to real parties (several political scientists have been discussing this development at length, often in positive value terms; see, for example, Gidlund 1992). Traditional transnational co-operation among parties has existed for decades. Now scholars – and politicians – expect it to develop further, being enhanced by European integration, and, in turn, enhancing that very same integration process. Fewer have argued like this since the traumatic events of 1992–93, but the dream of a Pan-European party system is by no means dead.

The existing 'party system' in the European Parliament is, however, still a far cry from being a supra-national structure. The national parties still dominate the scene in the individual nations as well as in the European Union. The traditional parties also largely control the MEPs. It is, however, already the case that the linkage between the national party and the European group, which is working through the individual MEP, pose some difficulties to the MEP as well as to the national parties. It can even be argued that the new Euro-parties constitute a challenge to the national parties in general – and their leadership in particular. Perhaps not a serious challenge at the present, but in the longer run this may change. In this chapter I will discuss some aspects of this challenge.

HOW PARTIES CAME TO THE EUROPEAN PARLIAMENT

When the Treaty of Rome created new European institutions, the former consultative assembly of the Coal- and Steel Union was transformed into a consultative assembly for the entire network of treaty institutions. From the early 1960s this assembly started to call itself a parliament. With the enlargement of the EEC in 1973 the European Parliament gradually took on a new role as a meeting-place for European politicians from many different parties.

In this 'parliament' the same development took place as in other institutionalising parliaments: politicians from various parts of Europe started to meet across national boundary lines, and the most daring among them even started to talk about the possible emergence of transnational parties. The use of the semi-circular format of the European chamber facilitated the creation of a familiar ordering of members from a left, through a centre, to a right tendency while avoiding the terms 'groups', 'party groups', or 'parties'. It was exactly these shared notions that made it possible within a few years to bring some order to the new European parliament.

During the 1970s members were appointed by their national parliaments, and it gradually became commonplace to send members to Strasbourg in numbers that reflected the strength of the respective parties in the national parliaments. In this way a certain 'mirroring' took place, even if the voters themselves were not involved. The 'semi-circles' of the various European parliaments were easily copied in Strasbourg.

With the introduction of the principle of direct election in 1979 another important step was taken. There were almost 4000 candidates for the, then, 410 seats in the European Parliament, and the members were elected by the voters in their respective nations, using the nationally appropriate electoral system, and – most important – as candidates representing the various national parties. In other words, the traditional parties were from the very beginning in control of the nominations. Only in Denmark was there an exception when a strong opposition movement against the EEC successfully put up its own candidates. It can be argued that Denmark from 1979 on had two, partly different, party systems: a national party system and another EEC-related party system which was only mobilised every four years (see, for example, Worre 1987; Pedersen 1987). Denmark is, however, the exception which proves the rule that national parties were in command. It could also be said that the Danish case represented a special type of potential conflict between the political order in a national parliament and an emerging European political order.

THE BASIC FEATURES OF PARTY SYSTEMS IN EUROPE

This story of the emergence of an ordering of representatives is one that has been heard before.

In 1789 the French *Etats Generaux* met in Versailles for a session that would soon change for good the political landscape, not only in France, but in all other European nations as well. During late summer modern parties were born in the sense that some of the most crucial aspects of the modern party system inadvertently were 'discovered' for the very first time. In September, when the assembly had already been turned into a National Assembly, the members gradually started to converge in some groupings in the assembly hall, and smart journalists soon gave these groupings the labels Left and Right. In this way the basic organising principle of party systems came into being.

From France these notions of a left side and a right side in politics gradually spread to most other European nations. In some countries in Scandinavia the labels Venstre (Left) and Højre (Right) even became the official names of some of the early parties which were founded around 1870–80. When new parties were grafted on the original nucleus of – mostly bourgeois – parties, the distinction between the two polar positions in politics was preserved. It was gradually becoming the major ordering dimension of all party systems in Europe.

In the classical analysis of the formation of parties in Europe it is argued that the modern party systems took their present form around 1920, in some countries with few parties, in other countries with a greater number (Lipset and Rokkan 1967). In any case, it was only possible to understand the formative period and the ensuing result, if one used the Left–Right dimension as the primary cleavage dimension in the national political systems. Along the same lines political historians have argued that it would be completely impossible to write the political history of European nations without resort to this distinction (see, for example, Rémond 1968).

Political scientists have since demonstrated the value of the distinction in numerous studies of voters, parties, parliaments, etc. (for example, Duverger 1951; Sartori 1976; Inglehart and Klingemann 1976; Laponce 1981; Castles and Mair 1984; Huber and Inglehart 1995). In later years another cleavage dimension has sometime been added to the description. It has been baptised the 'post-materialist' dimension, the 'green' dimension or something along these lines, but it is still the case that the older – socio-economic – 'left–right' dimension dominates.

The reason why this distinction has to be taken into consideration here is that it is fundamentally embedded in the mind of the European citizen. It is one of the few political images that all Europeans share. We are all taught how to make the distinction. Learning how to use the dichotomy for description as well as evaluation is a central part of the socialisation of the ordinary citizen (Percheron 1973). It thus happens to be one of the major shared cognitive dimensions in the politics of Western European nations. And consequently it is no wonder that it also plays an important role for the emergence of some kind of party system at the level of the European Parliament.

The pictorial presentation in Figure 2.1 of the political groups in the Parliament as of January 1995 reflects the old cleavage – with its two major groups at the left and right respectively. But it also suggests that other, complicating, political dimensions exist, not only the second cleavage dimension mentioned above, but others as well: it is these to which we will turn next.

THE 'FIT' BETWEEN NATIONAL PARTY SYSTEMS AND THE EURO-PARTY SYSTEM

To compare the system of political groups in the European Parliament and the various party systems in the member states, we will look at the composition of political groups after the two elections of 1989 and 1994.

The format of the party system in the European Parliament is a multi-party system with approximately 10 parties. Two of these – the Socialist group and the European People's Party – are fairly big groups with 150–200 members. The other parties are smallish in comparison. In this respect the format resembles somewhat the format of some of

Figure 2.1: *Political groups in the European Parliament, January 1995*

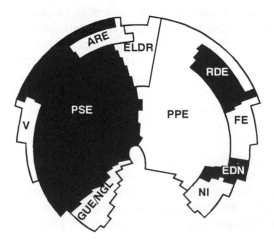

the national party systems.

But how good is the 'fit' between the two levels? A perfect 'fit' between the EP-format and the national format can be defined as a situation with total congruence between the two, meaning that: (1) each national party is mirrored into one of the groups in the European chamber; (2) two parties from a given nation will never register with the same European group; and (3) each European group will have one party member from each European nation. Conversely a bad 'fit' is any situation in which a high degree of incongruence occurs.

The problematic and embryonic character of the new Euro-party system is easily understood when we compare the 'fit' between the EU-system of political groups and the national party systems. Although the political groups relate to the classical left–right dimension as well as to newer – and 'greener' – dimensions, at least five important deviations from perfect congruence are observed (see Table 2.1).

Superficially, Table 2.1 suggests that the political groups are able to absorb most of the elected members. Thus, in 1989, the political groups encompassed 506 of 517 members of the parliament. Nine of the unattached members (NI) were elected in Italy and in Spain. Five years later, 540 out of 567 members affiliated with one of the political groups, and most of the non-affiliated were French (Front National) or Italians (Alleanza Nazionale and PSDI). In this limited perspective the fit between the two types of 'party system' can be said to be quite good.

Upon closer inspection the picture is different, however. Reading the two tables 'horizontally', we see, firstly, that only the two big groups – the Socialist Group (PSE/SOC) and the European People's Party (PPE) – attract members from all countries. Some – like the European Democrats (ED) only bring in members from two countries. In 1994 Silvio Berlusconi's Forza Italia decided to form its own group (FE). An intriguing question to ask is what it means to the working conditions of a political group that it has members from all countries? Even more interesting is the question about the effects of a nationally skewed distribution of members and the absence of some – or many – nations in the political group? Does it mean, for instance, that the members of that group more or less ignore the interests of the excluded nations?

Secondly, a 'vertical' reading of the tables indicates that in no case will a collective national representation cover all political groups. The fragmented Italian party system comes closest to all-encompassing coverage while in the nature of their national party systems, the British and the Germans fit into only a few of the political groups. These discrepancies have important consequences for the activities of – and activities within – the political groups.

Table 2.1: *the 'fit' between official groups in the European Parliament and National Parties in the twelve Member States*

(a)   July 1989

Group/Country

	B	DK	F	G	GR	IR	IT	L	N	P	S	UK
SOC	2	1	2	1	1	1	2	1	1	2	1	2
PPE	2	1	1	2	1	1	2	1	1	1	2	1
LDR	2	1	5	1	–	2	1	1	1	1	2	–
ED	–	1	–	–	–	–	–	–	–	–	–	1
VER	2	–	2	1	–	–	4	–	2	1	1	–
GUE	–	1	–	–	1	–	2	–	–	–	1	–
RDE	–	–	3	–	1	1	–	–	–	–	–	–
DR	1	–	1	1	–	–	–	–	–	–	–	–
CG	–	–	1	–	1	1	–	–	–	1	–	–
ARE	1	4	1	–	–	2	2	–	–	–	2	1
NI	–	–	1	–	–	–	2	–	1	–	3	1

Legend: '1'= Only one national party was affiliated with the European political group; '2'= Two national parties were affiliated, etc.
Source: Mackie 1990.

(b)   July 1994

Group/Country

	B	DK	F	G	GR	IR	IT	L	N	P	S	UK
PSE	1	1	1	1	1	1	2	1	1	1	1	1
PPE	2	1	1*	1	1	1	3	1	1	–	2	1
ELDR1	2	1*	–	–	1	2	1	2	1	1	1	
GUE	–	–	1	–	2	–	1	–	–	1	–	–
FE	–	–	–	–	–	–	1	–	–	–	–	–
RDE	–	–	1*	–	1	1	–	–	–	1	1	–
V	1	1	–	1	–	1	2	1	1	–	1	–
ARE	1	–	1	–	–	–	1	–	–	–	3	–
EN	–	2	1	–	–	–	–	–	1	–	–	–
NI	2	–	1	–	–	–	2	–	–	–	2	–

("*"= French UDF/RPR affiliated themselves with three political groups)

Legend: '1'= Only one national party was affiliated with the European political group; '2'= Two national parties were affiliated, etc.
Source: Doc. PE 182.789, final edition.

Thirdly, politics evidently also make strange bedfellows at this level. In only two countries, Greece and Luxembourg, did national parties fit into the European groups of 1989 in such a way that MEPs with different party affiliations also came together in different political groups. In some instances up to four or five national parties would be represented in one political group. For Italian and Spanish MEPs this was the rule, not the exception. This picture had changed somewhat in 1994. Now the 'fit' between national parties and Euro-parties has become considerably 'better'. We may choose to interpret this difference as an – albeit weak – indicator of convergence of the two systems.

Fourth, it should be noted that not all MEPs that cooperate in the political groups are from genuine national political parties. The 'fit' just mentioned is partly an effect of the increasing tendency for regional parties to seek and gain seats in the European Parliament. We are here speaking not only about the traditional bifurcated parties in Belgium, nor about the CDU-CSU combination in Germany. In 1994 the Scottish Nationalists, the South Tirolians, the Catalonian CDC-CIU and the Flemish Front in Belgium obtained seats alongside with traditional national parties.

Finally, mention should be made of the parties created by the anti-integrationist movements in Denmark, France, and The Netherlands. These groups do not necessarily participate in national elections, but play an important role in the European elections as well as in EU-related referenda.

So, even if there is some correspondence between traditional party 'families' in Western Europe and the EP political groups, the 'fit' between the 'party system' in the European Parliament and the various national parliaments is far from perfect. It never will be. At least not until the dream envisaged in the minds of a few federalists have come true. The great variety of party systems in Western Europe – ranging from '2½'-party systems to highly fragmented, even atomised multi-party systems – precludes the formation of a relatively simple system of political groups in the European Parliament. The relative lack of powers of the EP also dampens motivation among members to change the present situation. They are probably quite satisfied with a situation in which the groups are – just – loosely organised umbrella bodies, linking representatives from like-minded national parties, facilitating some practical activities, and giving the MEPs an arena for transnational socialisation – and a social life away from home.

THE STRATEGIC PROBLEM: TWO FUTURES

But even in the present situation the linkage between the two levels is a problematic one. Today the national parties – with few exceptions – still have a monopolistic position with regard to the European elections. They nominate the candidates, organise and finance the electoral campaigns. The expenses of the campaign are met by the parties, most of them at least. In return the national parties will also administer the corresponding flow of income from EU-sources.

But when a candidate has been elected in a national election slot and has become a MEP, something important happens to his or her political situation. The MEP has to establish and maintain a triple relationship in order to maintain a political profile in domestic politics, survive the next European election, and create for herself or himself a status and a platform within the European Parliament.

The first relationship is the one between the MEP and the 'national constituency' – the total national or regional electorate – back home. This relationship is vital, not only in a democratic perspective, but also because maintaining it is essential for the re-election chances of the MEP.

The other relationship is the one which the MEP establishes by joining one of the political groups – 'parties' – in Strasbourg. This relationship is vital for creating and sustaining working conditions and collegiate connections in the European Parliament. As we have seen only few MEPs decide to stay completely outside the 'political groups'.

The third relationship, and the one that will be the topic of the following discussion, is the linkage to the national party. The MEP depends for his or her nomination and re-nomination on a national party organisation. The MEP is supposed to serve the interests of this party alongside serving national or other more abstract interests. This relationship is not without its problems for the MEP, and for the party and the party leadership. For the latter the new supra-national level of representation creates several new challenges.

We will start the discussion by juxtaposing two extreme views about the future of political parties in the European context.

The first is the 'federalist' view which can be found in the very constitution of the European Union. At a late stage in the Maastricht process it was decided to include a new Article 138A in the treaty. It reads as follows:

> Political parties at the European level are important as a factor of integration within the Union. They contribute to the formation of a European consciousness and to the expression of the political will of the citizens of the Union.

This paragraph is without any legal content or importance. It reads partly as a high-flown declaration echoing the integrationist ideal of the founding fathers of the European Union, partly – and this is the interesting interpretation – as a hypothesis about the possible long term effects of the creation of parties at the supra-national level. It is suggested in this opaque paragraph 138A that trans-national parties may enhance the process of integration by creating a new European awareness which may supersede national and nationalist thinking. A new democratic structure may become superimposed upon traditional political structures, in the process invigorating political life all over Europe. The other side of the coin – not mentioned in the treaty text though – is the corresponding weakening of the national parties and of the various 'national consciousnesses'.

Put this ideal – or dreadful future – against the many bitter and frustrated discussions in the aftermath of the Danish referendum of 1992 on the Maastricht Treaty, when a majority of Danish politicians, representing most of the parties in parliament, had been severely beaten by a majority of Danish citizens, who were, quite simply, not willing to follow the advice of their party leaders. The Danish political elite – including most Danish MEPs – against whom this onslaught had been made, was paralysed. For some time it was discussed in earnest whether the Danish party system would be able to survive this crisis. How could one reconcile an emergent, alien European political system with the venerable Danish patterns of democratic representation and the many new attempts at local ('near') democracy that had developed during the 1970s and the 1980s? Would it not mean that European citizens in Denmark and elsewhere might become alienated from the traditional party system?

It is obvious that each of the two futures embodied in these scenarios call for new re-evaluations to be made by present-day political parties. In the short run they have to consider and deal with the uncontrollable splits within national electorates and the actual as well as potential loss of control over 'their' voters. In the longer run the older parties will have to consider the potential build-up of new trans-European parties or cartels of parties, based upon cleavage lines and platforms that do not necessarily fit well with those of the national party system.

In both cases, what makes the situation interesting from a theoretical perspective is the fact that it is the common EEC/EU-generated extension of the parties' required span of control that have created the recent turmoil. Parties all over Europe have discovered how important it is for them to control the voters in the domain of supra-national political issues, elections, policy matters, even including constitutional issues. There are good reasons to expect that this is not a problem that will leave the agenda for quite some time.

THE THEORETICAL PERSPECTIVE: PARTIES WISH TO CONTROL

Parties are linkage organisations. They link citizens and the political regime. Many political scientists will say that this linkage is a prerequisite for democratic representation in a modern society. Others will remember Jean-Jacques Rousseau's verdict that parties are parasites distorting the will of the people.

At this juncture I will abstain from dealing with these normative questions. I will instead state quite bluntly that parties are first and foremost organisations that try to control the relations between the citizens and the political regime. This, by the way, is a definition of the concept of party.

Thus, according to a textbook definition, 'a political party is a group of officials or would-be officials who are linked with a sizeable group of citizens into an organisation; a chief object of this organisation is to ensure that its officials attain power or are maintained in power' (Shively 1993: 204).

From this definition, it also follows that to survive and to thrive parties have to control the political regime in its various manifestations, all sorts of representational linkages, and, first of all, the citizens in their capacity of voters and political participants. To what extent are they able to do this?

Two political science contributions stand out as especially interesting in the context of this discussion. They can be used as a starting point, even if they deal with parties as early and emergent phenomena, not as century-old political institutions. Stein Rokkan introduced the concept of institutional thresholds (Rokkan 1970: 79ff.). These thresholds were 'barriers' which parties, qua new social movements, were passing on their long road towards control over the parliament and the executive.

Hans Daalder was thinking along similar lines when he introduced the concept of the 'reach' of the party system (Daalder 1966: 58ff.). By the 'reach' or 'permeation' of the parties he had in mind the ability to control the 'mainsprings of political power' – that is the political elites.

It is noteworthy that these ideas about the different ways in which parties penetrate the political systems take it for granted, firstly, that parties aim at increasing their control over society within the national borders, and, secondly, that the primary goal is to control the various political elites. Daalder and Rokkan stressed that parties were crucial actors in a political development sequence that would lead to a 'take-over' by parties of traditional as well as new elite positions, local as well as central positions: the voters would follow their leaders along.

The idea to be pursued in the following is a simple one: European parties nowadays are old and institutionalised structures, not the vigorous and flexible movements they were in older times. If parties are to thrive and survive well into the next century they will have to meet various new challenges, among which is the challenge from new political arenas such as the European Union. They will have to re-learn how to control the mind of the citizen in his/her capacity of voter, at a time when new channels of electoral participation are opening up. This challenge can also be phrased as a quest for control over various segments of the 'political mind' of the ordinary citizen. Or, in Daalder's terms turned upside-down: parties will have to 'permeate' or 'reach into' the mind of the citizen. The reader may wish to phrase the problem in another theoretical language as well: various electoral arenas – sites for encounters between parties (Sjöblom 1968:26–27) – exist at any given moment, and the parties will have penetrated these arenas to a varying extent. Parties will only control the electorate, if they are able to control effectively all electoral arenas in which citizens are active.

This task of controlling the voters' minds and the various arenas is becoming more complicated, since the modern voter is now being asked to vote and to participate politically in more political events than was the case a few decades ago. The European voter is no longer voting only in national and local elections. He/she is also being asked by politicians and bureaucrats to perform in relation to complicated national–supra-national linkages, be they EU parliamentary elections, or constitutional referenda. At the same time the voter is also being invited in several European countries to take part in the management of local public neighbourhood-institutions.

AN EXAMPLE : HOW DANISH PARTIES ARE PERFORMING IN VARIOUS ARENAS

These somewhat abstract remarks can be fleshed out by the example of recent Danish politics. As a Danish citizen I am asked to perform considerably more and more often than the average European voter. I am required to follow and to feel an obligation with regard to national, regional, municipal, as well as 'neighbourhood' and 'workplace' politics – and, on top of all this, also supra-national politics. No small requirement for a plain citizen, who, maybe, is more interested in cultivating his garden ....

Let us enumerate these electoral arenas and briefly look at the degree of control that the parties exercise in each one.

Until quite recently Folketing elections took place on average every second year, as against the constitutional minimum requirement of an election every four years. I am also asked to vote in municipal and county elections every fourth year and in the EU Parliament elections every fifth year. If that is not enough for me, I am also entitled, if a member of the Church, to vote in the Parish Council elections that are held every four years. If I am a parent with children attending school or other public child-care institutions, I may also vote in School Board elections, etc. In universities students, teachers, and other personnel are also electing members of various public boards that are supposed to take part in running the institution. University Rectors, deans and assorted other leaders are elected directly in contests that may resemble direct presidential elections in other political systems. On top of this, the Danish constitution contains a number of clauses that call for popular referenda to be held under certain conditions. The referendum option may also, from time to time, be used at the level of the municipality for special purposes.

Do the Danish parties control all these arenas? The answer is at the same time yes and no. The parties are only totally in command in the national electoral arena. Although there is considerable electoral volatility (Pedersen 1987), voters seldom defect for longer periods, and the level of political participation is high. In regional and in municipal politics the turnout is lower, and in some municipalities the national parties still find it difficult to muster 'their' voters since many voters prefer to vote for local 'lists' (Elklit and Pedersen 1995). The newer local-level elections and referenda have not yet been 'colonised' by the national parties, even if some traditions exist, for example Social Democratic participation in the politics of the church.

The most serious problem for Danish politicians springs from Danish membership of the EU. Danes are, as is by now well known all over Europe, not only asked to vote in the European Parliament elections. They have also been called to participate in four important national referenda since 1972. Even if the referendum in 1986 (on the 'Single Act') was only a consultative referendum, it was an important manifestation that should be put alongside the decisive referenda of 1972, 1992 and 1993.

Table 2.2 highlights the degree of party control over these events. These figures demonstrate abundantly the problems that Danish parties have to encounter. First, the voters evidently consider EEC-/EU-Parliament elections second-order elections (Reif and Schmitt 1980). Parties are not even able to bring out the vote to the same extent as in

Table 2.2: *Turnout and the share of pro-European votes in various types of elections and referenda, 1972–94.*

a) Turnout – Percentage of electorate.

EEC Referendum 1972	90.1
EEC Parliament Election 1979	47.8
EEC Parliament Election 1984	52.4
EEC Referendum 1986	75.4
EEC Parliament Election 1989	46.2
EEC Referendum 1992	83.1
EEC Referendum 1993	86.5
EU Parliament Election 1994	52.9

b) Comparison of the strength of combined incumbent parties/'yes-advocates' and the corresponding electoral support in elections and referenda.

	'Yes-parties' in the Folke-ting (%)	Percentage of voters supporting the 'yes-parties'
1972 referendum	90.2	63.3
1986 referendum	44.1	56.2
1992 referendum	84.9	49.3
1993 referendum	94.1	56.7

	Pro-EEC vote before election	Pro-EEC vote in election
1979 Parliament election	74.2%	61.7%
1984 Parliament election	81.7%	65.2%
1989 Parliament election	80.4%	66.7%
1994 Parliament election	94.1%	81.9%

municipal elections. But every time a referendum is called on a European topic, the very same voters participate to the same high degree as they do in Folketing elections. Even more critical for the parties is their inability to persuade the voters to support their views. The discrepancy between the standpoints of the parliamentary parties and the electorate is as considerable in the 1990s as it was as in earlier decades. In this connection it should be noted that at least one of the parties that have been counted as 'pro-EEC/EU' in the post-1992 figures, the *Socialistisk Folkeparti* does not fit too well into a dichotomised categorisation.

From the background of this illustrative story of a troubled EU-member nation, we will now turn to the general problem of the parties' control or lack of control.

THE TASKS OF POLITICAL PARTIES: THE OLD VIEW

Students of political parties have devoted considerable effort to the description of functions that parties are supposed to fulfil in a political system. The list of functions can be made very long (see, for example, Macridis 1967; King 1969; Wiesendahl 1980). If we drop the ambiguous vocabulary of functionalism, it is, however, possible to summarise the tasks of parties and their leadership in four simple points (Pedersen 1989 [1994]). The party leadership has to organise its strategic thinking around the following tasks:

(1)   How do we mobilise and socialise voters and cadres?
(2)   How do we select and train political leaders?
(3)   How do we attend to relevant political interests?
(4)   How do we formulate political goals and platforms?

In relation to each of these tasks the party will have to consider a number of strategic questions. In the following I have listed twenty such questions (see Table 2.3). The list could be extended almost at will. Twenty questions are, however, more than enough to deal with in this limited context.

These questions are familiar to party leaders and party secretaries at the level of the national party as well as in local and municipal politics. Answers have been developing incrementally since the nineteenth century, and, as a consequence, these strategic questions are seldom discussed openly. They are primarily, if not exclusively, raised in connection with intra-party conflicts between, for example, the national

Table 2.3: *Four sets of strategic questions*

Political mobilisation and socialisation	Selection and training of political leadership
– Who shall the party try to mobilise? – What kind of channels and means shall be used? – What shall be offered in return for support and activism? – What shall be demanded in return? – What degree of activity shall be aimed at?	– What type of politicians shall the party try to recruit? – How open shall the recruitment process be? – How comprehensive shall the training of aspiring recruits be, and how long shall it last? – How big shall awards and risks be? – Who shall control the nomination process, and how?
Attention to political interests	**Political goal formulation**
– Whose interests shall be attended to? – How closely shall interests be taken care of? – How exclusive shall the attention be? – What shall the party expect in return? – What kind of channels and means shall be used?	– How comprehensive shall the goal-formulation be? – How detailed shall the party formulate its goals? – How binding shall the formulations be? – How shall the communication of the goals be done? – Who shall control the formulation of the goals?

leadership and the local (nominating) party organisations.

As soon as new arenas or 'levels' are grafted upon this old and institutionalised system, two important things happen: firstly, a new set of strategic questions emerge for the national parties to deal with. Secondly, the meaning of the four older sets of questions tends to change.

NEW STRATEGIC QUESTIONS HAVE TO BE DEALT WITH

First and foremost the development of new arenas for party competition demand of the national parties that they decide whether to enter the competition or not. There is no legal demand on a national party to enter the competition for seats in Strasbourg. In local politics parties do not always put up candidates, even if they have organisations operating in the municipality. A decision to run candidates in a European election may of course be based upon some kind of idealistic notion of a 'European obligation'. It may be that a 'So ein Ding müssen wir auch haben' argument plays a role. The possibility of gaining points in the domestic political competition is probably more important than more lofty considerations. Nor should one forget that the mundane prospect of getting a considerable amount of financial support from the EU coffers could sometimes be a relevant factor in the decision to nominate candidates.

Next comes the decision about the amount of effort to be put into the electoral competition. A party may choose to run a low-cost, low activity campaign because the party does not consider the European perspective of primary importance for its main goal, i.e. to gain government positions and influence on the distribution of power within the national political system. The party may run its own campaign, or it may make a coalition with like-minded partners.

As soon as a party has decided to run EU-candidates – and especially when it has gained seats in the European Parliament – it will also have to set up procedures for the co-ordination of the national and the supra-national activities. As long as the supra-national body is not considered important by the voters 'back home' the party may leave it up to its MEPs to run their own business. But when a supra-national parliament is developing its own power – however slowly – it is vital that the national party decides, whether to let 'its' members handle their activities in an autonomous way, or whether to demand loyalty to a specific programme or set of guidelines. If European topics are, or become, critically important for domestic politics, co-ordination becomes essential.

Parties have two types of co-ordination problems. They have to co-ordinate 'vertically' between the national and the supra-national parliamentary groups, and they also have to co-ordinate 'horizontally' within the European arena.

The use of existing transnational collaboration among like-minded parties is one way to do the latter. The emergence of political groups in the European Parliament also makes such co-ordination easier, at least to the extent that the national party and its MEPs choose the right partners in Strasbourg. The frequent changes made by individual MEPs and national groups are indicative of the difficulty of finding like-minded partners on this level.

It is also important to establish co-ordination between the MEPs and the national party organisation back home. Unilateral connections can be taken care of by means of efficient recruitment and, sometimes, de-recruitment, if that is deemed necessary. The use of 'double-mandates' in the European Parliament and in the national parliament is a disputed, but often used means of co-ordination, even if the frequency of such double-mandates have decreased over the years. It can be quite efficient, but may sometimes not be so, because the strain on the representatives may force them to downgrade one or both activities. Other, less conspicuous and less burdensome, types of double-mandates are also in use. Thus many MEPs are active in regional politics for their parties. They may also serve in various non-elective capacities in the national headquarters.

Whatever method the party adopts to co-ordinate and control its members, the practical question is how to make sure that information is communicated from the national leadership to the members of the European Parliament, and how information is fed back from Strasbourg. It is vital for the party to set up an efficient communication network between the MEPs, the national party headquarters, the national parliamentary group, and, eventually, the governmental apparatus (in those cases in which the party is in power nationally). Equally important is the establishment of efficient channels back to the local party organisations, the national and the local press, to relevant sponsoring organisations and so on.

In one country, Denmark, the co-ordination and communication is made simpler by the operation of a special committee in parliament (e.g. the Danish Markeds-/Europa-udvalg) in which the national parties have a forum for the exchange of information and for creating joint policies, which may, eventually, also be of guidance for the members of the European Parliament, irrespective of party. This special procedural solution to the information problem is, however, *sui generis*, and its side-effects on the freedom of party manoeuvring are debatable. In other countries the individual party may to deal with co-ordination problems solely within its own organisational boundaries.

It is beyond doubt that many MEPs during the first decades of the European Parliament were pretty much left alone, as soon as they were elected. Only at re-election every fifth year did they have to report back on their actions and answer critical questions. In recent years, however, voters have become increasingly aware and knowledgeable, and the European Parliament has itself become more important with higher status and increased powers of scrutiny. The MEP has increasingly become accountable, not only to the public opinion and the voters, but also to the party organisation back home. As a consequence it has also become necessary for the party to develop guidelines for the degree of autonomy to be granted to the MEP, as well as guidelines for the resolution of conflicts among MEPs from a given party, or among the MEPs and the national party leadership, the national parliamentary group, and even the nominating organisation.

This development can be summarised in the five additional points/ questions (see Table 2.4).

OLD QUESTIONS NEED NEW ANSWERS

Most major parties in the EU countries decided long ago to take part in elections to the European Parliament and to participate in all EU-related arenas. They should therefore also already have explored the question whether the European Parliament is an arena of the same kind as a national parliament, or whether it is categorically different. Most discussions on this topic have, however, focused upon the constitutional questions about the relative lack of legislative as well as controlling/scrutinising powers. Much less have been said about the European Parliament as an arena of political competition among national political parties or supra-national parties in future.

As soon as a party decides to run candidates in the EU elections, it has to revise its strategic thinking because the answers that are appropriate within the national party and in domestic politics no longer suffice. Consider the Danish case once more. The process of political goal

Table 2.4: *Additional strategic questions for the party leadership*

Transnational arena co-ordination, communication and conflict resolution.

- Shall the party enter competition in the European arena? Why? Why not?
- How important is the European arena for the party, and how much effort shall be invested?
- To what extent – and how – shall the party co-ordinate its activities in the European arena?
- What kind of communication networks are needed in order to control the activities?
- How shall the party handle intra-party conflicts between the national and the European arenas?

formulation has become extremely complicated after the so-called 'national compromise', in which all parties but one participated. It is almost impossible to formulate a party specific platform on any EU-related issue without being accused of betraying this compromise. Consequently the major parties perform ritualistic acts of loyalty to each other and their past decision while trying on a modest scale to build up a profile of their own. In this situation the party leadership has to maintain strict control over the formulation of long-term as well as short-term goals, since even the slightest deviation from the 'national line' is reported and leads to criticism of the party and quite often within the party itself.

Under such circumstances the short-term way to handle the problem of policy formulation consists of behaving as if the problem either does not exist at all or is only important in European election years. This strategy of omission is facilitated by the fact that most voters, party members and activists still tend to consider the European institutions remote and not very important for their daily lives. Thus, although the MEPs belonging to a given party are formally connected with their colleagues in the national parliament, as well as with the voters back home, the constraints posed by national parliamentary groups, party members, activists and the electorate are negligible unless a European election is approaching.

In other countries such obstacles to goal formulation do not exist, and European questions can be discussed more freely. The extent to which Europe can be put on the political agenda for open discussion will, however, differ widely across EU member nations, and so does the freedom of manoeuvre for individual parties.

The European Parliament does not play any significant role in the mind of the average voter. Elections are only held once every five years. MEPs are in most cases not known to the voters. In many cases they are not allowed to campaign in a self-advertising way by their parties. It is no wonder, then, that voters are also difficult to mobilise, especially if the party uses traditional and old-fashioned methods. The electronic one-way media are bound to become the primary means of 'bringing out the vote', especially since the party finds it difficult to enter an exchange with prospective voters and members. Old-fashioned meetings in which candidates for the European Parliament meet and discuss do not draw much attention, and the candidates will find it difficult to establish local support outside their natural 'home base'. Only nationally known political figures, such as media personalities and former national political leaders are able to present themselves in an effective way.

All these obstacles, however important, are only part of the problem. In many cases the party will have decided that it is not worth while to spend too much effort on the mobilisation of the electorate. For decades the EEC was an elitist 'club'. The voters did not care. Hence it was of no use to waste energy and resources on the short-lived campaign in connection with the European elections every five years. After all, the European election was not viewed as a 'real election'. It was much more advantageous to mobilise the inner-circles of active party members, send them on delegation trips to Brussels, and expect them subsequently to communicate their experiences and viewpoints. Many parties in Europe managed their relations with voters in this superficial way, at least until a few years ago. The turmoil around the ratification of the Maastricht Treaty, however, brought an end to this innocent period. Nowadays it is dangerous – especially in countries with vigorous anti-European movements – to underestimate the voters.

The same problem of the long distance between the clients, the national party, and the European wing of the party is visible, when we consider EU democracy from the perspective of the interest articulation. The individual national party – unless it commands the governmental majority – is not able to promise much to national lobby groups in terms of European action. MEPs may promise to attend to specific requests from their national constituencies, but they are not able to do a lot, especially since, in major cases, they have to co-ordinate their efforts with the national party leadership. Since the Euro-parties are still weak structures, lobbying has to be done vis-à-vis individual MEPs or at the committee-level. But traditional lobbying by interest groups is much more efficiently done before the issue comes to the Parliament, that is, in the institutions of the Commission and the Council of Ministers. It is simply not efficient to deal with these institutions through party channels, be they national or European. As more and more interest organisations, municipalities, counties, and major private enterprises set up offices in Brussels to work directly with the European bureaucracy, the MEP will find it increasingly difficult to define his or her role in relation to the national electoral constituency and the party 'back home'. This tendency can only be broken if the European Parliament succeeds in strengthening its overseeing and controlling powers.

Finally, the recruitment of politicians for the European Parliament constitutes – or, rather, should constitute – a major problem for political parties and their leadership Ten years ago a Danish scholar produced a collective portrait of the MEPs. The typical MEP at the time was a middle-aged man, brought up in a politically active family; he had an academic education, mostly in law or economics. He had served his party extensively and loyally, in most cases including a long career in local politics or in the national parliament before election as MEP; he had also been active in various other organisational contexts, including various European movements (Sørensen 1984:28). This profile has changed somewhat since then, but some of the characteristics are still visible.

In a national party, a municipal or a national political career are to some extent self-contained: they may also be linked, in that a local political career can either be an end in itself or serve as a stepping stone to a national career. The same relationship does not exist between a seat in Strasbourg and the national career. The European Parliament is still a dead end for a national politician in his prime, especially for an ambitious minister-to-be. When such a figure is elected, it is unlikely that they will serve in a serious capacity, for example Michel Rocard, and in earlier times Francois Mitterand (who quickly gave up his seat) and Laurent Fabius (who kept the seat, but did not exhaust himself).

The kind of political personality that may serve well in a national parliament, such as a hard-working, no-nonsense 'party soldier', will not function well and may even be a disaster in the international circuit and in a 'legislature' which does not legislate. A slick media operator or a 'high-flier' will definitely serve much better in the European campaign, if not as an MEP.

A serious problem for the European Parliament is that the relatively well-paid, semi-glamorous, not too demanding service in Strasbourg has always attracted and may still attract former active politicians or national politicians. Sometimes the party wants to discard a member, and this is an honourable way out. Therefore the position of MEP has been often the final stop in a political career. The political patronage of parties also tends to produce MEPs who have only little incentive to put in an effort in Strasbourg, but who are, on the other hand, loyal to the national party leadership, upon whose good-will their position depends.

Increasingly, however, candidacy may serve as an attractive, not too risky, training ground for young men and women. The possibilities for creating a platform also makes nomination attractive to media professionals, who may see it as a short-cut compared to nomination for national elections. Many, younger Southern European MEPs combine their European seat with service in a regional council or assembly in their home country, two assignments that apparently are fairly easy to reconcile. In United Kingdom, some MEPs have subsequently proceeded to seats in Westminster.

It is obvious that recruitment patterns are undergoing relatively rapid change. So, too, is the relationship between the European candidates and members and their parties. Thus the UK MEPs, partly due to the special electoral system and a preference in constituencies for local candidates, apparently differ from other representatives by feeling themselves accountable to and responsible for their constituencies. Hence, they pursue European careers to a higher degree than MEPs from other member states (Westlake 1994). Another tendency, by now quite visible, is the professionalisation of the group of MEPs: they are apparently more and more recruited from the 'talking and writing' professions.

If a party does not want to see its group of candidates entirely composed of ex-politicians and professionals, it has to do some active planning or, as the British parties have done, choose to decentralise the recruitment process. If the party does not do the latter, it has to set up a *cursus honorum*, a proper training, and it has to balance risks and rewards of MEPs in such a way that free-riders and parachutists are avoided, while aspiring political leaders are encouraged to serve in the European Parliament for a while, or even permanently as a career. Turnover is still at a very high level, and this in itself makes it difficult to build up and maintain an effective linkage between the European Parliament and the national parties.

CONCLUSION

Any discussion of the possible convergence of West European party systems will have to do more than deal with the processes of integration and trans-nationalisation within the European Parliament. The European political groups may slowly become more cohesive (Attiná 1990). In some cases there may even come into existence a predisposition toward closer collaboration, programmatic as well as organisational (Ladrech 1993). But European political groups are still loose umbrella bodies. They remain in their composition extensions of national parties (Bardi 1992). The relative powerlessness of the European Parliament deprives the MEPs and their national party delegations of incentives to intensify transnational collaboration. Most important of all, European elections are still fought in a national context and on nationally defined European issues, the campaigns being in several cases even dominated by purely domestic issues.

But, even so, there exists a problem of co-ordination for national parties in relation to the voters as well as to the MEPs in Strasbourg.

Although some tacit co-ordination takes place at the European level as well as in the relationship between the MEPs and their 'home-parties', it is still possible to argue that co-ordination is defective. When this is the case, the parties find it difficult to follow and control the activities of their MEPs, but also difficult to persuade the electorate to support the integrationist route.

It has been argued in this chapter that national parties should not fear the creation of a Pan-European party system. They should rather be conscious of more mundane problems. If they do not carefully consider the strategic questions as they have been summarily outlined above, they run the risk of ending up in a situation similar to the one, the Danish parties had to face in 1992–93. That, in itself, may not be a disaster for democracy, but it would be dangerous for the national party as an organisation, whose 'chief object ... is to ensure that its officials attain power or are maintained in power.'

3
EU-Lobbying: Between Representativity and Effectiveness

Svein S. Andersen and Kjell A. Eliassen

Theories of representative democracies have several shortcomings, but they offer a fundamental critique of other forms of political authority. The democratic deficit in the EU has until now received only limited attention by the member countries, but it is gradually being moved up the agenda, particularly after Maastricht. Within Europe, there is a conflict between the federalists, who want an integrated Europe with strong supranational authority, and the confederalists, who want a Europe where the national governments retain much influence. Even if there are important nuances within this conflict, it is a dominant characteristic of the political debate.

If, in the future, the EU gains more independence from the member states, the demand for direct democracy is likely to increase. That will probably mean more influence for the Parliament. Meanwhile some maintain that the democratic problems of the EU are not that different from national systems with strong corporative elements. As Anderson (1977) has demonstrated, national systems have developed strong corporatist characteristics even when there cannot be found any clear normative basis for such institutions. The growth of such institutions has for the most part been accepted as a supplement to the voter's influence.

WHAT IS LOBBYING?

Lobbying is often discussed in relation to two major concerns: one approach sees lobbying as an informal mechanism of influence. What means do the lobbyists use to influence? It focuses on such questions as what is the relative importance of *cohesion* versus persuasion? To what extent do lobbyists supply information which improves the quality of public decisions and to what extent is the purpose of the activity mainly to affect the distribution of benefits? What distinguishes lobbying from other forms of informal influence in various parts of society?

While the first approach is concerned with the micro mechanisms of influence, the second major approach takes a more systemic view. Within this perspective a major distinction is made between liberal interest group theory and neo-corporatism, as lobbying is usually associated with the former. This perspective does not pay such close attention to the process of lobbying, rather assuming the existence of a mechanism of competition and selection to explain outcomes. Yet, it may be argued, in systems based on open competition, informal influence or lobbying in a relatively fragmented way is likely to be the major mechanism of interest articulation.

In contrast, corporatism emphasises hierarchic co-ordination and the articulation of interests through a small number of interest associations. Informal influence is, however, important, but it takes place in a different way. A major part takes place as intra- and inter-organisational bargaining and the degree of formal and informal regulation is higher. The number of access points for influence are fewer and the process is orderly and predictable.

If we give examples of countries according to these two major perspectives on interest articulation, the United States would come close to the liberal interest group model. This is no great surprise as the model has been developed mainly to account for the American system. If we look at Western European countries, the picture is less clear cut. Some small countries have historically come close to the corporatist model, for example, Austria, Sweden and Norway, but in most other countries we find a mix of these two systems of interest articulation, for example, in the UK, France and Denmark. Even in the smaller, corporatist countries there are also elements of informal interest group competition, such as specialised interest groups, firms, citizens, etc., in addition to the major interest associations. The major interest organisations were also engaged in areas outside their domains. Such types of influence introduced elements of interest group competition and lobbying into these corporatist systems. Such tendencies have strengthened over the last decade, particularly in Sweden.

We approach the concept of lobbying by contrasting it with the integrated corporatist participation in public decision-making. The definition of corporatism normally emphasises variations in the structure of interest representation. EU lobbying goes further than the conventional interest groups system with respect to fragmentation and specialisation, and the same goes for the processes of influence which are very issue and expert knowledge oriented. Representative associations engage in lobbying, but in principle anyone can become involved in lobbying directed at one or another of the EU institutions.

Will decision-making in the EU be subject to the same pragmatic acceptance of functional interest-representation that occurs in a corporatist society? An important difference seems to be that corporatism has developed within well-established parliamenty traditions. In some cases increased corporatist influence may have been part of a conscious parliamentary strategy (Slagtad 1986). Further strengthening of the EU is dependent on the system's capacity to demonstrate that it follows democratic traditions. This will require a movement towards a stronger parliamentary system.

The broadening of the Parliament's influence, for which the treaty provides, will strengthen the social dimension, and environment and consumer interests in the EU. Lobbying of the Parliament is therefore likely to increase dramatically. In that respect Maastricht represented an increase and strengthening of ongoing tendencies, particularly with regard to the social, environmental and consumer interests in the EU. Traditional labour interests will increasingly be channelled through the more corporatist structures in the economic and social committees, and not least in the three-tier system with the Commission, the 'social dialogue'.

Maastricht thus represents a small step towards a stronger Parliament, a federal solution, and a strengthening of the decision-making capacity of the Council. Traditionally, however, the Council represents the confederal authority. Pure confederal authority entails unanimity between members states but Maastricht increased the role of majority decisions. The Council is meanwhile still responsible to the fifteen national parliaments. This ambiguity in the EU's decision-making system weakens the prospect of promoting corporatist interest-representation within the system. Complex lobbying is perfectly suitable for an EU headed by the Council, not least in a situation with increased majority decisions.

The EU represents an interesting fusion of different democratic traditions. Firstly, the European national tradition, with the parliamentary chain of influence from the people through the parties to the parliament, government and administration. France is the only exception to this tradition of parliamentary democracy within the member states of the EU. The logic of a stronger Council, articulated in Maastricht, stems from the will to balance the EU's central institutions based on a power sharing principle. Yet this search for a balance between national and supranational authority will probably never result in the EU solving its 'democratic deficit' through a purely federal model. The EU is neither a confederal model of state nor a supranational federation, but something new in international co-operation with a binding majority in a Council of Ministers representing the member states.

THE GROWTH OF LOBBYING

A sharp increase in attempts to influence EU decision-making has been observed since the late 1980s (Andersen and Eliassen 1993: 37; Mazey and Richardson 1993: 5). This does not mean that lobbying was unknown in the EU previously, only that it has reached new proportions. This development is linked to a change in the nature of EU lobbying. While the growth of European interest organisations has been progressive, there has over the last ten years been a literal invasion of professional lobbyists, accounting firms, legal advisers and representatives of individual companies, counties and cities. The relative proportion of European associations among those lobbying in Brussels has consequently dropped.

In the years after 1957, Europe-wide pressure groups were established within the various areas of Community policy. By 1970 it was possible to identify more than 300 Euro-groups (Butt Philip 1987: 75). In 1980, Community officials created a register of all the formally recognised Euro-groups numbering 439 (Economic and Social Committee 1980). In addition there were some unrecognised Euro-groups and other lobbies active in Brussels (Butt Philip 1987: 76). A number of lobbying groups started at the national level, trying to influence Brussels as described in van Schendelen (1993). Until the late 1980s the national channel of influence was the dominant avenue of influence at the EU level. Despite the strong increase in direct influence upon central EU institutions, the national channel has continued to play an important role (Mazey and Richardson 1993: 29).

In some countries, such as Italy, the importance of domestic politics is consistently very high both in setting the agenda and as a key factor in linking up to EU decision-making (Bardi and Bindi 1993). Greenwood and Grant (1993) describe Britain as a case where the role of central government in relation to the EU is weakening, with a growing role for the business lobby. In Germany there seems to be less concern for concerted action through central government. Little emphasis is put on national policy co-ordination in relation to the EU and there is considerable room for direct influence from sub-governments, such as the Länder (Kohler-Koch 1993).

There are differences between EU member states in the formal arrangements for the national co-ordination of policy formulation at the EU level. Central responsibility usually falls onto the Ministry of Foreign Affairs, but in some cases upon the head of state (France) or the Prime Minister (UK). The degree of interest representation largely reflects variations in national state traditions (van Schendelen 1994).

Key political actors in Europe, such as companies, interest groups, governments and local authorities, increasingly direct their attention towards the EU. The increase in attention by organised interests is closely linked to the revitalisation of the EU through the successful launching of the internal market and the general expansion of EC legislation and other programs. One of the most striking consequences of this development is the explosive growth of direct interest representation, that is, lobbying.

The new pattern of lobbying is different from traditional national systems of interest articulation in Europe where elements of corporatism have been an important part, particularly in the Scandinavian countries and Austria (Katzenstein 1983). Fragmentation and specialisation characterise these new forms of direct influence and participation in the central EU decision-making processes. In countries such as Britain there has always been an element of lobbying in combination with major interest associations. Italy has been characterised by a high degree of interest group fragmentation, although with a co-ordinating role of parties until the traditional party system collapsed in the early 1990s. France differs from other EU members in that it has traditionally had a stronger element of technocratic politics and a weaker role for interest groups.

In some ways the EU system of lobbying may seem closer to what we associate with traditional US lobbying, focusing on competition between interests and specialised polities. Van Schendelen argues that EU lobbying is characterised by extreme complexity and openness. 'Lobbying in the EC machinery is much like playing chess', he even argues, except that 'EC lobbying is more complex than the game of chess.' Moreover, he states, 'There are many routes by which to approach any authoritative role player and always there is an indirect route. In addition to all these formal linkages there are the infinite informal ones every actor is free to develop' (van Schendelen 1993: 11). The result is a high degree of openness in terms of formal access requirements. However, openness is not the same as transparency. Both in terms of structure and process the system is complex and hard to understand for those who are not directly involved in the specific areas.

The internal environment affecting the policy formulation process includes such different factors as historical developments, party organisation, voters' opinions and interest organisation. Although national policy-makers find themselves more and more influenced by the external environment, that is the EU system and the interaction involving other member states, their loyalty first and foremost goes to protecting their national interests. EU policy formulation thus finds itself in a more and more delicate position between EU and domestic policy concerns.

The number of European pressure groups has increased in relation to the national arena. Many national groups joined forces with other groups in order to have more influence in the EU with regard to those matters that are decided at the EU level. One example of the latter is the question of professional rights, where national trade unions co-operate in order to put pressure behind the demand for increased recognition. Decisions concerning a minimum level of such rights is increasingly taken at the EU level.

Turning from the growth in lobbying and the changing weight of state-centric versus trans-European types of influence, we next discuss how patterns of influence themselves have been affected. It is important in any consideration of influencing the decision-making process, to remember that the Commission has the exclusive right to put forward proposals. If the Council or the Parliament want new legislation they must go to the Commission. Hence, the Commission is the most important lobbying target due to its agenda power.

There is a general agreement that lobbying should take place as early as possible in the decision-making process (Budd and Jones 1989: 61). For effective lobbying, contacts at the appropriate level in the Commission are a strong advantage: it is not necessarily the bureaucrats at the top of the hierarchy that are the best contacts. Proposals are often made at a lower organisational level, and the low level managers may be the most important people to lobby.

The members of the 'cabinet' of each Directorate of the Commission are also important actors in the decision-making process. Not only are they involved in the policy area of 'their' commissioner, but they are informed and involved in all policy areas of the EU. Consequently, claim many observers, these cabinets are extremely important targets for lobbying and interest representation in all policy sectors. This is particularly true regarding lobbying related to national interests and of more politically oriented lobbying in cases where the commissioner has a special interest.

Most people regard the Commission as the most important institution to lobby, especially if one wants to raise a question. Yet the Commission has only a limited staff and limited opportunities to propose new legislation. It is therefore also important to participate in the wider task of setting the agenda for the EU. Organisations such as ETUC and UNICE use this strategy.

The next step in the process is when a proposal is being examined by experts and working parties. The European Parliament plays an important role in the decision-making system of the EU today. Lobbying the Parliament is therefore seen as more and more relevant, because one needs to follow proposals from the Commission to the Parliament. Again, it is important to be active early in the process in the Parliament.

Attempts to lobby the EP have increased rapidly due to the increase in power accorded the Parliament in the Maastricht Treaty. Parliament's influence is, however, still weak in policy sectors involving a high degree of technical expertise. The sectors that offer more room for political argument, such as the environment, the social dimension, culture and education, are where the EP has increased its influence. The Maastricht Treaty gave the EP a right of veto on important questions. It can now not only suspend decisions but stop proposals viewed as unacceptable.

After consideration by the Parliament, a proposal goes to the Council. COREPER is the first institution to discuss the matter, and if there is no agreement reached, the matter is passed on to the Ministerial level. This is the last chance to influence a proposal before it is either accepted or refused. At this level it is more useful to lobby national governments than directly in the EU system.

Studies indicate, as is the case in the US, that business groups play a dominant part in influencing EU policy-making. It has been argued that other types of interests will never be able to assert themselves to the same degree (Calingaert 1994). The degree of access to and close relationships with central EU institutions reflect the difference between types of interests. While business interests have acquired a close contact with the Commission, the environmental and consumer lobbyists have been most welcome in the European Parliament (Andersen and Eliassen 1991).

STUDIES OF LOBBYING: THREE PERSPECTIVES

There has been a lack of systematic empirical research on EU lobbying. In contrast to the large body of literature which exists on interest articulation in national systems, most notably the models of corporate pluralism and societal corporatism (Rokkan 1966; Schmitter 1974 and 1977; Grant 1985; Williamson 1989; Scholten 1987; Damgaard and Eliassen 1978; Buksti and Johansen 1979; Johansen and Kristensen 1982; Heisler 1979). In the USA, there is a substantial number of studies on lobbying (Gable 1953; Epstein 1969; Hayes 1981; Birenbaum 1985). The growth of lobbying in EC decision-making and the development of new forms of lobbying requires scientific examination.

In the 1960s Meynaud and Sidjanski (1967, 1970) undertook one of the first serious studies of EU lobbying. They studied interest groups with enough resources to be heard by decision-makers and to establish relationships with them (Meynaud and Sidjanski 1967: 104). Later studies in the 1970s employed the interest groups approach to the study of EU lobbying (see, for example, Avery 1975; Auken, Buksti and Sørensen 1974; Sidjanski and Aybek 1974), a focus which corresponded to the general role ascribed to interest groups in theories of European integration.

In the 1980s there have been some attempts to understand the EU interest articulation within the corporatist framework (Grant 1989; 1990; Sargent 1987; Schmitter 1990). These have, however, often ended up by endorsing the pluralist hypothesis. On the other hand, studies associated with the neo-liberal school have pointed to quasi-corporatist relationships, for instance, between farming and DG IV (Agriculture) (Greenwood, Grote and Ronit 1992: 4–5).

The new forms of interest articulation associated with lobbying have received limited attention. Van Schendelen (1993) and Bindi (1994c) are among the few authors to discuss the various concepts of lobbying in relation to EU developments. Van Schendelen demonstrated the multi-dimentional and variable use of the concept of lobbying, but the discussion mainly centred on national lobbying towards the EU. Bindi discussed lobbying in the relation to interest group theories and provided a classification of EU pressure groups (Bindi 1994c).

Some studies have a prescriptive component but few are normative in the sense that they discuss the implications for democratic processes. The normative studies that have been undertaken focus on the European Parliament and the 'democratic deficit', with exceptions in Obradovic (1994) and Mazey and Richardson (1994a). Studies of the institutionalisation of EU interest articulation are rare. Schmitter and Streeck (1990) discuss macro aspects of the future inter-relationships between organised interests and central EU institutions. We are not aware of anyone who has applied a systematic institutionalisation perspective towards different sectors and policy areas.

Studies of lobbying can be divided into three major groups. A First group of studies looks at the role of national interest groups attempting to influence the EU decision-making-system as an extension of national policy-making. The first studies of this kind date from the late 1970s (Auken, Buksti and Sørensen 1974; Kirchner 1977). During the 1980s there were also a few similar studies (Kirchner 1981; Buksti and Martens 1984; Sidjanski 1989), and in the early 1990s the interest in such studies with a national focus has increased (van Schendelen 1993; Bregnsbo and Sidenius 1992; Bindi 1994b).

Van Schendelen made the first attempt to provide a systematic description of national differences in the attempts to influence EU policies. Although he discussed theories of lobbying and the development of EU lobbying, his focus was on the articulation of national interests in Brussels. His study covered most EU countries and a couple of the EFTA-countries, where the interest groups try to operate from outside. His chief conclusion is that the attempts to influence the EU are increasingly based on spontaneous lobbying rather than through national power systems (van Schendelen 1994: 275–288).

The past has set the pattern for the future in EU interest articulation. France represents one extreme, where the co-ordination of almost all EU related interests is centrally located in the hands of the SGCI reporting to the prime minister. Changes are, however, taking place (Lequesne 1994, Einarsdottir 1994). At the other extreme we find countries such as Belgium and the Netherlands. In Belgium regional communities and the business associations have considerable autonomy in relation to state interests. In the Netherlands major public and private actors prefer to take their sectoral issues directly to Brussels (van Schendelen 1994: 284–285).

A second group of studies focuses on both national interest groups' attempts to influence at the EU level and the overall pattern of interest articulation at the EU level. Butt Phillip made one of the first attempts to employ both a national and a European perspective on EU-lobbying (1985). Mazey and Richardson (1993) discussed both the European lobbying process and sectoral variations in the lobbying patterns; their book combined academic perspectives with contributions from experienced insiders in the EU decision-making process covering the EU level activities of national and European interest groups but not from a EU political system level. Mazey and Richardson (1993) examine the consequences of transferring power to Brussels for the EU policy processes and the activities of the European Commission as well as the behaviour of interest organizations at the national and European levels. They emphasise the novelty of the system, describing the system of interest representation at the EU level as in a state of flux. In this situation groups seek to develop new strategies for EU lobbying while EU policy-makers struggle to cope with these new forms of influence (Mazey and Richardson 1994a: 4). An interesting observation is that interest groups tend to shift their lobbying to Brussels in the early stages of national policy disputes. This interplay between national and EU level policy-making is of major importance.

One of the main conclusions that Mazey and Richardson (1993: 256) draw regarding the new forms of EU lobbying is that the sectoral, lobby nature of EU interest articulation will continue in a foreseeable future. This would imply a multiple model of EU policy-making in contrast to development of a trans-national neo-corporatism, which they consider is proposed by Andersen and Eliassen (1991), though that stretches our argument about a partial closure of the representation system too far.

A third group of studies focuses on the EU-level. This group includes several articles and books, published in recent years, which focus on the practical challenges for EU-lobbying in the 1990s (Mack 1989; Gardner 1991; Andersen 1992; Collins 1993; Stern 1992; Sasseen 1992) including a recent study by Club de Bruxelles (1994). These guides are often based on an anecdotal approach presented within the framework of strategic interaction and persuasion, though a few display a more systematic approach (C. Andersen 1992).

Of particular relevance here is *Organised Interests and the European Community* (Greenwood, Grote and Ronit 1992) which deals with lobbying at the EU-level, focusing on the relationship between organised business and the European community. Its aim is to explain how certain forms of interest organisation and inter-mediation emerge and how the articulation of interest affects the integration of European markets. It explores organised interests in a trans-national perspective, dealing with complex and reciprocal influences exerted between organised interests as well as processes of economic and political internationalisation.

The book identifies several ways to study interest intermediation in the EU. It stresses that the European level becomes increasingly more important as a target for interest intermediators, but that there are huge differences across industries. In general, sector associations seem to be more important than peak associations. Stressing the diversity of the system of EU lobbying, a disaggregated approach rather than one unitary theoretical framework is recommended.

None of the three types of groups that we have commented upon addresses the systemic aspects of the EU as a new political system, and EU-lobbying as part of it. The idea behind our article on European Community lobbying (1991) was to check some of the characteristics of the whole new system of interest articulation and decision-making by means of systematic interviews with key informers in Brussels and other national capitals. We concentrated on the ongoing processes related to the making of internal market directives, where the focus was on variations in patterns of mobilisation across types of actors and sectors identifying points of influence within an institutional framework characterised by rivalry and complex relationships between central EU institutions.

There are some limitations in this study. For instance, the internal market activities should have been contrasted more from traditional politicised bargaining, and going into how the central EU decision-making processes could shift/switch from relatively depolitizised majority rules to more traditional political bargaining would have strengthened the study. A good case study of this is the attempt to pursue an internal market in the energy sector (Andersen 1994). This perspective has been developed further in an analysis of the interaction between the EU and national level of policy-making (Andersen and Eliassen 1993). In addition to an insistence on the EU level of analysis, the argument about process is also pushed a little further: two distinctive elements of EU decision-making are emphasised – one is Europeification, the other is lobbying (1993: 43).

European Union interest representation in the late 1980s and early 1990s differs from the pattern in national Western European systems in two important ways. It is increasingly based on supranational authority, Europeification. Secondly, in the EU system, it is less corporatist and more lobbying-orientated than the national European systems. Whatever the national traditions are, each and everyone who wants to influence EU decisions has to engage in lobbying. In this way, lobbying reflects special features of interest articulation in the Community institutional set-up and decision-making models.

WHY HAS LOBBYING BECOME IMPORTANT?

Why has lobbying become so important in contrast to national systems of parliamentary government and interest articulation? The Single European Act represented a revitalisation of the decision-making system in Brussels. The 279 directives that were to be implemented before 1992 suddenly turned the EU's common policy formulation into an important political arena. The growth of direct lobbying of the EU's institutions has also contributed towards developing a European political system independent of the member states. All the important actors in European politics, e.g. businesses, trade unions and other interests groups, local and national authorities, have become more and more focused on the EU system. This increased interest in the EU's central institutions is closely linked to the establishment of the internal market and the general expansion of the EU's spheres of competence. The new forms of participation in the EU's decision-making system and the development of direct interest representation are characterised by a high degree of specialisation and fragmentation.

Definitions of corporatism tend to emphasise structural variables in relation to interest groups. EU lobbying is even more specialised and fragmented than traditional systems of interest representation. Professional expert knowledge is also a central matter. Highly specialised skills are an important part of lobbying in Brussels, where the Commission works on proposals for detailed laws and regulations. An executive officer in Brussels thus seeks contact with persons who are knowledgeable of the relevant problem area. There are approximately only 3500 higher administrative positions in the EU institutions (Greenwood, Grote and Ronit 1992: 24), and that makes contacts between the economic/interests organisations and EU bureaucrats particularly important.

Most studies of EU lobbying are descriptive and case or issue orientated. A majority of the research has focused on the lobbying of business regulation (Sidenius 1994; Greenwood, Grote and Ronit 1992; Calingaert 1993). There are, however, studies on 'softer' EU policy areas, e.g. consumer policy (Helenius 1994), animal welfare groups (McKinney 1994) and environment (Monfort 1994).

One reason why business lobbyists have paid little attention to the European Parliament is that it is considered less influential than the Commission. When business interests want to influence the Council they do it mostly through national governments (Calingaert 1993: 126–127). This pattern may change as a result of institutional reforms strengthening the role of the Parliament and the new priority given to unemployment and social issues in which national parliaments used to have a strong interest.

An important reason why lobbying plays a central role in the EU is the EU institutional system itself. It is different from those we are accustomed to from the representative democracies of both Western Europe and the USA in the following ways:

–   The EU is based on a *new form of supranational authority*.
     It is not a state in the traditional European sense. At the
     same time, the EU is also quite different from the federal
     state in the United States. The EU is based on strong na-
     tional systems, with virtually no independent sanctioning
     power.
–   *The Commission plays a key role*, with the exclusive right
     to initiate legislation. It plays the role of government. The
     Council is relatively weak because it is not a full-time rep-
     resentative body. The Parliament is politically weak.
–   *The role of the Commission and that of Council representa-
     tives are almost reversed*. The civil servants cultivate rela-
     tions with special interests.
–   *Since democratic representativity and legitimacy is of low
     importance* in the EU functional representativity linked to
     expertise in the Commission plays a central role.

In contrasts to national traditions, the EU stands out through a number
of unique features of interest articulation:

–   *New types of actors* can participate. For instance European
     consumer interests, individual firms and cities have all es-
     tablished themselves as lobbyists.
–   *There are very few procedures regulating participation*.
     Unlike the United States, it is not required that interest
     associations and lobbyists register, and lobbying is not
     professionalised.
–   *Interest articulation takes places on many levels*: regional,
     national and supranational. These levels can operate simul-
     taneously or actors can have another try at a different if
     their first attempt fails.
–   *The system is still in the formative stage*. This means that
     outcomes of particular decisions are important for the fur-
     ther elaboration of the system. The strategic implications
     of decisions are great.

The Commission and other EU institutions are, in many cases, dependent on information from outside the EU system. It is therefore important to be aware of matters under discussion in Brussels which may be
relevant to one's company, region, town, organisation, etc. At the same

time, it is important to know how to send one's information into the EU system.

So far we have discussed the growth of lobbying, changing patterns of influence and the factors driving the institutionalisation of an EU system of lobbying. Below, we comment on the relationship of EU lobbying to democracy and efficiency.

CONCLUSION

Few studies have systematically linked the analysis of lobbying to the more general question of democracy and legitimacy in the EU. To the extent that EU lobbying is viewed from the interest group or neo-corporatist perspectives this is not surprising. An exception is Anderson (1976, 1977) who demonstrates the lack of a positive underpinning of direct interest articulation. As long as interest group representation was regarded as a supplement to numerical democracy the problem of legitimacy was less acute.

A striking characteristic of EU lobbying is that it takes place in the context of a weak party system and a weak Parliament at the EU level (Mazey and Richardson, Eliassen 1995; Andersen and Eliassen 1995). Thus direct influence largely replaces the parliamentary channel as the most important means of influence, and this brings up the basic democratic problems in a more pressing way. As Mazey and Richardson state:

> Thus, although the Euro interest group system makes a major con-
> tribution to the system of representation and accountability, it re-
> tains exactly the same disadvantages that writers have long identi-
> fied at the national level. Firstly there is no guarantee that money
> and resources will not determine influence. Secondly, even the in-
> corporation of a wide range of groups into the policy process still
> means the private management of public business (1994a: 20).

On the other hand, the EU is in many important ways not a state in the same sense as the member states. Thus, there are many indirect ways parliamentary influence can be exercised at the EU level. The European Council, which is the locus of EU decision-making, is also a possible avenue for national parliamentary representation into the EU. This possibility does not, however, in any way eliminate the fundamental problem of legitimacy raised by EU lobbying. The increased importance of EU decision-making emphasises the need for a better understanding of EU lobbying with regard to influence as well as legitimacy.

Even if EU lobbying is problematic in relation to democratic theory, it is widely recognised as a key factor contributing to the efficiency of EU policy-making. In this pragmatic sense lobbying has contributed positively to the legitimacy of the system, and it has been an important precondition for the implementation of the 1992 program. The EU bureaucracy is small compared to member state bureaucracies and it has limited expertise and capacity. The paradox, however, is that because direct parliamentary influence is weak in the EU, there is a strong need for political reasons for consultation with affected interests. Thus, the independent legitimising aspect of lobbying is perceived as stronger rather than weaker in many quarters. However, the basic problem remains. The role of lobbying will be a recurrent theme in both public and academic debate as a context for further institutional reforms.

4

The Modern West European State and the European Union: Democratic Erosion or a New Kind of Polity?

Wolfgang Wessels

THE SEARCH FOR AN OPTIMAL DEMOCRATIC AREA

The European state system is in a dynamic evolution. Driven by the attempt to handle a twin set of basic dilemmas, the (Western) European states are forced to construct an effective as well as democratic system. The EC/EU as a 'mixed polity' is one of the major, yet incomplete, answers to these challenges.

This opening statement needs careful explanation:

(1)   We assume that – with due regard to the constitutional and territorial stability of Western Europe – in the post World War II period has witnessed considerable changes in the functions, procedures and thus the 'nature' of the 'state' (Poggi 1991).

(2)   We assume that this evolution is not accidental or circumstantial, but based on certain fundamentals; as one (not the only, but a highly relevant one) basic trend we identify the evolution of the European states towards welfare and service states (Tilly 1975; Flora 1986) which have to face an increasing degree of international interdependence affecting all sectors of traditional and new public policies.

(3)   This evolution is characterised by a twin set of dilemmas (Wessels 1992):

   (a) The 'multi-level-dilemma' indicates that for gaining and keeping national legitimacy European states have to guarantee sufficient effectiveness of their public policy instruments. For this end they have to open and thus to rely on positive inputs from the international or European arena. For the sake of political stability the state has to promote a process which leads to its very erosion.

(b) European states need efficient and effective institutions and procedures for preparing, taking and implementing decisions concerning the use of important public instruments and resources at the European level. The 'natural' instinctive reaction towards an intergovernmental co-operation is inefficient and ineffective. Federal constitutional solutions are, on the other hand, perceived as direct threats to the national constitutions. States thus get stuck between a *de facto* erosion (intergovernmental exit to the multi-level-dilemma) or a constitutional erosion (federal exit to the multi-level-dilemma) (Wessels 1994).

(4) As a consequence we assume that the states have to search for an optimal area which deals with the two major demands on states: to be effective but also democratic, i.e. that binding acts need to be subject to public control and participation in order to be accepted as legitimate. The dispute about the optimal size of a political entity is a classical issue which can be traced back to ancient political thought (Dahl 1989). It is generally held that the bigger a polity is, the higher are the costs for uniform regulations, the more numerous the minorities which cannot be satisfied, and finally the weaker the control by the individual citizen that can be exerted over the decision-makers (Sartori 1987; Dahl 1970; Dahl and Tufte 1973). We assume, however (though this is heavily disputed), that given the externalities of most public policies there is a trade-off between effectiveness and democratic participation and control (see Figure 4.1).

The larger the problem solution area (= Europeanization or internationalisation of policy solutions), the higher is the effectiveness in terms of scope, but the smaller proves to be the real influence of the 'people' in terms of political participation and accountability.

(5) We assume then that the EC/EU is the most prominent European answer to this search for a way out of the given dilemmas. By a 'fusion' (third exit to both dilemmas) of national and Community instruments major actors of the EU member states try to achieve both: an increase in effective-

Figure 4.1:

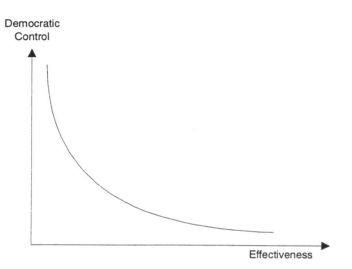

ness by applying public instruments for dealing with ineffi-
ciencies and to keep a major say by a broad and intensive
participation.

The complexity of the EC/EU procedures is thus not accidental but an unwanted result of this strategy. The product in the making – with the Maastricht Treaty as an inter-
mediate step – is a 'mixed polity' (Barker 1959: 477ff.). In
an analogy to the view of Aristotle, it combines several different national and communitarian elements to a political
system, describing thus a constitution which awards some
share of political authority to several levels of governance
and includes a multitude of different sources of direct and
indirect, functional, legal and democratic legitimacy. The
EU is thus a new stage in the history of Western European
states.

(6)   With a look to the future, we assume that the present state
of the EU is neither perfect nor stationary. The battle between direct participation and functional effectiveness will
continue. The debate about Maastricht and the 1996 IGC
offers a broad range of exits.

THE BASIC THRUST OF THE ARGUMENT: DILEMMA AND EXITS

The modern Western European state has since World War II been characterised by a high degree of political stability and economic prosperity – both elements proved to be mutually reinforcing. Acceptance by the citizens was generated not least by providing an ever-growing amount of social and welfare services (Flora 1986: xxi–xxv), thus increasing the legitimacy of the liberal democracies. This can be regarded as part of a 'universal tendency' (Ritter 1989: 193); the welfare and service state is made responsible for the material well-being of its citizens. For this, economic growth is deemed indispensable.

On the other hand, in order to achieve economic growth the (Western) European states increasingly need to open their markets and thus the frontiers of state action. A tendency towards the 'open state' (Vogel 1964: 33) can be made out which leads to an ever stronger interpenetration of national economies. Governments and administrations have to rely more and more on the joint management of social and welfare functions.

The growing interconnectedness and interference within the highly modernised western world leads to a loss of state autonomy – the independence of the nation state is eroded by global interdependence. Domestically, growing claims are launched by the public which have to be satisfied by the governments and administrations. A gap emerges between high demands for allocative (regulatory), distributional (welfare) and stabilisation (macroeconomic) policies (Musgrave 1959), accompanied by decreasing capacities for offering effective instruments and thus causing a vicious circle of mutually reinforcing elements.

The above mentioned change of basic conditions leads to a new constellation defining the limits and possibilities of the modern Western European state. In order to improve its economic capability and performance, the welfare state is forced to further open its boundaries to the global system, and, on the other hand, the negative consequences of this situation must again be countered by the increased use of public instruments, whose effectiveness is ever less striking and efficient in national terms (Cameron 1978: 1256; Katzenstein 1985). 'The hard shell of the social state' (Kaiser 1970: 66) is broken, and the absolute pretension of the parliamentary constitutional state succumbs to lasting 'eroding tendencies' (Scharpf 1991: 622). In order to work smoothly, the nation state must undermine its own foundations.

The notion of sovereignty becomes disputed, and even state functions such as internal security are now difficult to manage by the nation state alone (Held 1991: 224). Given this situation, it may appear necessary for governments and administrations to attempt to influence the use of public policy measures which lie outside their territory and constitutional sovereignty. The intensive and direct participation in the decision making at the European and wider international level seems to be the only realistic way to 'regain sovereignty or national political influence on the welfare of our citizens' (Kuhnle 1991: 20; Nugent 1994: 434).

This development can be described in short as the transformation of a virtuous circle into a vicious circle. A mutually reinforcing correlation between economic growth and political stability (of the parliamentary systems) could be made out, and which was translated into a high degree of public support and acceptance. This 'virtuous circle' was broken up by globalising tendencies, depriving the nation-state simply of the means to fulfil its role and maintain the equation between socioeconomic performance on the one hand and democratic legitimacy on the other. The stabilisation by successful policy-making gave way to the potentiation of incapabilities and insufficiencies; the nation state was caught in an accelerating dynamic revealing its lack of power to act autonomously and effectively. A chain reaction of growing, but unfulfilled, demands and increasing disappointment among the citizens was triggered off, leading to a loss of political support for governments and political parties. To counter this development, governments must find ways of tackling problems in the international and especially European arena. But the extent and quality of such action is highly disputed.

There are two major strategies offering alternative exits from the erosion process (Wessels 1994): to strengthen the intergovernmental co-operation or to build up a federal state.

Each of these options is pointing at specific problems: in the first case, following the 'lessons' of the regime school (Krasner 1984; Kohler-Koch 1989), it is the deficit in implementing and controlling common decisions which reduces the effectiveness of common or co-ordinated instruments to a degree which reinforces or at least keeps up the *de facto* erosion of national public policies.

The federalist approach (Spinelli 1958; Mayne and Pinder 1987; Wistrich 1994: 164), on the other hand, threatens the constitutional and national character of Western European states. Here, the question is to what degree the political public will accept paying the price of losing points of reference for national identification and also emotional links. The Maastricht debates have shown quite clearly that social and political sensitivity is widespread in Western Europe and that even politicians formerly regarded as convinced integrationists have ceased speaking of a federal political system as something like the 'United States of Europe' (Schneider and Wessels 1994: 7f.).

In the EC/EU case actors are looking for the 'third way'. National governments make a calculation which, in their own interest, is oriented towards a successful problem-solving; this calculation must go beyond the patterns of mere co-operation. The relinquishment of a state's autonomy is thus made at least tolerable. 'Viewed from a broader perspective, the EU is not only the cause of a decline in national powers, but it is also a response to decline' (Nugent 1994: 434; Milward 1993).

The states concerned are able to address domestic and other problems more efficiently through the specific procedures of the EU for preparing and taking binding decisions and more effectively through the common control of their implementation. This calculation of governments, however, does not go as far as traditional federalists expected. National actors within the EC/EU system still have an important say, a voluntary and complete loss of sovereignty does not lie in the self-interest of governments and administrations. The joint use of public instruments can be seen as a 'psychological compensation for the loss of national competence' (Oppermann 1991: 631). Thus, integration is the creative evolution of the state' (Isensee 1987: 630) and the multilevel game acquires a new dimension for economic and social actors.

AFTER MAASTRICHT: LEGITIMACY REVISITED – THE MEGA-BUREAUCRACY OF BRUSSELS OR A NEW POLITY?

The Maastricht Europe as the product of a fusion process evokes an increasingly intensive debate about its legitimacy. Two views oppose each other, both reflecting basic schools of thought about the optimal area for democracy and indeed about democracy itself.

One view – the more outspoken in the post-Maastricht period – perceives the complexity of the Maastricht Treaty – explained by us as the fusion process – as a direct threat to democracy. Two slightly different aspects are touched upon. One dimension is concerned by the attack on constitutionalism (see, e.g., Bundesverfassungsgericht 1993): by and through this system the competencies of the constituent bodies of the nation states are *de jure* and even more *de facto* substituted by non-national bodies; as there is no European people (only European peoples as the Treaty indicates), no direct democratic legitimacy can be claimed by the European bodies (Lübbe 1994: 100; Bundesverfassungsgericht 1993). Because of that, the directly elected European Parliament does not dispose of an 'unfiltered' legitimacy similar to that of national parliaments. The transfer of competencies can only be limited and must always be linked to the real sources of legitimacy, namely national politicians and especially national parliaments.

The citizens loose the feeling of loyalty towards 'their state' and, by this, also the notion of solidarity with other citizens. They see themselves confronted by a complex system of different layers of functional organisations on several territorial levels which cannot stimulate any kind of sufficient basic support (Delbrück 1987: 390). A second aspect of the critical view concerns the effects of the complexity on democratic accountability, transparency and participation. Two basic features characterising the relationship between decision-makers and the electorate in the national framework – congruence and symmetry – are severely questioned (Held 1991: 198). The 'average citizen' looses any possibility of following the political process and of influencing its outputs. Furthermore, the rational voter cannot sanction any single person or party for a positive or negative performance. The 'benevolent diffusion of responsibility' (Scharpf 1985: 349) is not compatible with the notion of democratic accountability. Both aspects create the image of a mega-bureaucracy in Brussels which is putting the major historical achievements of democratic evolution into jeopardy. The Commission was described in this sense by de Gaulle as a 'technocratic, irresponsible and fatherless' organ (de Gaulle 1965). This school of thought accepts the argument of effectiveness only to a limited degree. Indeed, a liberal economic strategy claims that larger units even reduce effectiveness. The (open) state guaranteeing an optimal game for market forces is the model to be pursued.

The opposite school of thought on the question of legitimacy stresses the highly differentiated participation of a multitude of actors from several territorial levels and functional groups. This view sees in the fusion process the Europeanisation of many 'representatives' of the citizen. From the highest political authorities in the European Council to the sectoral interest groups the actors within the EC/EU system bring their respective legitimacy into the new polity (Wessels 1992: 51). Thus several different functional, legal and political sources of legitimacy are fused. The procedures, by their very complexity, may lead to a broad 'permissive consensus' (Inglehart 1971) in the EU. In this sense, the EC/EU should not be regarded as 'an embryonic superstate and supernation, but as one organ in a system of complex governance, consisting of multi-tiered, geographically overlapping structures of government and non-government elites. There is certainly an increasing degree of co-operation, in vertical terms between different government levels, and in horizontal terms among several groups of actors' (Kirchner 1994: 264; Schneider 1986: 97).

Irrespective of some possibilities for majority voting the European Union is and remains in basic characteristics a 'concordance system' (Hrbek 1988), i.e. a system 'wherein actors find it possible to consistently harmonise their interests, compromise their differences and reap mutual reward from their interaction' (Puchala 1972: 277). The fusion implies a new exercise in indirect democracy and is, in this sense, a 'saut qualitatif' in democracy: a new kind of democracy for a larger area – not perfect but a major step forward, or as Robert Dahl puts it, 'a transformation on a larger scale: from democracy in the national state to democracy in the transnational state...freedom and control might be lost on one front, they could yet be gained on others' (Dahl 1989: 321).

In comparison, this view looks more promising in explaining one major feature of the evolution of the European Union. In spite of a widening and deepening in the last decades, the EC/EU has been characterised by an overall constitutional and political stability, and by a high degree of attractiveness, at least to those EFTAN and CEE states outside.

The 'mixed polity' is not yet complete: some groups of actors are still not involved. High on the list are national parliaments (see the Declaration on the Conference of Parliaments of the Maastricht Treaty), but also the idea of a new court by national supreme courts (The European Constitutional Group 1993) has been launched. If some of these proposals materialise the complexity but also the degree of indirect representation will increase even further.

A major condition for this school of thought is the attitudes of the population – what has been called 'permissive consensus' (Inglehart 1971). Within this set of attitudes the normal European citizen accepts the European Union as fundamentally 'good' (in the same way that 'peace' is accepted) and – on a low level of knowledge and interest – trusts his/her representatives to do the best for them in that complex process. Thus a major factor for the evolution of the EU is how far existing 'elites' involved in national and European policy making are 'real representatives'. The degree of trust between citizens and the political class (von Beyme 1993) is again determined by several factors partly dependent on each other. Image (e.g. reputation) and success, especially in economic terms, will certainly be crucial elements for this fundamental support.

Finally, the problem of legitimacy is not regarded as a minor point, but requires a careful and sober assessment: 'The legitimacy gap of the EU, like that of the individual traditional nation-states in Europe, is a major problem and needs to be taken seriously, but it should also be recognised as a virtually unavoidable part of an evolution in which member states merge and pool their public legal and budgetary means. A 'neo-medieval' situation of overlapping competencies is the product....' (Wessels 1994: 456).

SCENARIOS AND STRATEGIES IN THE POST-MAASTRICHT ERA

The Treaty on European Union is a 'package deal' (H. Wallace 1990: 238f.; Keohane and Hoffmann 1990: 285) characterised by an inherent dynamic with its own in-built logic of change and adjustment, resulting from its own shortcomings but also from the changes in its environment. One essential part of this need for reform is the still unsatisfied (and perhaps never adequately fulfilled) desire for more participatory and democratic structures and procedures. The EU finds itself in permanent tension, and thus cannot be a stationary and immobile phenomenon.

Some basic scenarios for the further evolution of the EU can be envisaged. The positive outlook will be based on the following assumptions:

(a) With an economic upswing the EU might regain some of its popular acceptance as it did in the second half of the 1980s when the plans for 1992 raised broad positive reactions.

(b) Real progress (even though slow) in implementing Maastricht and the new accessions will favour a renaissance of the permissive consensus.

(c) A group of 'fresh' national leaders could raise more trust than the outworn elites and personalities. The 1980s had a group of statepersons such as Kohl, Thatcher, Mitterrand, Lubbers and González, who each by him/herself inspired a sense of dynamics in the EU.

A negative outlook would assume:

(a) '1989' has not only changed dramatically the international and European environment but also withdrawn some implicit conditions for the fusion of European welfare states: with no threat from the East and a new internal equilibrium (German unification) new (=old) nationalistic perceptions will re-emerge.

(b)   The debate about Maastricht indicates a fundamental structural change: now that the EU becomes serious (high politics) citizens will not stay in a 'subject political culture' (Almond and Verba 1963: 17f.) of a permissive consensus.

(c)   The political systems of member states (irrespective of the EC/EU dimension) have been discredited by 'small' and 'high' corruption (Meny 1992), i.e. the present national elite is perceived more as a 'political class' (von Beyme 1993) oriented towards its own interests than as representatives of the public good. The complexity of the EC/EU can thus be explained as an extreme, though typical, way of self-immunisation. In this case the first step is to improve the means of direct democracy; a further step might be to dismantle the EC/EU altogether.

Closely related to these mentioned scenarios is a wide range of alternative options (see Figure 4.2) regarding the future of the Maastricht Treaty and thus of the European integration process as a whole. These are discussed as strategies of political orientation and action and will directly affect the issues of democracy and legitimacy (Wessels 1994).

Figure 4.2: *The Future of the Maastricht Treaty*

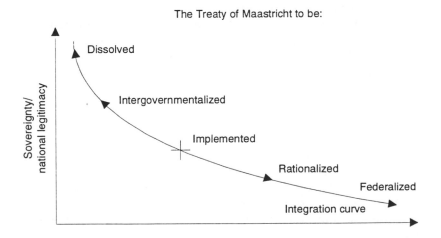

(a)   The first of these strategies can be called the solution of 'implementing Maastricht'. In this view it would serve best to apply fully the provisions of the Treaty on European Union which is regarded as the most attractive option available at the moment. As Maastricht reflects a compromise subscribed to by all member states it would not be desirable and might even be dangerous to put into question this agreement. Compared with the previous situation, Maastricht is considered as an important improvement. With regard to democratic accountability and legitimacy, major progress can be made out, especially concerning the increase in power of the European Parliament (procedure of co-decision; appointment of the Commission) and the stipulations on union citizenship. This might not be the final leap towards a federal Europe, but it can still be seen as an incremental step leaving open the future development of a more integrated Europe.

(b)   A second approach considers the reforms introduced by the Treaty as insufficient, particularly with regard to the democratic quality of the European Union. With a view to 1996, the demands for more democratic institutions are placed on the agenda, being inserted in a kind of European constitution drafted according to federal principles. The division of powers should be expressed particularly in a bicameral Parliament, with the existing EP as the first chamber and majority voting in the Council being the regular case; the Commission is envisioned as the future European government depending politically upon the will of the electorate channelled through the EP.

(c)   The last point of view finds its counterpart in the option of 'renationalising Maastricht'. The Treaty is regarded as a premature step overstretching the political will and capacities of the governments and especially of the citizens. Furthermore, an excessive centralisation and bureaucratisation is identified by this school of thought. Democratic quality can first and foremost be claimed by the nation-states, the European Union enjoying only a kind of derived and 'mediated' legitimacy. This view is characterised by hesitant and sometimes contradictory attitudes towards the integration process. The subsidiarity principle should serve as a regulatory idea which will lead to the transfer of competencies back to the national level where this is deemed necessary

by the governments. Instead of enhancing the role of the
EP, the Commission and the Court, it should be the European Council, the Ministers and committees of national civil
servants which control and determine the integration process.

d)   Even further, there is the strategy of 'abandoning
Maastricht'. The whole notion of integration and thus legitimacy on a European level becomes disputed and is rejected by the adherents of this approach. After '1989', the
stimulus of European unification and its main fundamentals have ceased to be valid, and this reinforces the nation-
state as the sole source of legitimacy and democratic accountability. The nation-state in Europe is – according to
this point of view – after some years of externally enforced
hibernation alive and well. The Maastricht Treaty is to be
abandoned or at least fundamentally revised in the sense
of a 'deconstitutionalization'. The existing institutions
should be submitted to a drastic revision, even allowing for
the cutting back of their competencies; the very principle of
supranationality is rejected.

THE EU: A NEW KIND OF POLITY?

In contrast to the preceding points of view, if the approach of 'rational-
ising Maastricht' is to be pursued it will need to take into account both
the major setbacks as well as the advantages of the Treaty on European Union. The first step would be to take Maastricht seriously; and
the second to propose significant reforms of the provisions. Maastricht
reflects the fundamentals of the integration process and has not become outdated after '1989'. It is in the first place not a threat to the
nation-state, but reflects a strategy of strengthening its role and functions and enabling it to face the challenges of an interdependent world,
without, however, leaving its character and nature unaffected. The price
of transformation has to be paid unless the nation-state is to be paralysed and even eroded by its own limits and incapacities. Legitimacy
and democratic responsibility cannot be 'counted in national currency',
i.e. that they are also included in the fundamental trends which characterise the whole process of European unification since its very beginning – especially the increase of procedural and institutional complexity and differentiation. A horizontally and vertically interwoven, multi-
level set of actors and structures cannot provide for the same degree of

transparency and participation as witnessed in national frameworks. New categories are required not only for scientific research, but also of perception by the average citizen and the political public. Neither a federal leap nor a nationalistic 'relapse' can be considered as being in line with the logic of European integration.

Taking these final considerations, it becomes clear that a new approach towards the system of the European Union is more necessary than ever. Especially with regard to its democratic quality, hitherto unused and even strange conclusions can be drawn. As the institutional setting of the EU does not correspond entirely to national models and realities, i.e. its character can be regarded as 'sui generis', it should not surprise the observer that democratic legitimacy is not to be found in familiar terms. But this does not mean that it does not exist at all. In analogy to Aristotle's concept of 'polity' and its specific connotations (and not only in the wider sense of a form of political organisation), the EU can be regarded as a unique phenomenon.

Aristotle defined his 'polity' as a 'mixed form of constitution in which elements are judiciously combined from oligarchy and democracy. Its social foundation is the existence of a large middle class composed of those who are neither very rich nor very poor' (Sabine 1973: 115f.). Our mixed polity called the EU is not the ideal, but a highly practicable and thus 'optimal' form of government. It combines several levels of governance and a wide range of actors, thus creating a complex and highly differentiated entity which can be regarded as a solution to the problems of modern Western European welfare and service states. This mixture is in a constant evolution, adjusting its components to the needs and demands from different directions. As to the Greek philosopher, the maintenance of a balance between the categories of quantity and quality can be regarded as essential. In the case of the EU, this equilibrium is in many ways more 'sophisticated' – on the one hand because of the larger dimensions of actors and levels of action included, and on the other hand due to the dynamic character of integration.

The European Union as a developing phenomenon reflects basic features of the integration process whose final outcome remains open and undefined. This is a chance and a threat at the same time. Discussions on the future of European integration will never come to an end, and proposals demanding an abandoning of the whole endeavour may always be heard. We think that, given the logics of European unification and its inherent dynamics, the task of finding accurate forms of assuring its democratisation and the reinforcement of its legitimacy will be on the agenda as long as this process continues.

Part II
EU Policy-making and National Institutions

5

The French EU Decision-making: Between Destabilisation and Adaptation

Christian Lequesne

For more than forty years, the emergence of the Community political system has confronted the French state with a gradual process of 'Europeanization' (Ladrech 1994). The changes taking place within France's institutions and political processes show this with an intensity that has increased after the entry into force of the Single European Act (SEA) on 1 July 1987. Since then, there has been an acceleration of the impact of the European unification process on the functioning of the state in France. French society at large only became aware of this phenomenon with the signing of the Treaty on European Union (TEU) on 7 February 1992.

GOVERNMENTAL CO-ORDINATION: THE LIMITS OF THE HIERARCHICAL MODEL

Numerous studies have shown that, in Western Europe, the nation state has become a complex and segmented entity and, further, that it is no longer the only organiser of the 'social piloting'. Consequently, the phenomenon of administrative co-ordination can no longer be analysed as a search for harmony between single politico-administrative actors; it has to take into account a broader social context. Nevertheless, this does not mean that specific forms of co-ordination, of which the objective remains the maintenance of coherence within the state, can no longer be distinguished. In France, there is governmental co-ordination based on a hierarchical mechanism – a legacy of the Jacobean nation state – which, for the most part, has been reinforced during the Fifth Republic: the interministerial realm. From a formal point of view, this mechanism appears as a combination of organs (the General Secretariat of the Government, etc.), meetings (interministerial committees, interministerial meetings, etc.) and procedures (e.g. the technique of arbitration) that supervise the cabinet of the Prime Minister and to some extent that of the President of the Republic in order to hierarchize the different public policies (Fournier 1987).

In a very 'idiosyncratic' way, the French government has projected this hierarchical approach of co-ordination into the treatment of Community policies. Since the creation of the European Coal and Steel Community (ECSC), the definition of every position concerning several ministries before a Community Council is subjected to the filter of an organ composed of officials of different state administrations directly linked to the Prime Minister: the *Secrétariat Général du Comité Interministériel pour les Questions de Coopération Economique Européenne (SGCI)* (Lequesne 1993). As an obligatory intermediary between the ministries and the French Permanent Representation to the European Union, the SGCI originally intervened only in the formulation phase of the Community policies. From 1986 onwards, it has also been entrusted with the co-ordination of the normative implementation of Community policies on the national level and, from 1994 onwards, that of positions related to the third pillar of the European Union, that is justice and home affairs. Nevertheless, due to strong resistance from the Quai d'Orsay, the co-ordination of the Common Foreign and Security Policy (CFSP) has not been entrusted to the SGCI, which only intervenes if a CFSP joint action calls on Community instruments or policies.

In most cases, the meetings within the SGCI allow for the definition of common positions through a bureaucratic bargaining process before negotiations in the EU Council. If a point of contest persists between the ministries, the SGCI submits it to the cabinet of the Prime Minister which attempts to organise a renewed co-ordination with the advisers of the ministers in *interministerial meetings*. Moreover, the most sensitive questions (like, for example, the issue of the General Agreement on Tariffs and Trade in 1993) may lead to a meeting of the concerned ministers under the presidency of the Prime Minister. This is thus known as the convocation of the interministerial committee or – in a more informal phrasing – of a meeting of ministers. Resuming a practice that had become obsolete during the 1980s, Prime Minister Edouard Balladur brought together an interministerial committee every month devoted to European affairs in order to get to the point with the members of his government on current 'big' issues and also to settle certain important positions. During these high level meetings in Matignon (i.e. the seat of the Prime Minister), the cabinet of the Prime Minister – knowing that the Secretary General of the SGCI often acts as an adviser – or the Prime Minister himself may *arbitrate* between the conflicting positions of the ministers when a consensus has not been reached. The dyarchic nature of the Fifth Republic provides only a single means to challenge this power of arbitration of the Prime Minister through the intervention of the President of the Republic. The conflictual atmosphere of the first 'cohabitation' (March 1986–March 1988) has reinforced this phenomenon on several occasions (Lequesne 1993).

As long as the scope of Community policies was limited to customs union, energy policy, competition policy, agricultural policy, commercial policy, social policy, and while the EC Council of Ministers was the dominant decision-making organ deciding by consensus, this hierarchical process of interministerial co-ordination produced policy coherence. However, the progressive widening of the Community agenda from the mid 1970s and the institutional reforms introduced by the SEA and the TEU have made the decision-making process more atomised, and in the process revealed serious limitations in the hierarchical process.

Even though the Prime Minister, in a circular of 21 March 1994, reinforced the procedure that contacts between representatives of the administration and the services of the Commission had absolutely to be prepared in concert with the SGCI, it is in fact impossible for the latter to co-ordinate all the exchanges that the officials of the ministries have daily with those of the Commission and the representatives of interest groups in order to explore sector by sector the orientation of the Community policies. Despite the creation of posts responsible for relations with the European Parliament within the main ministries whose activities have to be co-ordinated by the SGCI, the latter is, in the same way, no longer in a position to control all relations developing between the officials of the ministries and the members of the European Parliament since the SEA. Finally, it would be even more illusionary for the SGCI to pretend to exercise systematic control over the informal flows of communication between the local political and administrative actors, the representatives of local economic interests, the administrations of the prefectures and those of the Commission for the implementation of the EC regional policies.

The French government is coping with the new situation in which the European unification process imposes new ways of making decisions based on horizontal and informal networking, whereas the French internal decision-making system was built on the principle of vertical hierarchy. It has had to accept that the formulation of Community policies means that each directorate, each ministerial cabinet or simply each official expresses the interests of sectoral networks including elected members (local, national, European), officials (of the Commission, other member states, local communities) and the representatives of interest groups. If the SGCI is thus more than ever invited, in the official statements of the governments, to maintain the constraint of formal hierarchical co-ordination, this is because Community policies are more and more the product of an addition of 'micro-negotiations' and of 'micro-decisions' carried out in different political and administrative settings and no longer centrally controllable. In such a new configuration of decision-making, governmental co-ordination means monitoring various administrative autonomies more than exercising an absolute control on all the policy process from the centre.

THE LOCAL AUTHORITIES: MORE LINKS WITH BRUSSELS DOES NOT MEAN THAT THE STATE IS OUT

In France, no procedure provides a formal link between local authorities and the formulation in the central government of positions for Council negotiations. There are, however, numerous informal channels for regions and other local authorities – departments and communes – to be heard by the government or Community institutions, including representation by elected members in national and European parliaments and by the activities of interest groups.

Despite the decentralisation process which started in 1982, the twenty-two regions of France are not in charge in the negotiations for the inter-regional distribution of Community credits available under structural funds. It is the state, through the ministries, the *Délégation à l'Aménagement du Territoire* (DATAR), the SGCI and the permanent representation, that negotiates the targets of intervention and the areas of eligibility. The regions may, however, intervene later when the Commission presents the regional plans for which it fixes the criterias, i.e. the *Cadre Communautaire d'Appui*. Specialists agree that, when structural funds are implemented, the state administrations – particularly the regional prefectural services (SGAR) – play a decisive role in the co-ordination, monitoring and control of Community programmes because of their expertise and their neutrality vis-à-vis the local political arena (Balme and Le Galè 1995; Balme 1995).

Direct representation of regions and departments in Brussels has nevertheless increased noticeably following the SEA. In 1994 sixteen regions out of twenty-two had direct representation. Their offices are either individual (Nord-Pas-de-Calais, Rhône-Alpes), or represent groups of several regions (for instance, the office for the 'Grand Sud' represents the interest of the six regions of the south). All these offices use a 'lobbyist' type of approach, directed first and foremost towards the Commission. Their objective is to inform private and public regional actors of the funds and contracts offered by the different DGs, to follow the elaboration of proposals that might affect the local economy and, finally, to promote activities for crossborder co-operation which offer the most autonomy for French regions vis-à-vis the State. The Commission encourages this type of activity, for example through the INTEREG programme which contributed 800 million ECUs to French regions in 1990–93. The implementation of these programmes can create strong tensions between the prefects and the regional politicians, particularly because the latter have more difficulty in accepting state control of the credits when the state is not seen to add anything to them (Balme 1995).

The regions are also directing their lobbying activities to the European Parliament, as the cumulation of mandates – which French MEPs are used to – allows for local interest to be taken into account. An example is the 'Atlantic group' of the European Parliament, which is constituted of deputies from the Atlantic coastal area dominated predominantly by the French. This group seems to have played an important role in the widening of the criterias of eligibility of the STRIDE programme (development of regional capacity in research and technology) to rural and maritime areas. It has also contributed to the process of creating the TGV line from Paris to Madrid which crosses the Atlantic axis (Balme 1995).

THE NATIONAL PARLIAMENT: FROM INFORMATION TO CONTROL

In all EU member states, the growing interference of Community policies with domestic legislative activities has led the national parliaments to claim a closer association with the definition of positions negotiated within the Council. In France, this demand of the national Parliament has grown during the ratification of the TEU (La Serre and Lequesne 1993). Taking advantage of the reform proposed by the President of the Republic, with a view to rendering the Constitution more compatible with certain clauses of this treaty, the National Assembly and the Senate adopted in June 1992 a new article 88–4 which stipulates that:

> The government submits propositions comprising clauses of legislative nature to the National Assembly and the Senate as early as their transmission to the Council of the Communities. During or outside parliamentary sessions, resolutions may be voted upon [...], according to modalities established by the statute of each assembly.

Even if these resolutions are not legally binding on the government, the fact that Parliament can resort to them is a sign that its powers concerning Community policies are advancing progressively from simple information to control. A circular from the Prime Minister of 21 April 1993 completely reorganised relations between the French government and the national Parliament as a result of from the application of article 88–4.

The SGCI is instructed about all propositions from the Commission, and it has to distinguish between two categories of texts. Firstly, those which are susceptible of comprising 'clauses of legislative nature' (in the sense of the French law defined in article 34 of the Constitution of 1958) and are required to be specifically transmitted to Parliament according to the terms of article 88–4. Secondly, those that are, according to the terms of a law of 10 May 1990, for simple information, transmitted to the Delegations for the European Union that have existed within the two assemblies since 1979. The propositions susceptible of being dependent on the procedure of 88–4 are thus transmitted to the Conseil d`Etat which then has of fifteen days to render an opinion about their legislative nature. The ministries – theoretically alone but in practice together with the SGCI – have eight days to examine the legislative texts that have to be modified or repealed. After an examination by its different administrative sections (and, in some cases, by its general assembly), the Conseil d'Etat produces an opinion. It is then up to the SGG to formally apprise the presidents of the National Assembly and of the Senate. While for the government, the national parliament only represented a marginal constraint in the formulation of Community policies until 1992, the procedure of 88–4 has turned it into a binding 'link' of the interministerial work.

The transmission to the Parliament of Commission propositions containing dispositions of a legislative nature is based on a long bureaucratic procedure. It is, therefore, not surprising to find that a year after its introduction, an average of one month passed between the moment when the SGCI obtained the propositions of the Commission and when the SGG forwarded them to Parliament for the latter to examine them and, if necessary, to vote on resolutions. Some propositions were even transmitted while the EU Council had already adopted them in Brussels, an event strongly criticised by parliamentarians. The debate on the deeper association of the French parliament to EU affairs shows how difficult it is to reconcile domestic procedures for setting agendas and the speed of decision making with Community procedures. To avoid the situation where Parliament cannot comment on a text because it had not been consulted in time, a circular from the Prime Minister of 19 July 1994 introduced important changes. Under the pressure of the French MPs inspired by the British example, it invites ministers as far as possible to oppose the inclusion on the Council agenda of any proposition containing dispositions of legislative nature on which the national Parliament had not been able to comment or, else, to subordinate the passing of votes in the Council to a later opinion by the national Parliament. This reversed a long-standing French position: the principle of reserves for parliamentary examination had been for a very long time, completely unacceptable to French governments because it was considered to be contrary to their constitutional monopoly in the sphere of international negotiations. This development indicates that Community policies are no longer assimilated with foreign policy within the French government. It also perfectly illustrates how a domestic political process can gradually be 'Europeanized'.

THE INTERMEDIATION STATE-INTEREST GROUPS: TOWARDS MORE PLURALISM?

The neo-corporatist grid of analysis has never been applied to the case of France because institutionalised macro-negotiation between the state and the main social organisations never established itself there (Cox and Hayward 1983; Jorbert and Muller 1987). At the same time, a mediation of the sectoral corporatist type between the state administrations and the interest groups has, over a long period, allowed for the coherence of public action (Suleiman 1976; Jorbert and Muller 1987). Considered 'inappropriate as soon as the problems to be treated require an approach which no longer coincides with the existing cleavages', (Jorbert and Muller 1987), this kind of mediation has also been challenged by developments in European Community, particular by since the launching of the internal market programme.

By allowing national interest groups to use several channels of pressure in parallel (Commission, European Parliament, European professional federations), the European Community has contributed to making the French model of sectoral corporatism evolve toward a more pluralist character (Streeck and Schmitter 1991). This pluralism encourages competition and the fragmentation of interests, and less easily authorises *one* French administration (or *one* administrative 'corps') to claim to control the formulation or implementation of *one* policy in symbiosis with what were traditionally called in France 'les professions'. In their study of the 1992 reform of the Common Agricultural Policy, Francois-Gilles Le Theule and David Litvan show how the system of shattered representation of interests at the Community level is a factor (among others) that has contributed to the Ministry of Agriculture and the main French agricultural unions being incapable of producing a common position vis-à-vis the Commission and the other member states (Le Theule and Litvan 1993). Similar conclusions could be drawn, in the French case, from the import policy of Japanese cars (1991) or the reform of the Common Fisheries Policy (1993).

Secondly, because the European unification process relies very often on frame-objectives ('objective 1992' being the most obvious example) to stimulate its development, it forces the actors to consider the agenda in a more anticipatory way. Hence the expertise function which, in the Community realm, is, however, rarely the monopoly of a single actor. On the contrary, there is a competition of expertises which are carried out in parallel and often without any co-ordination within the Commission, the committees of the European Parliament, the socio-professional organisations and, of course, the national governments. For a long time concentrated within the SGCI, expertise on Community policies has, with the debate on the internal market, tended to diversify itself in France even if remaining within the state apparatus. One of the institutional translations of this evolution has been the development by the central administration of new mediating structures in order to hierarchize priorities with the interest groups. These structures have mostly associated high ranking civil servants with local representatives, heads of business, bankers, unionists, academics or else representatives of non-profit associations. Examples of this include the 'committee on economic reflexion for the preparation of the 1992 deadline,' chaired from 1987 to 1988 by Marcel Boiteux, honorary president of the EDF; the 'groups for study and mobilisation', (GEM) initiated in September 1988 by Edith Cresson, Minister for European Affairs, and revived in 1991–1992 during her short stay in Matignon. The analyst has nevertheless to be very cautious when considering the real effects of these new structures of intermediation. The need for more 'outside' expertise relating to the 1992 deadline does not allow the conclusion that the decisions taken by the French governments have taken more effectively into account the pressures of the interest groups. Besides, the effort to associate the social actors with the project of the internal market was not continued with the more political project of the European Union. During all the negotiations leading to the Maastricht Treaty, expertise was the monopoly of the central state administration (and within it, of a specialised network of ministers and high-ranking bureaucrats) which pursued it in a situation of splendid isolation. Parliament and the public *discovered and reacted to the treaty a posteriori,* during the ratification debate.

CONCLUSION

Even if the French state continues to be based on the Jacobean principles of hierarchy and dependency which have traditionally inspired it, it has not escaped from the tendencies, since the end of the Second World War, towards greater sectorisation and segmentation which the European unification process has reinforced. From this results a general evolution of the French policy style from hierarchy towards more inter-organisational negotiation. Political processes, such as the relations between the government and the Parliament, or the forms of mediation between the state and the interest groups, are all affected by this 'Europeanization', a process characterised more by incremental adaptations than radical change.

6
European Union Policy-making and National Institutions – the Case of Belgium

Cecilia Andersen

This chapter analyses the contribution which Belgium can make to more democratic decision making in the European Union.

In recent decades, Belgium has realised a far-reaching federalisation process with extensive consequences for the way in which the country deals with its rights and obligations in the context of the European Union. Belgium has also dealt in a very pragmatic way with a series of issues relevant for the further democratisation of the European Union. Information on the experience of Belgium can be very useful in the broader context of the analysis of ways to obtain more democracy in the European Union.

The chapter will deal with the following topics:

- the federalisation process in Belgium;
- the Belgian approach to democratic deficits in the European Union;
- reconciling Belgian regionalism with European Union obligations;
- Belgian pragmatism in handling of the Presidency of the Council of Ministers;
- what Belgium can contribute to the democratisation process of the European Union.

THE BELGIAN FEDERALISATION PROCESS

The Belgian federalisation process is a unique and very complex attempt to federalise a hitherto unitary state. Belgium has only been independent since 1830 but in its short history it has coped with serious threats of division. It has three official languages: Dutch, French and German. The Dutch and French-speaking population form the two major linguistic groups in Belgium, each living in geographically separated parts of the country: the Flemings in the north (Flanders), and the Walloons (French-speaking) in the south (Wallonia), with, since 1989, a 'mixed' bilingual zone (Brussels-Capital) in between. The German-speaking population forms only a small group located in the Eupen-Sankt Vith area in the east of Belgium.

In recent years, the country has beocome a federal state in which the role of national sovereignty is much less than in the other European Union countries.

Before 1980, the Belgian Unitary State had three levels of government: the national government level, which operated in conjunction with the bicameral parliament; the provincial level with nine provinces; and the municipal level of the 589 municipalities. Since 1980, however, two new sets of institutions have been positioned alongside the national government: three Regional and three 'Community-level' institutions. Today, Belgium is a federal state with a Central (Federal) Government, three Regions and three Communities.

The competencies of the Regions and Communities have constantly expanded in recent years and are expected to increase still further.

The Federal Government has substantially curtailed powers but remains responsible for matters such as defence, justice, the printing of money and foreign affairs.

The three Regions are Dutch-speaking 'Flanders', French-speaking 'Wallonia', and the bilingual 'Region of Brussels-Capital'. The Regions have far-reaching responsibilities. They are, for example, responsible for town and country planning, research, environmental protection, housing, foreign trade, energy policy, employment policy, public works and transport. Economic policy is in a special category. The division of responsibilities and competencies for economic policy between the different governments is not always clear. In principle economic policy falls within the responsibilities of the Regions. Nevertheless, Federal government is responsible when it concerns national interests or monetary policy. A special feature of Belgian regionalism is the fact that the three Regions have the right to sign treaties with other nations.

The impetus behind the three Communities is the existence of different cultural and linguistic factors. The Flemish Community operates in the Dutch-speaking region and in the bilingual region of Brussels. The French Community has its centre of activity in the French-speaking region and in the bilingual region of Brussels. The German Community deals with the German-speaking population.

The responsibilities and competencies of the Communities are the policy domains of culture, education and the so-called person-bound matters (healthcare, youth protection, and so on). The cultural policy domain includes, among other matters, the arts, cultural heritage, tourism, broadcasting and linguistic matters.

The Government and Assemblies of the Flanders Region and the Flemish Community have merged to form the so-called Flemish Government and the Flemish Council, both of which are based in Brussels. The Government and the Assembly of the French-language Community are also located in Brussels. The Government and the Council of the Walloon Region are located in Namur. Brussels also houses the Government and the Council of the bilingual Region of Brussels as well as two Community Commissions: the 'Commission Communautaire Française' (French Community Commission) and the 'Vlaamse Gemeenschapskommissie' (Flemish Community Commission). The French Commission groups the French-speaking members of the Council of Brussels-Capital. The Flemish Commission groups the Dutch-speaking members of the Council of Brussels-Capital. Matching the two Community Commissions are two executive authorities: the Colleges. There is also a joint Community Commission for Brussels-Capital which is responsible for those matters, such as health care, which cannot be divided between the two Communities.

Four special characteristics make the Belgian federalisation process unique (Delpérée 1993):

(a) Belgian federalism stresses dissociation and not association. Responsibilities are entrusted to entities which are specially created to that effect.
(b) Belgian federalism leads to a situation where all Belgian citizens are simultaneously subject to various layers of laws: Federal Laws, Community Decrees and Regional Decrees. To these must be added the provincial and communal rules as well as the European Union rules.
(c) Belgian federalism is confrontational and not collaborative. The Belgian federalisation process is dominated by two political streams of thought: those of Flanders and of Wallonia. Harmonious collaboration permits the smooth functioning of the Federal government but disagreements lead to block-

ages and to the inevitable need to resort to 'Belgian style' compromises. The new 1993 constitution contains such a compromise. Anxious to obtain the required support of the ultra Flemish party (the 'Volksunie'), the legislators accepted the following compromise: 'The Communities and Regions are competent in all matters excepting those which the Constitution and laws, adopted in virtue of this Constitution, formally attribute to the Federal Government.' (Delpérée 1993). The residual powers are therefore no longer federal but federated.

(d)   The Belgian federalisation process may not yet be a concluded process. For certain political groups and persons the ultimate aim is the complete independence of Flanders and Wallonia.

The Belgian federalisation process results in various 'governments' operating within the geographic context of Belgium and having the democratic right to be involved in European Union developments. As a consequence, the unique Belgian federalisation process affects the European integration process and thereby contributes to democratic developments in the European Union.

THE BELGIAN CONTRIBUTION TO THE DEMOCRATISATION OF THE EUROPEAN UNION

The main democratic deficits of the European Union are:

–   the absence of a meaningful European-level citizenship for the citizens of Member States;
–   the limited Parliamentary involvement in the processes which are determining the further integration of Europe.

The Treaty on European Union contains the first provisions for the ultimate emergence of a meaningful European citizenship over and above national citizenship in that the notion of European citizenship is recognised in the Treaty. Additionally, the Treaty accords to residents, who are citizens of other Member States, the right to vote and be eligible for election in municipal and in European Parliament elections in the country in which they reside.

Belgium ratified the Treaty on European Union but did not, prior to this ratification, adapt its internal law to make possible the participation of foreign residents citizens of other Member States in Belgian municipal elections. Belgium must take the necessary steps to adapt its law before 31 December 1994. As Belgium held municipal elections in 1994, the consequences of the European Union innovation will only be effective in the next Belgian municipal elections to be held in six years time.

At the Essen Summit (1994), Belgium sought and obtained the agreement of other Member States to refuse the right to vote and to be eligible for municipal elections to citizens of other Member States, residing in a Belgian municipality in which more than 20 percent of the eligible residents do not have the Belgian nationality. This included the condition that it would apply only to those who had lived for less than six years in the municipality concerned.

Parliamentary involvement in European Union activities takes place at the level of the European Parliament and at the level of the Member States' parliaments. Belgium has taken various steps with respect to the involvement of the Belgian Parliament. In 1985, the Chamber of Representatives of the Belgian Federal Parliament created an Advisory Commission for European Affairs consisting of ten deputies and an equal number of Belgian European Parliamentarians. The Commission of the Senate, which dates from 1990, consists of 22 Senators. Belgian Euro-Parliamentarians can assist but cannot vote (Nagant de Deuxchaisnes 1994).

The Commissions provide opinions, either on request or on their own initiative. They inform themselves by participating in the meetings of the representatives of Parliaments of Member States. These meetings have, since 1986, been held twice a year. The Commissions and the Belgian Parliament influence Belgian participation in European Union developments in various ways. Parliament adapts internal Belgian legislation, which falls under its competence, in accord with European Union developments. Parliament also plays an important role in the control of the implementation process of European legislation. Parliament also participates in the determination of Belgian positions at the European Union level (Delpérée 1994). It holds general debates prior to the meetings of the European Council and also follows closely the activities of the Council of Ministers.

Moreover, the Federal government has the obligation to inform Parliament from the outset about negotiations concerning modifications of the Treaties or other of Acts of the European Communities. Parliament must be notified of the content of a Draft Treaty before the draft is signed. The Federal government has the discretion to decide whether or not to sign a Draft Treaty but Parliament can, at all stages of the process and at its own discretion, adopt non-binding resolutions to inform the Federal government of its standpoint with respect to issues covered in a Treaty.

The positive evolution of the involvement of the Belgian Parliament in European affairs is illustrated in the following example. In July 1986, the Chamber of Deputies received a report on the Single European Act and adopted a resolution. This was after the signing of the Act in February 1986. The Chamber received a report on the activities of the two Intergovernmental Conferences which prepared the Treaty on European Union and adopted a resolution before the 28–29 July meeting of the European Council in Luxembourg. The resolution influenced the determination of the further Belgian position in the ongoing negotiations leading to the Treaty of Maastricht.

Parliament is also notified of proposals for EU legislation concerning matters falling within its jurisdiction. This is done as soon as these proposals have been transmitted to the Council of Ministers. This process leads to increasing Parliamentary scrutiny of EU regulations, directives and other normative acts.

Parliament may make recommendations to the Federal government but there is no binding parliamentary scrutiny reserve. The Federal government and/or the governments of the Federated Entities can – after mutual consultation – express an opinion in the EU Council of Ministers even if Parliament has not expressed its opinion or is, through delay, attempting to block decision-making in the Council of Ministers.

When Member States decide to discuss treaty revisions, the Councils of the Communities and the Regions must also be informed. Commission proposals on matters which, pursuant to the federated structure of Belgium, affect their jurisdiction must be transmitted to the Federal Councils once the Commission has transmitted them to the Council of Ministers. This formal process does not preclude prior informal consultation within Belgium.

RECONCILING REGIONALISATION WITH EUROPEAN UNION OBLIGATIONS

The Belgian example provides an important example of how to meet legitimate regional aspirations in a Union which is constantly increasing in size and complexity.

The reconciliation of Belgium's regionalisation with European Union obligations will be discussed through the analysis of the following topics:

- the recognition of regions at the European Union level;
- the role of Belgian Regions and Communities in decision-making in the European Union;
- the role of Belgian Regions and Communities in the implementation of European Union legislation;
- the standing of the Belgian Regions and Communities with respect to the European Court of Justice

In the European Union, the term 'region' covers two kinds of regional configuration. Specific geographic areas in the European Union are eligible for assistance through regional programmes and structural funds on the basis of objective criteria determined by the European Union. The Belgian Regions and Communities as well as the Belgian provinces and local townships play a role in the committees which supervise the implementation of the Commission and European Union's decisions with respect to these policies.

Although there is no Community definition of a region in the context of article 198A–C of the Treaty of Rome, the recent creation, through the Treaty on European Union, of a 'Committee of the Regions' represents an important step in the recognition at a European level of the existence and special interests of geographic regions in Member States.

In the case of Belgium, the Communities have been assimilated with the Belgian Regions and, in 1993, the Belgian Council of Ministers agreed that the Belgian delegation would consist of six Flemish Ministers, one Dutch-speaking member of the Government of the Region Brussels-Capital, two Ministers from the Government of the French Community, two members of the Government of Wallonia and one French-speaking member of the Government of the Region Brussels-Capital. The representation of the German-speaking population is guaranteed by the following solution: a minister of the government of the German Community would occupy the seat of a Dutch-speaking representative for the first two years while and would then occupy the seat of a French-speaking representative for the last two years (Delpérée 1994).

It is specifically with respect to the standing of regions in European Community decision-making that Belgium is having to innovate and accommodate so that the far-reaching federalisation of Belgium can be reconciled with smooth participation in European Union activities.

The following points will be examined:

- the association of the Regions and Communities in alterations of Treaty provisions;
- the participation of Regions and Communities in Belgian representation and voting in European Union decision-making processes

Belgium signed the Treaty of Rome as a Unitary state but it has since evolved to a Federal State. The Belgian Federal State is markedly different from other European Federal States. Contrary to the German 'Bundesrecht bricht Landesrecht', for instance, there is no hierarchical approach to legislation in Belgium. Moreover, when the Belgian Communities and Regions receive competence they also exercise these competencies on the level of external relations. This is not the case in other countries such as Spain where the Spanish constitution explicitly allocates external relations to the federal level.

The current Belgian situation is determined by article 167 (amended article 68) of the Constitution and by the Special and Ordinary Acts on the International Relations of the Communities and Regions of 5 May 1993 (*Belgische Staatsblad*, 8 May 1993). The King (by which is always meant, the King together with his Ministers, who are accountable to Parliament) is in charge of foreign relations, and this without any prejudice to the powers of the Communities and Regions to regulate international co-operation, including their treaty making power, within the scope of their competencies. This provision of the Constitution does not grant any implicit residual powers to supervise Communities or Regions on international co-operation to the Federal State. However, Communities and Regions have the obligation to keep the Federal government informed about their international relations. The King also has the power to block treaties.

In 1992, the President of the Government of Flanders has stated that the right to sign treaties 'will do much to stimulate and facilitate relations between Flanders and its international partners' (*Financial Times*, June 1994). Today, Flanders is working on a treaty on water with the Netherlands and has already set up a network of 70 economic representatives over five continents. It also has its own representation in important locations such as Vienna, The Hague, Washington, Tokyo and Brussels.

Various consultative procedures are necessary to ensure the smooth functioning of the federated system. There is an information requirement so that advisory committees can examine if the draft treaties of Federated Entities conform with Belgian foreign policy. Nevertheless, the treaties of Federated Entities cannot be revoked; only their implementation can be suspended. If a Government believes that another Government is exceeding its powers, it can refer the matters to either the 'Council of State' for executive rules or to the 'Court of Arbitration' for legislative rules. If one Government believes it is itself seriously disadvantaged by a draft decision of another Government, it can refer the matter to the 'Concertation Committee' of the Federal and the Community and Regional Governments. Draft treaties signed by Communities and Regions must be approved by the Council concerned and must receive the assent of the Government of the federated entity.

In compliance with the 1980 'Special Institutional Reform Act' (SIRA), the executives of the Regions and the Communities had to be associated with the negotiations on the Treaty on European Union because these negotiations covered areas of their competence. This association can take various forms, including prior consultation on the instructions to be given to the negotiators, prior advice before signature and ratification, and direct involvement of the executives (or their representatives) in the negotiations leading up to the drawing up of a treaty (Lejeune 1992).

In the case of the Treaty on European Union, Belgium fully associated its Regions and Communities in the process. The Regions and Communities participated, as part of the Belgian delegation, in the negotiations preceding the Treaty on European Union and its signature in 1992.

However, the federalisation process in Belgium can lead to very complex results for the country at the European Union level. This can be illustrated by the following example. In 1993, Belgium made a unilateral declaration when signing the Treaty of Accession with the newly adhering States (Austria, Finland, Norway, Sweden): 'By signing this Treaty on behalf of the Kingdom of Belgium, both the Belgian Federated authorities and the French-speaking Community, the Flemish Community and the German-speaking Community of Belgium, the Wallonian Region, the Flemish Region and the Brussels Region have entered into an undertaking at international level.' *(Official Journal of the European Communities*, C241, 29 August 1994).

The other States signatory to the Treaty of Accession made the following declaration: 'The other States signatory to the Treaty of Accession understand that Belgium's unilateral declaration is an explanation of Belgian constitutional law, which cannot prejudice the fact that the Kingdom of Belgium is the contracting party to this Treaty on its own and therefore alone responsible towards the signatory States for fulfilling the obligations which it has assumed in this Treaty as a Member State of the European Union.' *(Official Journal of the European*

Communities, C241, 29 August 1994).

When Belgian participation in European Union decision-making is examined, three issues are of importance: participation in the representation of Belgium and participation in, and influence over, the Belgian voting position.

THE REPRESENTATION OF BELGIUM

The federal representation of Belgium in the European Union is reflected in the composition of both the Belgian Permanent Representation to the European Union and the Belgian delegation at meetings of the Council of Ministers, official committees and working parties. These meetings may deal with matters which are either the sole responsibility of the Communities and Regions or which involve mixed responsibility.

The staff of the Belgian Permanent Representative includes a representative of, respectively, the Flemish, Walloon and Brussels-Capital Regions. The Permanent Representation is responsible for the defence of the Belgian position in the more than 150 committees of COREPER. The Permanent Representative informs the various Belgian governments about matters in their area of competence and ensures that the Belgian position in specific circumstances reflects what various the Belgian Governments have agreed upon or expect.

In the Foreign Ministry, this process is facilitated by the existence of structured 'co-ordination meetings' in which representatives of the Federal, Regional and Community-level Governments participate. There also is an 'International Co-operation Commission' which deals with the involvement of the Federal and the Federated Entities governments in international and supra-national scientific research including their representation in the EU's Programme Committees.

The 'Inter-Ministerial Conference on Foreign Policy' also plays an important role. It consists of the relevant members of the Federal, Community and Regional governments. Its purpose is to keep the governments of the Federated Entities regularly informed of foreign policy. The Federal government must do this either at its own volition or at the request of a Community or Regional government. Since European Union policy is part of foreign policy, the Inter-Ministerial Conference on Foreign Policy can serve as the ultimate means to obtain agreement on deadlocked issues.

Generally, practical solutions to representation have been worked out. For example, since 1982, the Belgian delegation to informal meetings of the European Ministers of Culture and Education has always included a member of each Community Executive. At formal meetings, the country has been represented by the national Minister, accompanied by the two respective Ministers from the Communities.

Today, the issue of representation has become easier because Belgium obtained a modification of article 146 of the Treaty of Rome. Ministers of the Belgian Communities and Regions can now formally attend, vote in and chair meetings of the EU Council of Ministers.

Before the modification of article 146 of the Treaty of Rome, only a national government representative could act for Belgium in the Council of Ministers. This severely limited Belgium's capacity to make its Regions and Communities directly participate in its representation at the EC level. However, the country has dealt pragmatically with this issue by developing a layer of formal and informal arrangements to ensure that the various Belgian governments take part in the preparation of Belgian positions at the decision-making level of the Council of Ministers.

Before the modification, the first paragraph of article 146 was 'The Council shall consist of representatives of the Member States. Each Government shall delegate to it one of its members.' Today, after the modification, it reads as follows 'The Council shall consist of a representative of each Member State at ministerial level, authorised to commit the Government of the Member State.'

The new article 92 (bis) of the 'Special Institutional Reform Act' (SIRA) states that the Federal government and the Federated Entities must sign one or more co-operation agreements for Belgium's representation in international and supra-national organisations, for procedures to exist to reach common decisions on policy issues, and for what must be done in those cases when no common viewpoint can be worked out.

The new article 81 of SIRA states that the Community and Regional governments are empowered to enter into binding agreements on behalf of the Belgian state in the Council of the European Union where one of their members represents Belgium under a Co-operation Agreement as defined in article 92 of the SIRA. Co-operation Agreements have as yet (1994) not been adopted.

Until such co-operation agreements are signed, a transitional rule provides that, at the European level, representatives of the Regions sit on technical committees in addition to Federal representatives. Nevertheless, these representatives can speak only when the committees deal with matters which fall under Belgian Regional responsibility. Agriculture is an exception to this: the Federal Minister of Agriculture remains the negotiator with full responsibility for agricultural matters but with a consultation requirement.

In 1993, the Inter-Ministerial Conference negotiated a draft accord whereby four forms of representation are distinguished in function of the respective competencies of the federal or federated institutions in Belgium. If there is exclusive federal competence, there will be exclusive federal representation. If there is mixed competence, but if the competence is mainly federal, there will be federal representation but there will be an assessor from the Federated Entities. If there is mixed competence but the matter mainly falls under the authority of the Federated Entities, then the Federated Entities will settle the matter between themselves but there will be an assessor from the Federal government. If the Communities or Regions are solely competent, they will have to come to an agreement between themselves. The assessor's role is to assist the Minister so that there is adequate representation when it concerns mixed areas of competence.

On 10 September 1993, the Belgian Council of Ministers approved the report of the Inter-Ministerial Conference and further specified that the Minister, present at the deliberations of the Council of the Ministers of the EU, represents Belgium. For this reason, horizontal co-ordination meetings must systematically be organised by the Ministry of Foreign Affairs before each EU Council Meeting.

Before Belgium votes in a decision in the Council of Ministers in the European Union, there must be discussion (concertation) between the concerned parties in Belgium to reach agreement on a common standpoint. When voting in the Council of Ministers, the Minister, who actually participates in the Council deliberations, can in principle not divert from the common standpoint. The current understanding is that Belgium abstains and does not participate in the formulation of a point of view of the Council if the concertation process has not led to a common agreement between all the Belgian parties.

From the European Community law perspective, this way of working is not a viable long-term solution. Abstention is not a neutral position. If unanimity is required, abstention is equivalent to a 'yes' vote; if a qualified majority is required, abstention is equivalent to a 'no' vote.

Moreover, one must not forget that the incapacity of a Member State to vote affects the overall capacity of the Council of Ministers to play its role effectively in the balancing of powers between Community Institutions. In the past, the Belgian staightjacket has occasionally meant that the Council has not reached a required qualified majority. Nevertheless, from the Belgian perspective, adequate consultation is absolutely necessary.

In December 1989, an Education Minister of one of the Communities represented Belgium in the Education Council. The other Belgian Ministers, responsible for education, were not present. The Council voted on the Commission proposal to augment the ERASMUS budget from ECU 80 million to ECU 180 million. This meant that the Belgian contribution increased by BF 160 million over a period of three years.

The above example illustrates that prior consultation and agreement within Belgium are vital and that the complex co-ordination activities of the Ministry of Foreign Affairs are more than justified. In addition to these co-ordination activities, continuous disagreements should be discussed and settled by the 'Inter-Ministerial Conference on Foreign Affairs' so that Belgium can fully exercise its European Union voting rights.

Today, the internal Belgian consultation and consensus processes work reasonably well. However, caution is also justified. As mentioned earlier, the federation process in Belgium is ongoing and it is thus possible that in the future a Minister of a Community or a Region will take a position in a Council of Ministers which could cause difficulties for the Federal government. For this reason, clear agreements and a willingness to respect these agreements, are necessary.

THE ROLE OF THE REGIONS AND COMMUNITIES IN THE IMPLEMENTATION OF EU LEGISLATION

In this section three points will receive attention:

- the implementation of European Union legislation;
- the representation of Belgium before the European Court of Justice;
- the Belgian responses to Commission positions.

These issues are important for understanding the current role of the Belgian Regions and Communities in the European unification process.

In the European Union, European legislation takes priority over national legislation and legally only Member States are 'acknowledged' as decision entities in the unification process. In Belgium the federalisation process has given the Belgian Regions and Communities exclusive responsibility for a whole range of policies which are affected by European Union legislation.

The jurisprudence of the European Union Court makes the Belgian Federal state liable for breaches of European Union law caused by Belgian Communities or Regions. This applies to both the non-implementation of European Union measures as well as to the implementation of actions which are counter to European Union legislation.

Over the years, the Federal State of Belgium has on numerous occasions been held in default by the European Court of Justice because one or more of its Federated Entities had not taken the necessary measures for matters falling under their exclusive competence. Because of this, the 1993 institutional reform introduced a substitution mechanism and the possibility of having eventual financial sanctions incurred by the Belgian state assumed by the responsible Federated Entities.

The revised article 68 (par. 7) of the Constitution and the amended article 16 (par. 3) of the SIRA create a substitution mechanism whereby the Federal legislative and executive powers can temporarily act on behalf of the Federated Entity to carry out the executory part of the judgement of an international or a supra-national court. There are various limitations. The substitution mechanism cannot be applied in the case of a preliminary ruling by the European Union Court of Justice. The substitution mechanism does not apply to a motivated opinion of the Commission on the basis of article 169 of the Treaty of Rome. There must be a judgement by the Court of Justice condemning Belgium. It is also essential that the Community or Region has been associated by the Federal State in all the procedural steps undertaken to settle the dispute, including the final litigation, so that its point of view is fully taken into account in the procedural defense. The substitution mechanism can also only be applied if the Federal government has itself fully respected the provisions of the future co-ordination agreement on the modalities of co-ordination between the Federal government and the Federated Entities in Belgium.

The federal measures cease to take effect as soon as the Federated Entities comply with international and supra-national law as stipulated in the executory part of the judgement. A Federated Entity can apply for annulment to either the Court of Arbitration or to the Council of State, depending on the case. This can happen if the Federated Entity considers that either the legal preconditions for the substitution have not been completed or the limits of substitution have been exceeded.

The Federal State has the right to deduct in advance the costs of the non-respect of an international or supra-national obligation from the transfers affected to the Communities and Regions. This arrangement is a consequence of the new article 171 of the Treaty of Rome which provides that the Court of Justice can impose the payment of a lump sum or a fine when a Member State has not complied with a judgement of the Court of Justice. The application of this right can politically be

Table 6.1: *State of implementation of measures of white paper by Member States at 10 December 1993*

	Implemented measures	Derogation	Measures not implemented	Not relevant
Belgium	188	0	25	6
Denmark	204	0	8	7
Germany	178	0	35	6
Greece	177	2	35	5
Spain	178	2	36	3
France	178	0	36	5
Ireland	175	1	37	6
Italy	191	0	24	4
Luxembourg	185	0	26	8
Netherlands	187	0	26	6
Portugal	190	2	25	2
UK	194	1	18	6

Source: Belgian Permanent Delegation, July 1994.

very delicate, especially in cases where joint responsibility of the Federal State and the Federated Entity could be deemed to exist.

Table 6.1 shows that the Belgian record with respect to implementation has improved in recent years. This can in part be attributed to the overall support of Belgians for the European unification process as well as to a pragmatic interest in improving the reputation of Belgium prior to having the country assume, in 1993, the Presidency of the Council of Ministers.

The Regions and Communities are associated by the Federal State of Belgium with actions brought before the Court which deal with their areas of competence. The Communities and Regions can also oblige the Federal State to resort to its supra-national standing on their behalf.

The 1993 changes to the special law of 1980 provide that there should be a Co-operation Agreement between the Federal State and the Federated Entities when it concerns cases that are brought before the Court by Belgium itself. The law does not require any agreement when it concerns Belgian actions brought before the European Court of Justice by third parties.

Member States and the Commission regularly have to discuss over differences in the interpretation of Community obligations. 'Aquafin' will be used as an example to illustrate how a dispute concerning a

Belgian Federated Entity of Belgium can be settled.

The Flemish Region gave a contract for the construction and exploitation of the regional infrastructure for the treatment of waste water to the private Flemish company 'Aquafin' without any open bidding and without publication in the Official Journal.

The Commission received a complaint about this, and it informed Belgium that a contract of such a size is subject to the European transparency rules. It should thus have been published in the Official Journal so that other bids would have been possible. In response to this, the Flemish Region clarified that Aquafin would be responsible for the coordination of the project while the actual work would be sub-contracted to other firms. This response did not satisfy the Commission especially since Aquafin, created by a decree of the Flemish Region, was a private company. The Commission proposed two alternative solutions: either the statutes of Aquafin were modified making it a public institution subject to the relevant European Directives or the Flemish Region would be held to be the awarder of the contract and conform to relevant European Union Directives. The Flemish Region opted for the first alternative. Acquafin ceased to be a private firm and the agreement between the Region and Aquafin was modified. The Belgian Authorities also undertook that Aquafin and all other public entities would respect European rules with respect to public contracts (*Europe Agence International d'Information pour la Presse*, 29 July 1994).

BELGIAN PRAGMATISM IN THE HANDLING OF THE PRESIDENCY OF THE COUNCIL OF MINISTERS

Belgium assumed the Presidency of the European Communities on 1 July 1993 and relinquished it on 31 December 1993. Belgium managed its presidency with typical Belgian pragmatism. Prime Minister Jean-Luc Dehaene (a Flemish Christian Democrat) was an active, informed and concerned president. Foreign Minister Willy Claes (a Flemish Socialist) presided at the General Affairs Council and Minister of Finance Philippe Maystadt (a Walloon Christian Democrat) served as president of the ECOFIN Council. The three politicians worked well together. In the Councils dealing with issues falling under the competence of Regions or Communities, the Presidency was assumed by a member of the Belgian government but Belgium was represented by a member of, as the case might be, a Regional or a Community-level government.

The Belgian Presidency concentrated on the smooth implementation of the Maastricht Treaty on 1 November 1993. This involved the interpretation of the Treaty and its completion by practical implementation measures. The Belgian Presidency succeeded in obtaining the consent of the European Parliament and of the Council for these measures.

The following indicate the steps needed to bring into force the Treaty on European Union:

– The Council of Ministers and the European Parliament reached agreement on the organisational arrangements for the proceedings of the Conciliation Committee. This forum for direct dialogue between the members of the Council (or their representatives) and the Members of the European Parliament is essential to ensure agreement on joint legislative texts.

– On 25 October 1993, the European Parliament, the Council of Ministers and the Commission reached agreement on a Draft European Parliament Decision concerning the regulations and general conditions governing the performance of the duties of the ombudsman.

– There was agreement between the Member States Government Representatives, meeting at Head-of-State and Government level, on the location of various new organisations dealing with European Union activities.

– The necessary steps were taken to ensure that the new 'Committee of the Regions' could meet for the first time not later than 15 January 1994.

– On 4 October 1993, there was political agreement on the arrangements for exercising the right to vote and to stand as a candidate in elections to the European Parliament for citizens of the Union residing in a Member State of which they are not nationals. This enabled the Member States to initiate the necessary preparatory work so that this part of European citizenship could be effectively exercised in the 1994 European Parliament elections.

– The meeting of the European Council on 29 October 1993 adopted an 'Inter-Institutional Declaration on Democracy Transparency and Subsidiarity'. This declaration was adopted to improve public access to information concerning European Union activities.

– The European Council agreed on practical steps necessary for moving from political co-operation to the Common Foreign and Security Policy (CFSP). These steps deal with instruments of the CFSP as well as with the co-operation between COREPER and the Political Committee. There was also agreement on practical steps to implement the provision on co-operation in the fields of justice and home affairs.

WHAT BELGIUM CAN CONTRIBUTE TO THE DEMOCRATISATION PROCESS OF THE EUROPEAN UNION

The current Belgian federal structure is unique and essential for the continued existence of Belgium as a Federal State. The ultimate success of the approach will depend mainly on the Federal government, the Regions and the Communities respecting the spirit and letter of the agreements in a commonly shared loyalty to the Belgian Federal State.

For the European Union, the ongoing process of federalisation in Belgium many suggest ways to meet the challenging democratic aspirations of regions at the European Union level. Some of Belgium's innovations can serve as examples for the future determination of the role of Federated Entities in a European Union where subsidiarity should play a key role. It must be remembered that the Belgian situation is exceptionally complex, but nevertheless, Belgium has been obliged to find solutions to specific issues which inevitably come to the fore when a Member State accords more powers to its regions. This is, in particular, the case for regional participation in EU decision-making and for the implementation and the application of EU legislation.

Reference to the Belgian case is, however, not facilitated by the ongoing nature of the Belgian federalisation process: while the main outlines of its current situation are clear, many details still need to be negotiated and approved.

The very complexity of the Belgian situation makes it essential that, on a European level, the Belgian situation continues to be considered as an internal issue of Belgian constitutional law. Nevertheless, the Belgian solution and its practical application can provide valuable information on increasing the democratic participation of regional entities in the ongoing integration process in Europe.

7
Italy: in Need of More EU Democracy

Federiga Maria Bindi

'Managers in Italy tend to be more flexible. Rules and regulations (where they exist) are often ignored....' (*The Economist* 7 December 1991). In Italy, at least until now, membership of the EC has been perceived as having a vital role in bringing order into the national system. The demand for supranational structures is in fact a demand for repairing the inefficiency of the Italian system itself. At times, the EC's name has even been used by Italian politicians to legitimise their actions (Cotta 1992: 211): European constraints are used to justify otherwise unpopular fiscal and monetary measures, as the headlines of leading Italian newspapers show: 'The Twelve ask us tears and blood' (*La Repubblica* 5 May 1992); 'Privatisation? It is imposed by the EC' (*Corriere della Sera* 3 August 1992). However, Italy's failure to implement EC legislation and to respect the obligations arising from the EC Treaties are well known. There are cases in which Italy is brought before the European Court more then once, even on a single case. And even when EC rules are implemented, this does not mean that they are enforced.

The Italian case is a peculiar one, and has been described as a 'blocked democratic regime'. Former President of the Council (June 1992–April 1993) and Constitutionalist Giuliano Amato describes it: 'My predecessor as Prime Minister, Giulio Andreotti, was already in government in 1946. Not even Andrej Gromiko lasted for so long.... Italy is an excellent example of the theory of involution, expounded by Mancur Olson: a vital system that becomes progressively rigid, incapable of correcting its increasing entropies, and unable to keep up with the need of change, that is finally destroyed by the impact on its corrupted tissues of newly emerging counter-forces.' (Amato 1994a: 225). The problem is to understand how such a system developed and how it is evolving today.

What follows is based on the literature mentioned, on a comparative examination of the main Italian newspapers and on about 80 interviews – carried out between February 1992 and October 1994 – with both Italian and EU officials and politicians. For reasons of confidentiality, the names of the interviewees are not given; however, all information obtained was cross-checked so far as possible to avoid inaccuracy.

THE ITALIAN SYSTEM

Italian unity was declared in 1861 but it was only with the 1954 *Memorandum d'intesa* that Italy defined its actual geographical borders. Thus, the Italian political system is the result of three fundamental historical experiences: *political unification* in the nineteenth century (liberal era); *fascism* (1922–43); *resistance and reconstruction* (mid–1940s). To this, a *transition period*, started in 1990 and still under its way, has to be added.

The monarchy was abolished by popular referendum on 2 June 1945, and on 1 January 1948, the Republican Constitution was promulgated. According to the Constitution, Italy is a parliamentary democracy, based on equal bicameralism: the *Senato* (Upper Chamber) and the *Camera* (Lower Chamber) in fact perform identical functions and are together attributed the legislative power (art. 70 Italian Constitution). This, however, diminished the Parliament's performances and effectiveness. Furthermore, the pure proportional electoral system produced a very fragmented party system, with at least eight national parties represented in Parliament at any given time and very little stability. Although elections are due every five years, the last regularly scheduled elections were held in 1968, while all the subsequent parliamentary terms were shortened and early elections called (respectively in 1972, 1976, 1979, 1983, 1987, 1992 and 1994).

Italy's *partitocrazia* (the dominance of political parties in the political and the economic systems) is widely known, as is the so-called *lottizzazione* (the allocation of posts between and among political parties). This, however, has an historical and thus a juridical explanation. After 8 September 1943, when the Allied troops landed in Southern Italy, the King slipped away by car from Rome and escaped to Southern Italy, leaving the Italians with the impression that the State no longer existed to perform its duties: there was nobody to tell them what they were supposed to do; no-one to instruct Italian soldiers. At that point, a new authority entered into the political arena: the political parties, whose members served on the liberation committee, the 'Comitato di Liberazione Nazionale'. They filled the vacuum and effectively became the voice of the State: as the only recognised and visible authority, they undertook the task of getting Italy back on its feet; of dealing with everything from the immense problems relating to Italian identity, to the small day-to-day problems. The parties appointed Ministers, as well as people to run the municipal companies, thereby taking care of public services in all the towns of central and northern Italy. The parties thus got used to sending their appointees on to the public services boards at a time when nobody else was prepared to do it: the 'lottizzazione' began at that time (Amato 1993a). Not surprisingly, the Italian Constitution assigns to the parties the key role in shaping politics. Article 49 states that 'all citizens have the right to freely get together in parties in order to contribute in a democratic manner to the shaping of the national politics'. In addition, the Prologue of the text – introducing the philosophical foundation of the State – establishes that sovereignty is owned by the people who 'exert it in the manners foreseen by the Constitution'; in other words, through the parties. This stood in opposition to fascism's disavowal of multi-partism and the progressive substitution of the State by the Party (Corneli 1993). In other words, the 'original sin' was to create deliberately weak institutions and strong parties, as it was believed that the system would work because of the strength and the authority injected from outside by the parties. The parties were in fact not only involved in policy-making, but they also appointed the Ministers, decided upon Under-secretaries, Chairmen and members of the boards of any public company or highly important public body (and even of those of small importance) including the appointment of the top executives of public departments (Amato 1993a).

As a consequence, the Italian government was much weaker than most of its European counterparts. The 54 Cabinets Italy has had, have been large and unstable, supported for most of the post-war period by four or five-parties, centre/centre-left coalitions, normally including Christian Democrats (DC), Liberals (PLI), Republicans (PRI), Social-Democrats (PSDI), and, since the early 1960s, Socialists (PSI). The President of the Council is appointed by the President of the Republic and in principle selects the members of the Council of Ministers (s/he is, however, allowed to take office only after having obtained a vote of confidence of the Parliament). However, as mentioned, in the choice of Ministers, the President of the Council was forced to respect the 'suggestions' of parties' leaders. The Council of Ministers is in principle a collegial body but, in practice, has not been considered to be an effective centre for policy co-ordination: the level of collegiality was extremely low (as were expectations in regard to the Cabinet's role in formulating or reviewing overall and sectoral policies), while inter-ministerial competition has been always high (Hine 1993: 213). This has contributed to the creation of a major gap between the 'formal' and the 'actual' significance of the constitution (Criscitiello 1993).

Initially ruled by the Piedmonts administration, on a Napoleonic-model, the new Italian State faced a process of 'southernization' when the capital was moved to Rome in 1870. As a consequence, economic leadership remained in Northern Italy, while the administrative centre was located in Rome. Today, Italy is characterised by a policentric urban and economic structure; yet, the institutional framework is highly centralised (Fondazione Agnelli 1994). However, the Italian bureaucracy is mostly of a low standard: poorly trained, badly motivated and of a low moral standard. Moreover, it is badly distributed: over-staffed in the South and short of personnel in North. In Italy, unlike in France for instance, there is very little cross-fertilisation and transfer from the private to the public sector (and vice versa) (Hine 1993: 223–242). A *Carta dei servizi pubblici*, a sort of 'Bill of public officials' was introduced in 1993 (*Sole 24 Ore* 30 November 1993). However, a 'culture' of public service still has to be formed.

Italy has three tiers structure of elected government below the national level: *regions, provinces and municipalities*. Regionalization was written into the 1948 Constitution but – except for the five 'special status' regions (Val d'Aosta, Alto Adige – further devised into two autonomous provinces, Bolzano and Trento – Friuli, Sicily, Sardinia) – it took as long as until 1970s to implement (partial) administrative decentralisation and even longer to draft regional Charters, transfer administrative responsibilities and work out financial arrangements. Nevertheless, the twenty regions – which are indeed important organs for articulation of demands and for public policy implementation – were not attributed fiscal autonomy.

Each regional authority consists of a directly elected assembly (called *Consiglio regionale*) which enacts regional legislation and elects the executive, i.e. the *Giunta* and its President. The *assessori* forming the *giunta* are organised following the patterns of the central government (Hine 1993: 257–272). The same kind of administrative asset is used at the provincial level (*Law 142* 1990) and at the municipal level. Municipalities are in fact run by a directly elected *Consiglio Communale* and by its *Giunta Comunale*. In particular, the Mayor (*Sindaco*) has – as from the electoral reform of 1993 ((*Law 81* 1993), introducing a majority one-or-two-rounds electoral system) – a leading political role.

A reform of the regions is also foreseen, concerning both the electoral system (from a proportional to a majoritarian one) and the role of regions and local entities. It should be emphasised that it is the Constitution as a whole that is in question and likely to be changed. In such view, a 'Comitato di saggi' (Sages' Committee) composed by 16 academicians was created by Minister for Institutional Reforms Speroni (*Il Sole 24 Ore* 9 September 1994).

Industrialisation came relatively late to Italy. By 1950 – despite the Marshall Plan and some years of economic recovery – the Italian economy was still industrially backward. Unemployment stood at 10.8 percent, while 40.8 percent of the labour force was employed in agriculture (Quartermaine and Pollard 1987: 21–22). From the 1950s onward, Italy's economy was progressively transformed, in essentially three phases: *the economic miracle* (1950–63); *transition* (1963–75); *stabilisation, adaptation and a cautious return to the Market* (Hine 1993: 33–58). Today, Italy is the EU's third largest economy, roughly on a par with the UK and the activities are divided as follows: 32.3 percent industry, 8.5 percent agriculture and 59.2 percent services. However, the unemployment rate is high at 10.3 percent (of which 15.9 percent are women and 48.7 percent are youths), while the 'underground economy' is still underestimated and higher than in the rest of the EU (Feron and Thoraval 1993: 572). Business is extremely fragmented: more than 95 percent of firms have less than 100 employees and are mainly producing for export (Mucci and Savi 1992: 103–116).

As for interest representation, Giuseppe Are speaks about an Italian form of 'negative corporatism', founded on corruption and the inefficiency of the administration (*Il Sole 24 Ore* 4 April 1994). In fact, major interests were often in symbiosis with the political system. Around 60 percent of former Ministers were reported to be linked to major national interest groups, and of them 31 percent were concerned with trade unions or the *Confindustria*, the Italian owners' association (Cotta 1991: 185–187). Not surprisingly, in a situation of declining political parties, some leading economic figures decided to get directly involved in policy-making: the most notable case is Finivest's owner, Silvio Berlusconi, previously a close friend of former Socialist leader Bettino Craxi, who become leader of *Forza Italia* and President of the Council, thanks to a campaign based on his own TV companies and other media (Fininvest owns among others the three major private national TV channels: *Italia 1, Canale 5* and *Rete 4*, the Mondadori publisher and several radio networks) (*The Economist*, 26 November 1994; Currias, Gramellini and Maltese 1994).

Trade unions and patronage have played an important role in the Italian Republic. Their actions were crucial in the transition from fascism to democracy during the late 1940s and early 1950s (Morlino 1991). Concerning trade unions, the three main ones – the *CISL, CIGL* and *UIL* – were linked respectively to the DC, PCI and PSI, as the interchange of careers between politics and trade unions also testifies (Feltrin 1991). The CGIL, CISL and UIL today organise about 42 percent of the active population and contributed greatly to reducing industrial conflict since the 1970s. However, they are presently suffering from the challenge of newly-created grass-root workers' committees, known as COBAS, which organise workers belonging to very limited sectors or even employed in very specific jobs.

As for business, the major industries soon gained the status of co-decision-makers with the government in the field of industrial policy, mainly through the patronage's association *Confindustria* (Cohen 1992: 85–102). However, Confindustria never became a mass movement, preferring to develop close personal relationships with decision-makers (Mattina 1991). Confindustria has been, since its origins, in a symbiotic relationship with the Liberal Party (PLI), though it developed a relationship of neutrality with the other centre-right parties, lobbying them when needed.

Finally, the judicial system: a division between enquiring magistrates and judging magistrates does not exist, and magistrates are grouped into para-political streams. Thanks, though, to the 'clean hands' affairs, magistrates have gained the full support of public opinion.

A challenge to this undoubtedly corrupted system started in the early 1990s. On 9 and 10 June 1991, a single preference-vote in legislative elections was introduced by referendum; on 18 April 1992, the electoral law was also abrogated by referendum, thus opening the way to a mixed system. Under the new electoral law, 75 percent of the MPs are to be elected to the Camera on a simple majority system, while the remaining 25 percent continue to be elected on a proportional basis.

In April 1993, at the crest of the *tangentopoli* investigations which put under investigation a relevant part of the political, administrative and economic elites, majority parties' positions were defeated on eight referendums, in what was described by analysts and commentators as the end of a regime (Bardi 1994: 11). In March 1994, legislative elections were held. The new electoral system turned out to penalise the more ideological 'traditional' parties, as it required coalitions to be built *before* the elections, thus opening the way to the *Forza Italia (F.I.)/ Lega Nord (L.N.)/Alleanza Nazionale(AN)* coalition.

The election of the new majority, led by *Forza Italia*, the movement created by Fininvest's leader Berlusconi, was judged by many as a victory for anti-partyism (Bardi 1994: 1), although the legitimacy of such a view is doubtful: *Alleanza Nazionale* substantially coincided with *MSI* (*Movimento Sociale Italiano*), a – since then – minority but highly structured party (Bardi 1994: 12), while *Forza Italia* suffers from a lack of internal democracy and mainly coincided with the Fininvest organisation (*Il Sole 24 Ore* 31 May 1994). Moreover, the coalition appeared to be built more on the basis of electoral convenience than on convergent programmes.

As for the formerly powerful parties, the Socialists, Liberals and Republicans are today almost non existent as such. Some of their leaders were elected as 'new political men' under the banners of *Forza Italia* or *Alleanza Nazionale*, while the remaining ones joined the progressive (Left) groups. The (previously Left) *Radical* party became a member of the (Right) majority coalition, its leaders having being elected under the *Forza Italia* flag, too. The Christian Democrats have reshaped the party and changed it into the *PPI (Partito Popolare Italiano)*; they suffered from a split into the *CCD (Centro Cristiano Democratico* – a small party now in the majority coalition) and from individual departures to *Forza Italia* and *Alleanza Nazionale*. Despite these realignments, party membership collapsed in the early and mid 1990s, and today it is estimated at no more than 2.5–3.0 million people in total (Bardi 1994: 8).

Social partners are playing an important role in the transition period. In the beginning, *Confindustria* seemed to adopt a neutral stance *vis-à-vis* the new *in fieri* political actors, whom it in fact briefed on *Confindustria*'s priorities (*Sole 24 Ore*, 11 February 1994). Later, however, the association sought and obtained consultation on crucial legislation such as the *Finanziaria*, the law regulating the economic life of the country. The trade unions – CGIL, CISL and UIL – soon declared their willingness to collaborate with the new government. Yet, when negotiations over retirement pensions broke down, they reacted sharply by calling for a general national strike (14 October 1994). An agreement was finally reached on 1 December 1994.

ITALY AND THE EU

The Italian government is based on vertical departments. The main role in EU matters has been played by the Ministry of Foreign Affairs (MAE). The Ministry of Foreign Affairs is divided into six Directorate-

Generals (DGs): Economic Affairs, Political Affairs, Culture, Emigration, Personnel, Co-operation for Development. Under the leadership of former Foreign Minister Beniamino Andreatta, the MAE has undergone unprecedented reorganisation, a process which is continuing today. However, the reorganisation of the DGs according to geographical – rather than sectoral – criteria is still under discussion and far from being achieved, as remarked the Italian Ambassador to the OTAN, Giovanni Jannuzzi (*Il Sole 24 Ore*, 2 September 1994).

Each DG has its own EU desk; however, most of the EC work was traditionally done by the Economic Affairs and the Political Affairs DGs. All information concerning EU matters is sent by the EU Commission and by the Italian Permanent Representation to the DG Economic Affairs, which further spreads it to the other EU desks in the MAE and to the EU Task Forces in other Ministries, as well as to the EU Committees and the two Chambers of Parliament, to the Regions and to relevant national groups.

In 1980, a new non-departmental Ministry was created and attached to the Presidency of the Council of Ministers, the *Ministero per il Coordinamento delle Politiche Comunitarie* ('Ministry for the Co-ordination of EC Policies'), whose aim was to co-ordinate EC-related activities. However, due to the lack of resources and opposition from the MAE little was achieved (Ciriolo 1991) and Grottanelli de Santi (1992: 186) described it as the Cinderella of the Italian Ministries. In 1987, the so-called 'Legge Fabbri' (law 183/87) introduced a new Department for the Co-ordination of EC Policies, again within the Presidency of the Council of Ministers. The aim of the *Dipartimento* was to secure more effective action, especially with respect to the implementation of EC directives and the completion of the single market. The *Dipartimento*'s role – only operative since June 1990 – was further specified by Law 139/90, which established how it should co-ordinate the EC activities of the government with those of the public administration and of the Regions. The *Dipartimento* was also supposed to develop better relations with EC institutions and to supervise the correct implementation of EC law and the use of EC funds. Law 183/87 had, in fact, also established a *Fondo di Rotazione* – operative (only) as from June 1990 – charged to collect and re-distribute all EC subventions to Italy. The experiment was not successful and under threat of the suspension of EC funds to Italy, a new inter-ministerial taskforce (formed by the Ministers for Industry, Balance, EU Politics) was created and charged with of the management of EU funds (*Il Sole 24 Ore*, 22 June 1994).

The post of Italian Permanent Representative (RPI) in Brussels has assumed great importance, so that the Ambassador to the EU is now considered of equal importance as the Ambassador in Washington. The RPI comprises the Ambassador and his Deputy, a legal Counsellor, and representatives from the most important Italian Ministries, including Agriculture, Internal Affairs, Finance, Treasury, Transport, Industry, Health, Work, External Trades, as well as from the *Banca d'Italia*.

Both the Parliament and the Regions have expressed on several occasions their wish to contribute to the shaping of EC policy. In the Italian Parliament, both the *Senato* and the *Camera dei Deputati* had an EC Affairs Committee.

The first to be established was the *Giunta per gli Affari Comunitari* of the *Senato,* in 1968. Its composition reflected proportionally the political spectrum of the Senate itself. Among the competencies of the *Giunta* were the right to give advice on EC law and on its implementation, to screen the reports of the government relating to EC matters, as well as the acts of the European Parliament or of any other international Assembly where Italian MPs sat. The *Giunta* could also vote on resolutions concerning future Italian policies in relation to the EC. Nevertheless, its functions were only consultative, and did not bind the government's action. The Parliament elected in 1994 had only a standing Commission for International Affairs (*Il Sole 24 Ore*, 3 June 1994).

The *Commissione speciale per gli Affari Comunitari* was established in the *Camera dei Deputati* in July 1990. As for the *Giunta*, its members, named by the President of *Camera* at the beginning of the legislature, reflected its political spectrum. The *Commissione* is competent to examine the annual *Legge comunitaria* (EU law) and all other EU-related legislation. However, the *Commissione*'s advice is also only consultative (Parliament Europeen 1990).

Concerning the role of the regions in the making of EC law, the relationship between the central Government and the regions was traditionally not an easy one, and EC matters were especially contentious. In 1989, the 'La Pergola' law introduced a bi-annual State/Regions conference called *Sessione Speciale Comunitaria della Conferenza Stato-Regioni* which was to give the regions the opportunity to discuss with the Government about EC regional policy-making and its implementation (art. 10). In addition, the law states that the five autonomous regions can directly enforce EU law – when the topic of the legislation is included in their exclusive competence – while, on subjects where competence is shared with the State, both ordinary and autonomous regions can implement EU law as soon as the annual 'EC law' enters into force (art. 9). However, the *Conferenza Stato-Regioni* did not take place as regularly as it should have done.

From the internal organisation point of view, almost all regions now have a special EU *desk* attached to the *Consiglio Regionale* and/or the *Giunta Regionale* (for past situation cf. Bindi 1994). However, Italian regions do not seem able to fully benefit EU funds. The situation is particularly critical in Lazio, in the islands (Sicily and Sardinia) and in other southern regions like Calabria, the extreme case being Campania: here in 1991 only 1.7 percent of the attributed money was used (*Il Sole 24 Ore* 2 August 1991)! Moreover, Italy has the lamentable reputation of organising the greatest number of frauds. For example, in 1991, 56 cases of agricultural frauds to the FEOGA were discovered in Italy, for a total of 2.27 million ECU (out of 9.37 for the whole EC, *Il Sole 24 Ore* 10 June 1992). The responsibility for this situation is not clear: from the one side the central government affirms that the regions are not able to deal with the power they have: on the other side, regions blame the government for not adequately defending them in Brussels. For instance, structural funds concerning Objective n. 2 were usually dealt by the Minister of Industry. Then, the CIPI stated that it was in fact the Ministry for Balance which should be charged for it. As a result, confusion was created and several times neither one of the two Ministries mentioned, nor the *Ministero Politiche Comunitarie e Regioni*, attended the COREPER meetings discussing structural funds (*Inserto Europa*, 31 May 1993). The situation may improve with the introduction of the taskforce mentioned above, as well as the creation of *Eurodéveloppement*, a European Economic Interest Group created by Italian regions through *Assofir*, the *Associazione Nazionale delle Finanziarie Regionali*, which is charged with helping southern European regions in planning and using EU funds (*Inserto Europa* 5 July 1993). Further help is also expected to come from the Regions' Committee created by the Maastricht Treaty in which the Italians have participated effectively, for instance electing, in the September 1994 session, Vannino Chiti (the President of Tuscany) as one of the Committee's Vice-Presidents.

Finally, the implementation of EU law has always been problematic for Italy. It is the reason why the 'La Pergola' Law established the duty of the government to report to Parliament every six months on Italian participation in the EU policy-making process. 'La Pergola' Law introduced the principle by which, each year, a so-called *legge comunitaria* (EU law) is voted by the Parliament. In the *legge comunitaria* dispositions must be included in order to abrogate Italian rules and laws in favour of EU ones, to implement EU Council or Commission acts and to give the government authorisation to adopt EU directives and ECSC recommendations (Paolo 1990; Caretti 1991).

In such a situation, Italian interest groups may sometimes achieve better results by by-passing national politics and present their own demands directly at the EU level rather than at the national one. 'All too often, Italian politicians' ability to talk about problems has been the direct opposite of their capacity to solve them' *(Financial Times*, 7 July 1992). Therefore, today, all big industrial (both private and public) groups are present in Brussels, among them Alfa Romeo, Alitalia, Fiat, Fininvest, Olivetti, Pirelli, E.N.I., I.R.I., ENEL, ENIMONT, ILVA, banks like Commerciale, Nazionale del Lavoro, San Paolo, Santo Spirito, Banco di Roma or Popolare di Novara and, of course, Banca d'Italia, or associations like Coldiretti, Confagricoltura, Confcoltivatori, Confcommercio, Confcooperative, Confesercenti, Confindustria, Lega delle Cooperative and Union Camere.

Major groups have easy direct access to Italian Ministries and therefore to the Council. Hence, their Brussels activities are mainly focused on the Commission and, to a smaller extent, on the European Parliament. Representatives of major (again both private and public) Italian groups also sit in the Economic and Social Committee: in Group I sit for instance, *Confindustria, Confcommercio, Confagricoltura, Intersind* and *Cida*; in Group II (Workers), there are representatives from the three major national trade unions CGIL, CISL and UIL; while in Group III (Various Interests) there are representatives come from *Confcoperative, Confartigianato, Confcoltivatori, Federconsorzi, Lega Nazionale Cooperative, Agenzia Difesa Diritti dei Consumatori, Comitato Difesa dei Consumatori, Federazione Terziario Avanzato*. In addition, Italian groups in Brussels contribute to the work of the European Association(s) they belong to: for instance, former CISL leader Gabaglio is the Secretary General of ETUC; Confindustria's Mondello leads the UNICE's working group on small and medium enterprises (SME); former ENEL Vice President Alessandro Ortis created and led EUROELETRIC. It is not unusual, in fact, to find Italians in the top positions of European organisations. Conversely, small Italian groups – lacking in resources – are practically absent in Brussels, thus mainly relying on the (little) information given by local/national bodies or by the Eurosportelli network (Bindi 1994).

CONCLUSIONS

Until now, EC law has been adopted in Brussels without any Italian action in the preparatory phase....', declared the then Minister for EC Affairs, Mr Romita *(Sole 24 Ore*, 12 April 1990). Two studies, one conducted by the Italian Senate's *Giunta per gli Affari Comunitari* (Senato 1991) and the other by the Camera's (1993) *Commissione speciale per gli Affari Comunitari (Commissione speciale per gli Affari Comunitari* confirmed the absence of Italy in the shaping of EC law, as well as the deficiency of proposed Italian action. According to former Commissioner Pandolfi, 'the weakness of Italy does not concern the big choices of the European political life but, on the contrary, its participation in the day-to-day EC work'. In the experts' committees (the so-called '*comitology*' system) Rome's emissaries are often not sufficiently qualified, nor interested in the work they are supposed to do. The case of milk quotas, a case still subject to continuous fines and re-negotiations with the Commission, was, typically, originated by a mistake of the Italian bureaucracy (Bindi 1993: 12).

It was expected that positive change would be brought about by Berlusconi's Government. In practice, this was not achieved, although Berlusconi declared in his Speech to Parliament that Italy was to act 'in a leading role' in the framework of the European Union (*Il Sole 24 Ore*, 17.5.1994); on the same lines went moreover the declarations of Minister for Foreign Affairs Antonio Martino (*Il Sole 24 Ore*, 24.5.94), probably the least pro-European of Italian politicians, being the only Italian member of Mrs Thatcher's Club de Bruges! Similar also the intentions expressed by the Minister for Agriculture, Mrs Adriana Poli Bortone, who in fact affirmed that 'Italy is going to play hard in Brussels' (*Il Sole 24 Ore*, 16.7.94). Italy indeed 'played hard' in the EU scene, even in rather sensitive areas such as the renegotiation with Slovenia of the Osimo Treaties, so much so that Slovenia was prevented from asking for EU membership because of the Italian opposition (*Il Sole 24 Ore*, 17.7.94 and 31.8.1994). But no improvement can be reported in the day-to-day work in EU matters. In fact, what Forza Italia, Alleanza Nazionale and Lega Nord really lack is the experience of working in an international environment. This is for instance why Forza Italia is trying so hard to get admitted into the PPE political family.

Silvio Berlusconi also declared himself and his Government to be independent of the old party logic. However, the never-ending fights among members of the majority coalition suggested that the old *partitocrazia* rules were still present (see, for instance, Piero Ignazi's article in the leading newspaper, *Il Sole 24 Ore*, 3 August 1994), while continuous contradictions, stop and goes, and delays characterised the government's action (*Il Sole 24 Ore* 18 August 1994). Even the Magistrates' Higher Council (CSM) showed in its last election how the para-political streams in which it was divided were still present, with only a slight change in names: the 10 elected Magistrates were divided into: 2

to *Forza Italia*, 2 to the *Lega*, 2 to *Alleanza Nazionale*, 3 to the *Progressisti* (United Left), 1 to the *Popolari (Sole 24 Ore*, 28 July 1994).

Efficiency was also an excuse for issuing law decrees: the use of law decrees by the government was so high that it was denounced by a worried President of the Camera, Irene Pivetti, and was the object of a closed-doors meeting between the President of the Camera, Pivetti herself, the President of the Council, Berlusconi, the President of the Republic, Scalfaro, and the President of the Senate, Sconamiglio. Law decrees have been used by the government even in sensitive areas such as judicial activity. For instance, law decree 140/94 – also know as *Decreto Biondi*, from the name of the Minister of Justice who promoted it – was perceived in Italy, as elsewhere, as a real 'invasion' of the Executive into the competencies of the Legislature, thus violating the principle of the public law establishing the division of powers. Law decree 140/94 furthermore ignored arts. 70 and 77 of the Italian Constitution. Art. 70 establishes that 'the legislative function is of the two Chambers of the Parliament', while art. 77 specifies that the government cannot issue decrees having the value of ordinary law, unless there is a case of extraordinary urgency; in such a case, the government must submit the decree to the two Chambers for conversion on the same day. In the given case, however, the justification of urgency was not present, the attempt by the government to impose conditions on the Judiciary by means of limiting preventive imprisonment was strongly criticised by legal scholars (Calussi 1994: 7–9).

The excessive use of law decrees constitutes a major additional, problem in the Member States/EU relationship. As mentioned earlier, one way to compensate for the lack of EU parliamentary legitimacy is to rely on the control of national Parliaments both of their representatives in the Council and on EU legislation. However, law decrees have the contrary effect of expropriating prerogatives of Parliament.

Moreover, the insignificant role of the Italian Parliament in the shaping of EU politics is confirmed by the consultative-only role played by the EU committees within the Parliament and by the deficiencies in the implementation of EU law. In fact, even though the *legge comunitaria* has enabled Italy to reduce the delay in the translation of EU directives into national law, this does not mean that the directives are enforced. Moreover, a higher degree of delegation (most especially through administrative norms) would further help a quicker implementation and respect of EU law (*Inserto Europa* 26 July 1993).

Similarly, the role in the national/EU policy-making process of the regions and the *Dipartimento* for EU politics is characterised by its irrelevance.

Italy's role in the Council of Ministers, the main EU decision-making body, still suffers from a lack of co-ordination *in* Rome and *with* Rome, even though the Italian Permanent Representative (RPI) in Brussels is considered one of the most important diplomatic bodies despite its dependence on the political changes in Rome. For instance, just a few months before the beginning of the Italian Semester of EC Presidency, the then (socialist) Minister of Foreigner Affairs, Gianni De Michelis, decided to replace the Italian Ambassador to the EC, the highly estimated and competent Pietro Calamia, with (socialist) Federico Di Roberto, certainly a bright person, but not as acquainted with EC affairs as an incoming EC Presidency would have required. These are, however, problems with which the Italian diplomatic body – in itself highly prepared – constantly has to deal with, as Ambassador Ferraris explained in a recent, brilliant article (Ferraris 1994). As Altiero Spinelli (1991: 618) noted in his Diary: 'Bisaglia [Minister of Agriculture] made concessions he was not authorised to'. Envoys from Rome are in fact too often little acquainted with the topic they are supposed to discuss in Brussels. Also, the credibility of Italy is threatened by the fast turnover of its Ministers, which makes foreign counterparts unsure of ever meeting the same person at the following meeting and that, in case of a change, engagements previously under taken will be respected. Italy is, in fact, one of the countries with the higher degree of élite circulation and where a ministerial career is characterised by a low average duration of cabinets, a high mobility of ministers through posts, and a low average *per* post. Moreover, in Italy Ministers tend to be politicians (i.e. generalists) rather than specialists, hence often little acquainted with the specialised topics discussed at the EU level (Frognier 1991; Bakema 1991).

In addition, one should mention that Euro-positions are often seen as well paid, interim jobs, to be taken on while waiting for the best occasion to go back in to the national political arena: 'Nenni [then PSI leader] ... asks me to help find an international post with a good salary for Cattani, who lost the elections ....', noted Spinelli (1991: 314) in his diary; but one could also recall sudden departures from the Commission to the National political arena like Malfatti's in 1972 or Ripa di Meana's in 1992. (Boudant and Gounelle 1989: 136). Not surprising, the two Italian Commissioners – previously nominated one each by DC and PSI, now by *Forza Italia* and *Radicali* – were not always chosen on the basis of pure merit. On the contrary, at the lower – but still very important – administrative levels, Italian EU officials, differently from the French or the Germans, do not feel they are sufficiently 'backed' by the Italian government, this help being of crucial importance in the passage from A4 to A3 level, when the nominees are mainly of a political nature.

Finally, concerning the European Parliament, Italian MEPs were traditionally not known for their regular attendance, further enhancing the problem of the democratic deficit. The 1994 Italian delegation was appeared very different from previous ones: 27 MEPs belonged to *Forza Italia*, 8 to *Partito Popolare*, 5 to *Rifondazione Comunista*, 3 to *Patto Segni*, 2 to *Socialists/Alleanza Democratica*, 11 to *Alleanza Nazionale/Movimento Sociale,* 2 to *Radicals*, 3 to the *Greens*, 6 to *Lega Nord* and 1 each for some minor or regional parties. However, when one reads among the 'new' MEPs, 'old' names, such as the newly elected EP Vice President Sandro Fontana – a former Christian Democrat Minister, now a 'new man' under the *Forza Italia* umbrella – any hope of change is blurred.

Italy does not seem, thus, to be of a great help in reducing the EU democratic deficit. On the contrary, its own internal contradictions seem to enhance it. The problem is thus twofold. On the one hand, the full application of democratic principles in the national framework still has to be assured. This is especially crucial in a time and in a country where, like in Italy, *metacommunications* (the tendency or capacity to create a kind of communication which has as a content the rules and the nature of the communicator itself) wins. The National and European electoral campaigns held in March and June 1994 showed clearly how the media, and most especially TV, constitute nowadays the real centre of the political debate. The entering into of the political competition of a media-champion such as Berlusconi has therefore opened a (not yet settled) debate about democracy and the communication industry (*Il Sole 24 Ore*, 27 March 1994; *Il Popolo*, 4 November 1994).

On the other hand, a re-thinking of how to deal with foreign policy is required. As Alessandro Corneli recalled, foreign policy has never been, in Italy, a matter of public interest. Rather, it has been an affair in the hands of a 'close circle of diplomats and journalists'. (Corneli, *Il Sole 24, Ore* 26 August 1994). The only difference is that EU politics have, and will have, a greater impact on internal affairs.

Part III
European Institutions: Legitimacy and Democracy

8
The Role of the Commission

Finn Laursen

It is commonplace to argue that the institutional set-up of the European Communities (EC), and now the European Union (EU) established by the Maastricht Treaty, is *sui generis*. The institutions established in the European Coal and Steel Community (ECSC) in 1951, later in the European Economic Community (EEC) and the European Atomic Energy Community (EAEC or Euratom) in 1957 were neither purely inter-governmental nor fully federal. They constituted a complex system of interacting institutions, where first the High Authority of the ECSC and later the Commissions of the EEC and Euratom have played important roles. These 'executives' were merged into the Commission of the European Communities in the so-called Merger Treaty which took effect in 1967. The Commission is more than a typical secretariat of an international organisation and less than a normal national executive. It has more powers than the UN Secretariat, but less powers and political legitimacy than most governments in democratic countries.

This chapter will explore what exactly the Commission is supposed to be, what it is, and what it may become, especially if the arguments in favour of a further 'democratisation' of the European Union lead to further changes after the intergovernmental conference in 1996 and beyond. We shall relate these questions to the ongoing discussion about a 'democratic deficit' in the EU, although that debate has mainly been concerned about the role of the European Parliament, and to a lesser extent the Council and national parliaments. It is more difficult to relate the role of the Commission to this debate. To the extent that the Commission has been a part of the debate, various reform proposals have tended towards making it more like a federal executive appointed by and politically responsible to the directly elected European Parliament, possibly retaining some role for the Council, which could become more like a second chamber in a bicameral system. Such a federal solution of the problem of a democratic deficit would appear be the most logical one. However, the electorates of some of the member countries, especially the UK and Denmark, are not ready for such a solution (Laursen 1994). The more minimalist political circles within the European Union seem willing to accept only small incremental reforms.

The question of legitimacy is complex and many-faceted. One important aspect of it is to create a link to the wishes of the electorates. But the notion of a European electorate is still very much a fiction. The most important inputs are still channelled through national systems, even though the power of the European Parliament has been formally increased over the years. Other important inputs at the European level come through the increasing amount of lobbying that takes place in Brussels (Andersen and Eliassen 1991; Mazey and Richardson 1994).

To the extent that the Commission is a bureaucracy, its legitimacy is also a question of capacity to produce results, especially welfare gains. Legitimacy thus has both formal and utilitarian aspects. To a certain extent, the Commission can be compared with a government in the member states. It takes political initiatives, it proposes legislation, it has a bureaucracy at its disposal, it gets involved in policy implementation. However, it depends less on the European Parliament (EP) than most national governments depend on national parliaments. The Commission is appointed by common accord of the member governments. It is still the Council of Ministers which plays the most important role in providing legitimacy for the European Union, albeit in an indirect way. The role of the EP has been increased over time. According to the Treaty of Rome the EP could vote on a motion of censure and force the entire Commission to resign, but this power has never been used. Since the Maastricht Treaty the Commission President and the entire College of Commissioners must be approved by the EP (art. 158). The EU has thus taken a small step towards 'parliamentary democracy' through the Maastricht Treaty. As we shall see later, however, the Maastricht Treaty did not improve the 'image' of the Commission. The expected welfare gains of the internal market programme, on the other hand, do seem to have improved the 'image' of the Commission through the late 1980s.

As we shall argue in the following, the main impetus for creating the Commission was one of efficiency. Its legitimacy was to follow from its expertise and knowledge. The founding fathers were concerned about the institutional capacity to solve common problems. 'Democratic' checks were added during the negotiations of the original treaties: first by, the Treaty of Paris established the ECSC, which included the Council of Ministers and some other institutions. The Treaty of Rome reduced the powers of the Commission in relation to the Council somewhat. Later the Single European Act (SEA) and the Maastricht Treaty increased the EP's involvement in legislation through co-operation and co-decision procedures, though without fundamentally changing the role of the Commission.

THE FOUNDING FATHERS AND THE HIGH AUTHORITY

To understand the special nature of the Commission it is useful to go back to the beginning. The ECSC had its immediate origin in the Schuman Declaration of 9 May 1950, in which the French foreign minister called for 'a new high authority whose decisions will be binding on France, Germany and the other countries who may subsequently join'. Such an authority was seen as 'the first concrete foundation for a European federation which is so indispensable for the preservation of peace'. It would be 'composed of independent personalities' (quoted from Patijn 1970: 47–53).

The key figure behind the Schuman Plan was Jean Monnet who prepared the text with a few friends, Etienne Hirsch, René Mayer, Paul Reuter and Pierre Uri. It went through a series of drafts. What was first referred to as 'an international Authority' was described as 'supranational' in the fourth draft, but Monnet disliked the term, so it became the 'High Authority' (Monnet 1978: 288–298).

The Schuman Plan was quickly accepted by the West German Chancellor Konrad Adenauer and, with some hesitation, by the governments of Italy and the Benelux countries. The British objected to the idea of setting up 'an authority, with certain supreme powers'. The French sensed, however, that according to the British concept, 'there would be no common rules and no independent High Authority, but only some kind of OEEC'. So France and the five other countries went ahead without the British. Monnet emphasised at the time that 'what must be sought is a fusion of the interests of the European peoples and not merely another effort to maintain an equilibrium of those interests through additional machinery for negotiation' (*ibid.*: 298–317).

The institutional details were worked out at an intergovernmental conference that started in June 1950 in Paris. 'We are here', Monnet told the government representatives, 'to undertake a common task –

not to negotiate for our own national advantage, but to seek it in the advantage of all'. Monnet and Walter Hallstein, who negotiated for the Federal Republic of Germany, insisted on the High Authority's independence. The other countries, in particular the Netherlands, sought various controls and safeguards or means of appeal.

It was the Dutch representative Dirk Spierenburg who asked the question: 'Why should these means of appeal not consist of a majority decision – perhaps a two-thirds majority – taken by a committee of Ministers from the countries concerned? This would give the Governments back their proper role' (quoted from *ibid.*: 327). Monnet reminded Spierenburg that 'intergovernmental co-operation had never led anywhere' (*ibid.*: 328). Eventually, however, Monnet agreed that there would be areas expressly entrusted to the High Authority and other areas where the Governments would be empowered to intervene (*ibid.*: 332). Thus the Council of Ministers was born. Less controversially, the negotiators also agreed on the establishment of a Consultative Committee representing interested groups, a Common Assembly of parliamentarians, and a Court of Justice, the former two consultative, the latter one with real powers. So it was through a political bargaining process that the ECSC got its elements of checks-and-balances, with the High Authority being a powerful 'executive'. There is an interesting parallel here to the way the origin of federal systems can be studied as political bargains (Riker 1964).

The ECSC Treaty of Paris was finally signed in the spring of 1951 and entered into force in 1952. The High Authority had nine members. A central stipulation was the following one in article 9:

> The members of the High Authority shall be completely independent in the performance of their functions, in the general interest of the Community. In the discharge of their duties they shall neither seek nor take instructions from any Government or from any other body. They shall refrain from any action incompatible with the supranational character of their functions.
> Each Member State undertakes to respect this supra-national character and not to seek to influence the members of the High Authority in the performance of their task (quoted from Van Panhuys et al. 1968: 660).

The treaty clearly stressed the independent and supranational character of the High Authority. In a number of areas it could act alone, in some areas it needed to consult the Council of Ministers, in others it needed the agreement of the Council of Ministers, sometimes by simple majority, sometimes by two-thirds majority, and sometimes by a unanimous vote (Haas 1958: 52–550). All in all, the High Authority that emerged from the negotiations was not as independent and strong as Monnet had wanted, but still a substantially more powerful body compared to the secretariats of typical intergovernmental organisations.

In some ways it is more instructive to compare the High Authority – and later the Commission – with the American Presidency. Both are supposed to represent the interests of the whole. The Council – like the US Senate – was intended to represent the interests of the member states, and the EP – like the House of Representatives – the interests of the peoples of the member states. However, whereas the American president is elected directly by the American people, the High Authority (later the EC Commission) is appointed by the member governments. It can therefore not claim the kind of popular mandate which an American president can claim. In a formal sense, the democratic legitimacy of the Commission is still mainly indirect, through the legitimacy of national governments, even if its capacity to solve problems can also provide it with some legitimacy.

THE TREATIES OF ROME AND THE MERGER TREATY

Many students of the institutions of the EC have noticed that the EEC institutions were less supranational in character than those of the ECSC. This may be explained by a change in the political mood after the debacle of the European Defence Community (EDC) in 1954, but might to some extent follow from the fact that the ECSC treaty is what the French call a 'traité loi' while the EEC treaty is a 'traité cadre' (Lasok and Bridge 1987: 188). To the extent that the EEC treaty set various objectives that were to be attained gradually over a number of years more involvement from national governments was considered necessary.

In the EEC treaty (1957) the Commission was the equivalent to the High Authority, but the Commission's powers were more circumscribed and limited than those of the High Authority (Hallstein 1962: 20). The functions of the Commission were listed in article 155 of the Treaty of Rome. The Commission shall:

– ensure that the provisions of this Treaty and the measures taken by the institution pursuant thereto are applied;
– formulate recommendations or deliver opinions on matters dealt with in this Treaty, if it expressly so provides or if the Commission considers it necessary;

- have its own power of decision and participate in the shaping of measures taken by the Council and by the European Parliament in the manner provided for in this Treaty;
- exercise the powers conferred on it by the Council for the implementation of the rules laid down by the latter (EC 1987: 366).

It is clear from this general description that, for a full overview of the functions of the Commission, one has to consult both the complete treaty (or rather treaties) as well as the legislation that empowers the Commission to implement and make decisions in individual cases.

An important function of the Commission is that of initiative. Many treaty articles outline procedures whereby the Council will adopt legislation on a proposal from the Commission – often after consulting the European Parliament and in some cases the Economic and Social Committee. Examples of such articles are article 43 on the Common Agricultural Policy and article 75 on the Common Transport Policy. This exclusive right of initiative in normal Community policy making has been a central aspect of the so-called 'Community method' since the Treaty of Rome. Emile Noël, the Commission's long-time Secretary General, wrote in 1973:

> The organization of the power of initiative in the Rome Treaties is one of the most striking characteristics of the Community system. The power of initiative is reserved almost exclusively by the Treaties to the institution whose task it is to express the general interests of the Community – the Commission – an institution whose independence was guaranteed by the Treaties, which established its political character when they stipulated *inter alia* that the Commission alone was responsible to the European Parliament. The Treaties also gave a political significance to the power of initiative, when they laid down that the proposals of the Commission or at least the most important – would be submitted to the European Parliament for their opinion – that is to say, that they should be publicized and made the subject of a public debate by the representatives of the peoples of the Community (Noël 1973).

Whether the European Parliament was able then or is able now to play that role is of course an important question when one tries to evaluate the degree of 'democracy' in the EC or EU. But Emile Noël went on to say:

> The power of initiative is exercised in an organized institutional system, in fact, in a constitutional system. The Treaties set up a particular form of separation of powers; where one institution – the

Commission – alone exercises the power of initiative, while another institution – the Council – alone has, as a general rule, the power of decision (except for delegation to the Commission in the case of derived law), until an increase in the powers of the European Parliament allows it to play a full part in the exercise of this power (*ibid.*)

A dialogue between the Commission and the Council was central to this system. Duties linked to the power of initiative of the Commission were those of 'reflection, preparation and thinking ahead'. By giving the role of initiative to the Commission the power of decision of the Council became less arbitrary. Words used to describe the system included co-ordination, conciliation, conviction and encouragement. Said Noël, 'Negotiation or dialogue is the normal rule in all modern democracies'. And he claimed that the system had established 'a modern and efficient system' (*ibid.*).

The Commission's first president, Walter Hallstein, described the Commission's role as being threefold:

> First, it has the task of drawing up proposals to be decided by the Council of Ministers; ...
> Second, it has the duty of watching over the execution of the treaty, and calling member governments and enterprises to account if they fail to respect it; ...
> Third, the EEC executive has the role of helping to bring about agreement in the Council of Ministers, by using its overall viewpoint, its skill, and its power of advocacy, to secure the acceptance of measures which are in the interest of the whole Community, even if they mean temporary sacrifices of purely national interests (Hallstein 1962: 21).

He summarised this by saying that the Commission was 'at once a motor, a watchdog, and a kind of honest broker'. He dwelled on the function of helping to bring about agreement between the member states. 'In a sense, this is one of the main purposes of the whole institutional structure of the European Community' (Hallstein 1962: 22). In this connection Hallstein also emphasised the importance of majority voting in the Council as well as 'democratic supervision' exercised by the European Parliament, and the 'directly enforceable' verdicts of the Court of Justice (*ibid.*: 23–29).

The concrete functions of the Commission are many. It engages in rule making, especially under the ECSC treaty, but also under the EEC treaty. It means that a lot of Regulations, Directives and Decisions are adopted by the Commission. Art. 48(3), for instance, enables the Commission to lay down the conditions under which workers have a right to live in a member state in which they have been employed. Within different policy areas the Council has also delegated wide rule-making powers to the Commission. This, for instance, is the case within the Common Agricultural Policy, where the Commission adopts hundreds of Regulations each year (Lasok and Bridge 1987: 190).

The Commission also applies the rules to specific cases in a number of areas. The most important area where this happens is competition policy, which involves individual companies as well as states. The Commission plays an important role vis-à-vis third countries, in representing the EC and in negotiating various agreements. This has included successive rounds of GATT negotiations as well as the negotiation of trade, trade and co-operation, and association agreements with third countries. It is also the Commission which negotiates accession treaties (Smith 1994).

The Commission has an important role in the budgetary field, in making and giving effect to the budgets adopted by the European Parliament. It administers the European Social Fund, the European Development Fund, the European Agricultural Guidance and Guarantee Fund, and the European Regional Development Fund.

Finally, the Commission has the role of guardian of the Treaties. This is the watchdog role. The Commission investigates alleged infringements of Treaty obligations and can take individual member countries to the Court of Justice (see especially. art. 169/EEC) (Usher 1994).

The composition of the Commission was specified in article 157 of the Treaty of Rome. At the beginning it had nine members with at least one per member state and a maximum of two; in practice France, Germany and Italy had two members and each Benelux country had one. Later enlargements added Commissioners from the new member states: in 1973 there were added two from the UK, one from Denmark and one from Ireland; one from Greece in 1981; two from Spain and one from Portugal in 1986.

Article 157 was replaced by an essentially identical article 10 of the Merger Treaty of 1965, which entered into force in 1967. A single Commission took the place of the High Authority of ECSC and the Commissions of the EEC and Euratom. It stipulated, inter alia:

> The members of the Commission shall act completely independently in the performance of their duties, in the general interest of the Communities.
> In the performance of their duties, they shall neither seek nor take instructions from any Government or other body. They shall refrain from any action incompatible with the nature of their duties. Each Member State undertakes to respect this principle and not to seek to influence the members of the Commission in the performance of their duties (quoted from Van Panhuys, et al. 1968: 796).

This article resembles art. 9 of the ECSC treaty, but we notice that the adjective 'supranational' has disappeared (Stein, et al. 1976: 38).

The Commissioners are appointed by common accord between the member states. In the past they were appointed for four years; Commissioners from January 1995 were appointed for five years to synchronise the life spans of the European Parliament and the Commission. The Maastricht Treaty now requires that the President of the Commission and the whole Commission must be approved by the Parliament (art. 158).

In cases of serious misconduct individual members of the Commission may be compulsorily retired by the Court of Justice (art. 160). The whole Commission can be forced to retire by the European Parliament by a motion of censure adopted by a two-thirds majority of the votes cast, representing a majority of the members (art. 144). As mentioned, this power of the European Parliament has never been used in practice (Lasok and Bridge 1987: 185).

A government cannot recall a Commissioner it has nominated, but can of course refuse to renominate a Commissioner, as for instance happened in the case of Lord Cockfield, who was not reappointed to the second Delors Commission in 1989. He had become too 'European' for Margaret Thatcher (Nugent 1994: 87).

REFORM PROPOSALS

The nature and respective roles of the EC institutions have been the subject of much discussion since the beginning of European integration in the 1950s. The 1960s witnessed a major conflict between General de Gaulle's France and the other five member states and the Commission about the nature and powers of the EC institutions, with General de Gaulle stressing the intergovernmental aspects and the consensual nature of the decision-making process. The conflict was brought to an end with the Luxembourg Compromise in 1966, where France insisted on having a right of veto whenever important national interests are at state. This mainly affected voting in the Council, but another outcome was a relative weakening of the Commission, whose first President Walter Hallstein had played too active a role for General de Gaulle's liking. The merged Commission that took effect in 1967 also saw a less active President than Hallstein, namely Jean Rey, and most Commission presidents, until Jacques Delors in 1985, played a less active role than Hallstein.

After the first enlargement in 1973 a special need to discuss the role of the institutions was felt. The December 1974 summit in Paris invited Belgium's Prime Minister Leo Tindemans to submit a report to the Heads of Government before the end of 1975. The Tindemans Report was submitted to the European Council in December 1975. It dealt with both policies and institutions. In his letter to his colleagues Tindemans said that he was 'personally convinced that Europe will only fulfil its destiny if it espouses federalism' (Tindemans 1976: 5). The report itself made more modest proposals. The section on 'strengthening the institutions' was based on four criteria: authority, efficiency, legitimacy and coherence. With respect to the Commission the main proposal was for the Council to use art. 155 more to confer on the Commission powers for the execution and administration of common policies. In order to increase the authority and cohesion of the Commission the report proposed the following treaty amendments:

(a) The President of the Commission will be appointed by the European Council.
(b) The President when appointed will have to appear before the Parliament to make a statement and have his appointment confirmed by vote.
(c) The President of the Commission will then appoint his colleagues in consultation with the Council and bearing in mind the number of Commissioners allocated to each country (Tindemans 1976: 31).

Efficiency seemed to be the main guiding principle in respect to the Commission. The concept of 'democratic legitimacy' was only explicitly applied to the Parliament by Tindemans. But having the President confirmed by the EP would presumably increase the Commission's democratic legitimacy, especially if the EP itself was considered legitimate.

Two other reform proposals followed in 1979, the Spierenburg Report which dealt with the Commission, and the Three Wise Men's report, which dealt with the EC institutions in general.

The first part of the Spierenburg Report dealt with the Commission's fundamental role and its effectiveness. This included the statement that 'over the last ten years the Commission's influence, effectiveness and reputation have declined' (Spierenburg 1979: 4). The main recommendations in the second part were that the number of Commissioners should be kept to a strict minimum, the presidency should be reinforced and the number of administrative units within the Commission should be reduced. The third section proposed measures to improve administrative efficiency, mainly in the area of personnel policy.

The Three Wise Men, Barend Biesheuvel, Edmund Dell and Robert Marjolin, also mentioned 'the declining authority of the Commission', saying that there had been a 'trend to fragmentation and loss of central control'. They also talked about the 'excessive load of business' (EC 1979: 11). They partly blamed the nationalistic attitudes of governments and the prevalence of consensus procedures in the Council for the difficulties, but also recognised some problems of internal organisation. In general they endorsed the proposals of the Spierenburg Report. This included reducing the number of Commissioners to one per country, reducing the number of Directorates-General within the Commission, strengthening the authority of the President, achieving a more homogenous college of Commissioners, more co-ordination, and better personnel management.

Reform discussions continued in the 1980s. The directly elected European Parliament produced a Draft Treaty proposal in 1984. Government representatives produced the Dooge Report in 1985. Eventually some reforms were introduced with the Single European Act (1986), which, however, only marginally affected the Commission.

The most radical reform proposal in the 1980s came from the European Parliament. Under the leadership of Altiero Spinelli it adopted the Draft Treaty establishing the European Union on 14 February 1984 with 237 votes in favour, 31 against and 43 abstentions. The Draft Treaty proposed a kind of parliamentary government at the Union level, attributing, however, an important role to the European Council in appointing the Commission. Art 25 stipulated:

> The Commission shall take office within a period of six months following the election of the Parliament.
> At the beginning of each parliamentary term, the European Council shall designate the President of the Commission. The President shall constitute the Commission after consulting the European Council.
> The Commission shall submit its programme to the Parliament. It shall take office after its investiture by the Parliament. It shall remain in office until the investiture of a new Commission (European Parliament 1984: 19–20).

Article 28 said that 'the Commission shall be responsible to the Parliament'. And, 'the members of the Commission shall resign as a body in the event of Parliament's adopting a motion of censure by a qualified majority'.

The Dooge Report called for 'efficient and democratic institutions' (EC 1985: 9). The Commission's powers should be increased and its autonomy confirmed. The President should be designated by the European Council, and the other members 'appointed by common accord of the Governments of the Member States, acting on a proposal from the President-designate'. The Commission should not include more that one national from any Member State. 'At the beginning of its term of office the Commission should receive a vote of investiture on the basis of its programme'.

Comparing the reform proposals of the 1970s with the proposals of the 1980s we notice a shift towards an increased involvement of the European Parliament in appointing the Commission. Implicitly this suggests a greater concern for the democratic legitimacy of the Commission. The ideal model was clearly that of a federal parliamentary system, even if most reform proposals did not go to the logical extreme. The multinational nature of the EC put limits on what was considered possible.

THE SEA AND MAASTRICHT TREATY

Substantively the SEA dealt with the internal market. Institutionally it introduced the co-operation procedure and made qualified majority voting in the Council the general rule in respect to internal market legislation. It also introduced the assent procedure for association agreements and accession treaties. More specifically, concerning the role of the Commission, it included in art. 10 a supplementary provision to art. 145 of the EEC Treaty concerning the Council's delegation of rule-making powers to the Commission. The Council can confer such powers to the Commission in the acts it adopts, but it can also impose certain requirements (EC 1986: 10).

Art. 10 of the SEA was accompanied by a declaration asking the EC institutions to adopt principles and rules concerning the Commission's rules of implementation. This led to the adoption of a Council Decision on comitology in 1987. This decision streamlined existing procedures into three kinds of committees: advisory committees, management committees and regulatory committees (Docksey and Williams 1994).

The Commission had started using management committees within the Common Agricultural Policy (CAP) in 1962 and regulatory committees in customs, health and veterinary legislation in 1968. Through these committees the member states got involved in the execution of policy, and could, depending on the exact nature of the committee, control the Commission. For this reason the Parliament has been critical of these committees (*ibid.*).

The difference between the three committee types listed in the 1987 decision, put briefly, is this: advisory committees give opinions, but the Commission is not bound by an opinion. A management committee can force a referral of a Commission proposal to the Council by adopting an unfavourable opinion by qualified majority. Under the regulatory committee system the Commission can only introduce measures approved by the committee. There is thus an increasing degree of control through these three kinds of committees (*see also* Usher 1994).

The Maastricht Treaty affected the role of the Commission more than the SEA, partly by introducing the co-decision procedure, partly by giving the Commission a non-exclusive right of initiative in Common Foreign and Security Policy (CFSP) and Co-operation in Justice and Home Affairs (JHA) (Laursen and Vanhoonacker 1992; Nuttall 1994).

The co-decision procedure (art. 189b) introduces the possibility of a third reading in the EP for some legislation, additional to the second reading introduced by the SEA (Westlake 1994). If, after the second reading there is no agreement between the Council and the EP a Conciliation Committee can be established between the Council and the EP. Art. 189b(4) stipulates, inter alia, that 'The Commission shall take part in the Conciliation Committee's proceedings and shall take all the necessary initiatives with a view to reconciling the positions of the European Parliament and the Council' (EC 1992: 77). But the Commission will not have its traditional exclusive right of initiative at this stage. During the negotiations of the Maastricht Treaty the Commission expressed concern about its role under co-decision and some changes were introduced (Wester 1992). But it still remains to be seen what kind of role the Commission will be able to play under this new procedure. Presumably it will still be able to play an important role as honest broker, at least.

Extending the Commission's right of initiative to the second and third pillars of the Maastricht Treaty, CFSP and JHA, expanded the scope of activities of the Commission. The Commission was associated with the work of European Political Co-operation (EPC) in the past, but had no right of initiative. Now it has a Directorate-General IA, which deals with External Political Relations. DG I still exists, dealing with External Economic Relations.

The Maastricht Treaty also included other innovations which affected the relationship between the EP and the Commission. Although the EP did not get the right of initiative, which it asked for, it may now request the Commission to submit a proposal (art. 138b). More importantly, the Member States shall consult the EP when nominating the

President of the Commission. This President-nominate is consulted on the other nominations to the Commission. Finally, all Commissioners must be approved by the EP:

> The President and the other members of the Commission thus nominated shall be subject as a body to a vote of approval by the European Parliament. After approval by the European Parliament, the President and the other members of the Commission shall be appointed by the common accord of the governments of the Member States (art. 158 (2)).

From January 1995 the period of office of the Commission is five years like that of the EP.

THEORETICAL PERSPECTIVES

The first major political science analysis of the ECSC was Ernst Haas' *The Uniting of Europe* (1958). A central concept in Haas' early work was that of 'spill-over', the suggestion that sector integration had a certain built-in logic that would make it expand from coal and steel to other sectors. The High Authority played an important role, but not necessarily as important as some would think. It is probably indicative that Haas wrote about the role of interest groups and political parties before he wrote about the role of the High Authority in his book. But the High Authority could contribute to finding compromises in the Council by establishing the facts:

> Negotiations are thus freed of the preliminary issue of the reliability of the facts alleged by the parties. Continual prior contact among the personnel engaged in the talks reduces the possibility of bluffing, idle speechmaking and bargaining in defiance of the technical demands of the issue at stake (Haas 1958: 524).

Terms like 'the technical demands of the issue' suggest a certain functional determinism, but Haas linked this with 'the symbiosis of interministerial and federal procedures' which had activated 'socio-economic processes in the pluralistic-industrial-democratic milieu in which it functions'. It all led to 'a highly specific, and certainly corporate, series of techniques whose tendency to advance integration is patent' (*ibid.*: 526–527).

The first major political science analysis of the EEC was Leon Lindberg's *The Political Dynamics of European Economic Integration* (1963). Lindberg continued on lines similar to those of Haas. Integration, according to Lindberg required the following four conditions: central institutions and policies, elite activation, inherently expansive tasks and continuity of national policy aims. In respect to institutions Lindberg said: 'Central institutions are required in order to *represent* the common interests which have brought the Member States together, and in order to *accommodate* such conflicts of interest as will inevitably arise' (Lindberg 1963: 8). In his general conclusions he said:

> Policy-making, or the pattern of bargaining and exchanging of concession that it has come to mean, involves not only six governments, but also an autonomous representative of the interests of the Community as a whole, the Commission. The Commission enjoys some unique advantages by virtue of its ability to embody the authority of a Community consensus. It can claim to speak for the common interests of all six countries, and has repeatedly demonstrated its capacity to precipitate unity by taking divergent demands and breaking them into their constituent parts, thus obliging each party to a conflict to re-examine its position in the perspective of the common interest (Lindberg 1963: 284).

The conflict between the Hallstein Commission and the French President, General De Gaulle, in 1965, and the ensuing Luxembourg compromise in January 1966, created certain problems for early neofunctionalist integration theory. But Lindberg tried with Scheingold to put forward a revised neofunctionalist theory in *Europe's Would-Be Polity* (1970). In this theory the Commission retained or was possibly given an even more important role and the problem of leadership was dealt with for the first time in an explicit fashion:

> ... leadership is a crucial activator of coalitions that conduce to system growth. It is the function of leadership to aid in the identification of problems; to evaluate, store, and retrieve information; to see to it that differences are handled in acceptable ways; to articulate goals for the collectivity and to symbolize them effectively; to build up support in the legitimacy of the system; and to engineer consent by organizing bargaining and the exchange of concessions (Lindberg and Scheingold 1970: 128).

The Commission can play such a role of leadership. When considering the Commission Lindberg and Scheingold talk about supranational leadership. But national leadership can also play an important role in the integration process.

Lindberg and Scheingold offered a general description of the ideal Commission. They listed the following as necessary for the Commission to realise its optimal potentialities:

1. *Goal articulation.* The Commission can articulate long-term goals for the Community that can in turn be legitimated in terms of some belief in a European common interest.
2. *Coalition building.* The Commission can take the initiative in identifying problems to be solved by joint or co-ordinated action, and in making specific proposals.
3. *Recruitment and organisation.* The Commission can recruit its staff so as to maximise prior national contacts and experience, technical expertise, and, at the higher levels, political experience and prestige.
4. *Expand scope.* The Commission can be alert to the possibilities of convincing governments and present or potential client groups to redefine their goals and purposes in the direction of more joint activity.
5. *Brokerage and package deals.* The Commission can play an active and constructive role in intergovernmental bargaining at all levels and stages of the decision-making process (Lindberg and Scheingold 1970: 93–94).

The Commission thus plays a role in articulating interests and goals but especially in aggregating interests through proposing package deals and creating the necessary coalitions. According to Lindberg and Scheingold the skills required of the Commission are political skills *par excellence*. Also, the relationship between the Community and the national governments, between the Commission and the Council are 'more nearly a symbiotic relationship than a competitive one'.

In 1970, another important study was published, David Coombes' *Politics and Bureaucracy in the European Community*. As the subtitle *A Portrait of the Commission of the EEC* indicates it is a book specifically about the Commission, and it remains one of the few major studies of the Commission. Coombes contrasted the relatively optimistic analysis of Lindberg in *The Political Dynamics of European Economic Integration* with the critical, federalist analysis of Altiero Spinelli in *The Eurocrats* (1966), according to which the process of European integration will fail if it does not succeed in mobilising a mass political movement in support of European federation. Co-opting national civil servants through *engrenage*, as the French call it, was clearly insufficient (Coombes 1970: 91–100).

Coombes went on to develop a conceptual framework which contrasted the different functions of the Commission. These included the function of initiative and, closely linked with that, what he called a normative function. This includes being the 'guardian of the Treaty' and an honest broker in the Council. These functions are clearly very important: '...the Initiative and Normative functions of the Commission are interdependent and together give it the role of political leader and promoter of the Community interest' (Coombes 1970: 236).

But the Commission also has an important administrative function. This includes taking regulatory decisions based on delegated authority. Coombes' central question, then, was whether the initiative and administrative functions call for different kinds of organisation. Further, the Commission has a mediative function, 'which arises from its duty to bring about agreement between the member States in the Council of Ministers'. Again, would the mediative function be incompatible with the normative function?

> The mediator who initiates too frequently runs the risk of seeming partisan or at least making enemies by accident. The initiator in his turn must have the backing of some legitimizing, norm-setting authority, whether this be a representative assembly, or a mass political movement, or whether the authority is in some way vested in himself (as is the case of the Commission). The mediator does not require such authority and may well find it an embarrassment, for his role depends on his unimpeachable independence and impartiality (Coombes 1970: 239).

The Coombes' thesis is illustrated in Figure 8.1. As the Commission has become more 'bureaucratised', it has become more difficult to fulfil

Figure 8.1: *The Functions of the Commission*

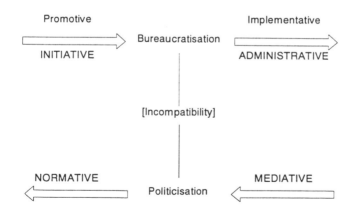

Source: adapted from Coombes (1970), p. 20

the more political, promotive functions. If the political functions are about 'upgrading the common interest' then the implementative functions are oriented towards 'splitting the difference'.

Commissioners are not political leaders. 'First of all, the members of the Commission are not elected by any popular majority with any mandate to govern, nor are they responsible to any directly elected representative assembly' (Coombes 1970: 251).

Although the Hallstein Commission had initially been 'a relatively united, committed partisan organisation, ideally suited to the Commission's promotive functions', by the time of the merger of the executives in the mid–1960s 'a bureaucratic vicious circle had begun to set in'. The Common Agricultural Policy (CAP) was in place. Now it had to be implemented. Also, the common culture in the Commission was constantly being threatened by the recruitment of nationalistic and technically-minded officials. Jean Rey who took over as president of the merged Commission in 1967 was a less 'charismatic' figure than Hallstein. He was 'expected to play a 'backseat' role as chairman and broker rather than the active one of promoter and instigator' (Coombes 1970: 265).

THE CASE OF THE DELORS COMMISSION

To what extent has the Coombes' thesis stood the test of time? While the problems singled out by Coombes are still central ones, the EP is at least now directly elected and does get involved in appointing the Commission. More importantly, the Delors Commissions have proved that determined Commissions can still carry out the promotive-normative functions.

The Delors Commissions have played an important role in the integration process since 1985 (Dinan 1994: 203–205; Grant 1994). The Commission played an important role in giving the integration process a new momentum in the mid 1980s (Laursen 1990). It put the completion of the internal market on the agenda with its White Paper. It contributed very actively to the Intergovernmental Conference (IGC) that negotiated the SEA. It helped achieve in 1988 important budget reforms, which gave more financial substance to the notion of 'economic and social cohesion'. It then helped put Economic and Monetary Union on the agenda and Delors himself chaired the Committee which produced the blue-print for EMU (EC 1989). There was clearly both intellectual and entrepreneurial leadership in all this (Laursen 1994).

When it became clear that the internal market had not been fully realised – that important non-tariff barriers to trade still existed – the Commission took the initiative in overcoming national 'defections' from agreed goals through renewed efforts to reach optimal outcomes (Laursen 1991). It outlined the plan, set the deadlines, engineered the required institutional changes, built the necessary coalitions and supervised the efforts, producing annual reports on national implementation of directives. The Delors Commission masterfully played the role prescribed by neofunctionalist theory in connection with the internal market and the SEA, thus in a way creating some problems for David Coombes' theory.

The logic of defection, which was such a problem for the internal market, also applies to monetary matters. You can defect – through competitive devaluations – and in the end we will all be worse off. 'One Market, One Money', the Commission reasoned, and helped push the EMU part of the Maastricht Treaty (EC 1990).

The Commission was less successful on other aspects of the Maastricht Treaty, especially the fact the CFSP and JHA stayed basically intergovernmental. And the No vote in the first Danish referendum in June 1992 was clearly a shock for the Commission. The permissive consensus about integration which had existed at the beginning of the process clearly no longer existed (Laursen 1994). The Commission, and national political leaders, clearly needed to think about the strategy for the future.

The appointment of the Delors Commission in 1984 showed that the Member States can appoint a powerful Commission, when they so decide. Changes in French policy under Mitterrand in 1983 have been singled out as being especially important (Moravcsik 1991). However, the appointment of Jacques Santer as President of the Commission from January 1995 suggests that governments can also decide to go for a less powerful Commission, when they so decide, although it is too early to tell what role that Commission will play.

The history of the role of the Commission, with the powerful Hallstein Commission being broken by De Gaulle's France, and the proposals for a powerful Dehaene Commission to follow the Delors Commission being vetoed by the UK, suggests the continued importance of neorealist-intergovernmentalist theories of integration. The least integrationist Member States can still largely determine the speed of integration. Although the EP is now more involved in appointing the Commission, it cannot by itself determine who forms the 'government' of the Union. Each Member State retains a veto. Those who think that democratic legitimacy only can exist at the national level will find this natural.

Federalists, who would like to see more transparency and democracy at the level of the European Union as well as efficiency, will deplore it.

LEGITIMACY: MODELS AND OPINION DATA

Legitimacy has different sources. To most people in Europe a government is democratically legitimate if it has the support of a democratically elected parliament (or at least not a majority against it). This concept can be applied nationally, but is more difficult within the EC/EU. National governments, which presumably have democratic legitimacy, and the European Parliament, which is supposed to have some kind of European legitimacy by being directly elected, now get involved in appointing the European Commission. But legitimacy is determined by more than formal rules alone. A bureaucracy is supposed to be efficient. The Commission has tried to increase its efficiency in various ways, including involving national experts in policy preparation and national officials in the implementation of policy. Indeed, the Commission employs an elaborate system of committees for theses purposes (Nedergaard 1994). Involving interest organisations also increases legitimacy and efficiency.

In reality we have conflicting concepts of what the Commission should be. Rometsch and Wessels (1994) outlined four different models: (1) the Commission as a dynamic and enlightened technocracy; (2) the Commission as a federal government; (3) the Commission as an expert and administrative secretariat to the Council; and (4) the Commission as the 'promotional broker' within the Council. According to the first model, associated with Monnet, the Commission's legitimacy is based on its expertise. In a way it could be compared with Plato's wise men. According to the second model, associated with Altiero Spinelli and other European federalists, the Commission should draw a democratic mandate from the directly elected European Parliament and become a real government. According to the third model real legitimacy lies with national governments. The emphasis will therefore be on the roles of the Council and European Council; the powers of the Commission will be circumscribed, *inter alia* through comitology. The fourth model is based on the concept of dual legitimacy, i.e. both the Member States and the European Community/Union has legitimacy. The Commission is a co-player in a co-operative game. It plays an independent role promoting the common European interest. It acquires influence partly from its expertise, partly from support from other institutions, including the EP and interest groups. This fourth model, according to Rometsch and

Wessels, is the one that best fits the current reality.

We do not have good measures of the actual legitimacy of the Commission, but the opinion polls conducted by the Commission and published in *Eurobarometer* usually include the question 'Has what you read or heard given you a generally favourable or unfavourable impression of the European Commission?' If we take the answer to this question as an indication of legitimacy we will notice (see Table 8.1 and Figure 8.2) that an increasing number of people answered 'generally favourable' from the mid–1980s until 1991 or so. Between the spring and autumn of 1992 the figure fell from 47 percent to 39 percent. In between we had had the 'No' vote in the first Danish referendum on the Maastricht Treaty. The figure fell further in 1993. This suggests that the Commission's image is linked with wider developments in the European integration process. When the internal market programme created new optimism in Europe, the Commission's image improved. Integration was expected to produce economic welfare gains. When the Maastricht Treaty ran into ratification problems, the image of the Commission deteriorated. In many ways it was made a scapegoat for a Treaty which it felt obliged to defend, but which it did not really like (Edwards and Spence 1994: 19). Apart from promises of more money for the structural funds, which would benefit the so-called cohesion countries (Greece, Spain, Portugal and Ireland), it was more difficult to defend the Maastricht Treaty with claims of economic gains. On the contrary, it deepened integration in such a way that it started to touch on the

Table 8.1: *Public Opinion of the European Commission (EC 12)*

Question: Has what you read or heard given you a generally favourable or unfavourable impression of the European Commission?
(A=Autumn; S=Spring; answers in percentages)

Year	A87	S88	A88	S89	A89	S90	A90	S91	A91	S92	A92	S93	A 93
Generally favourable	41	38	47	47	51	52	52	50	46	47	39	34	35
Generally unfavourable	27	24	17	22	15	14	17	19	22	18	25	28	25
Neither/Nor	27	32	28	24	27	27	24	25	25	27	30	32	33

Source: *Eurobarometer: Trends 1974–1992* (April 1993) and *Eurobarometer*, No's 39 (June 1993) and 40 (December 1993).

Figure 8.2: *Public Opinion of the European Commission (EC 12)*

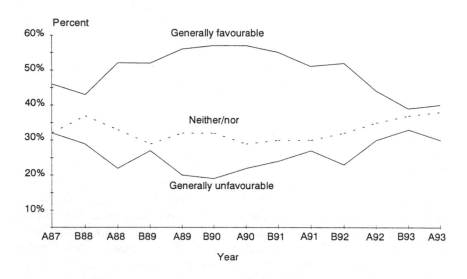

hard cores of national sovereignty, through plans for a single currency, common defence policy, etc. Whereas economic integration hitherto had been seen as a positive-sum game it now entered 'high politics' areas where the perceptions were more those of a zero-sum game.

STRATEGIC CONSIDERATIONS FOR THE FUTURE

The Santer Commission came into office in January 1995. Among the immediate tasks facing it were steering the EU through the adjustments required following the EFTA enlargement at the same date, the next IGC in 1996, where the whole problem of 'deepening versus widening' will again have to be considered in anticipation of one or more future enlargements with countries from Central and Eastern Europe and the Mediterranean area. Will the new Union have the requisite institutional capacity to solved the added and increasingly complex problems a much wider Union will face? The risk of institutional overload is clearly present. At the same time the Union must become more open and democratic, and leaders must explain the purposes of integration better, to assure the vital popular support without which the whole process will not be legitimate. Further advances in the role of the European Parliament will be one of the answers offered. Others will call for increased roles of national parliaments. However, the dilemma here is that too much 'democracy' in the form of too many veto-points will decrease the Union's institutional capacity. Will the future then be a wide, but weak union? Or will a core group of more 'federalistic' countries finally break the logic of intergovernmentalism? France, potentially, has a key role in determining the outcome. Put differently, the future will depend a lot on national capacity and leadership. But the Commission will continue to have an important role to play as a 'promotional broker'.

9
The Role of the Council

Fiona Hayes-Renshaw

Early protagonists of European integration liked to think of the European Communities (EC) as a sort of nation writ large, as suggested by the title of Friedrich's *Europe: An Emergent Nation?* (1969), implying the creation of a state-like body at a level above that of individual nations and invested with all the attributes of nationhood. Current citizens of the European Union (EU), however, attempting to understand how its supranational legislative system works by means of comparison with their more familiar national systems, are apt to be confused and disappointed. The greatest confusion and disappointment, arguably, is occasioned by an analysis of the role of the Council, the EC/EU's version of a 'cabinet' or 'government'.

In traditional nation states, where the notion of the division of powers results in a well-defined legislature, executive and judiciary, democracy and sovereignty are enshrined in the government which is directly accountable to the national parliament and, through that body, to the citizens of the state. Consequently, the government is endowed with legitimacy to take sovereign decisions relating to issues directly affecting the state and its citizens.

The case of the Council in the EC/EU is somewhat different. The members of the Council are neither drawn from nor directly answerable as a body to the European Parliament (EP), although the practice has arisen of Ministers, particularly those of the Presidency Member State, appearing before Plenary Sessions of the EP to give reports on the outcome of Council and European Council meetings, as well as participating in the work of EP Committees. Rather, the Council's accountability is indirect, in the sense that its members are individually responsible to their national parliaments and electorates, whose interests they are expected to articulate and defend at European level.

The Council's legitimacy, therefore, derives, in the first place, from the Treaties and, secondly, from the links of its individual members with the citizens of the Union and of the Member States. The question as to whether the latter have retained at least some measure of that most basic attribute of nationhood – sovereignty – is a moot point, given the level of interdependence of the Member States today. The European Communities were established in large part in order to achieve supranational solutions to common, cross-boundary problems, but the shift of authority from national to supranational level has been carefully packaged and presented as a 'pooling' rather than a ceding of national sovereignty on the part of the Member States and their governments.

Consisting as it does of the self-proclaimed guardians of national sovereignty, the Council has long claimed to be the legitimate representative of the interests and concerns of the Member States, and there is some force in this argument, as will be shown. When the notion of democracy is applied to the Council, however, the assessment becomes less positive and allegations of a democratic deficit at the heart of the EC/EU are difficult to counter, despite recent reforms which will be outlined below. The alleged irreconcilability of efficiency and democracy in the Council evokes little sympathy from citizens of a Union which daily affects their lives with increasing immediacy. A greater understanding of the composition and functioning of the Council might be beneficial in the context of current discussions on democracy and legitimacy as they relate to this central institution in the EC/EU's legislative process.

By *legitimacy* is meant the ability of an institution or system to articulate the interests and provide for the needs of a particular group, and to fulfil these two functions with authority. The two basic concepts underlying the notion of legitimacy are *representation* and *efficiency*. Legitimate systems and institutions must therefore reflect the views and interests of the group they represent, they must be open to influence from them and they must be able, at a reasonable speed, to produce policy outcomes which cater to the needs of the majority of the people they govern and represent.

Democracy, or government by the people, may be direct or representative. Given the size of most modern states, direct democracy on all issues is impracticable, with the result that some form of representative system is the norm. The EC/EU differs from the general pattern, in the sense that the European Parliament has only gradually managed to ease itself into the position of co-legislative authority with the Council, and still has some way to go until they are perceived as equal partners in the process. The two basic concepts underlying the notion of democracy are *popular sovereignty* and *majority rule* (Ball 1979: 119).

THE COUNCIL AS INSTITUTION

The Council hierarchy may be depicted in the form of a triangle (see Figure 9.1) and is made up of a number of different levels, ranging from the European Council at the top to the large number of working groups which form the base of the triangle. These various levels are composed of representatives of each of the Member States who are either attached to their respective Permanent Representations in Brussels (Hayes-Renshaw, et al. 1989) or travel to meetings from their respective capitals. Over-arching each of the levels is the Presidency, which is exercised by each of the Member States in turn for a period of six months. The system of rotation has been altered a number of times over the years in order to take account of new members (see Annex I). Underpinning and assisting the entire Council hierarchy is the Council Secretariat, a relatively small, politically neutral body of some 2000 international officials who are recruited by open competition from among the nationals of the Member States.

Much has been written on the decision-making process of the Union, and that of the European Communities which preceded it. The EC/EU has been described as a *sui generis* system, and is characterised by unique institutions, elaborate voting rules and procedures and complicated inter-institutional relationships. As a result, comparisons with national systems and institutions are not always helpful. In essence, the Commission makes a proposal, which is discussed at all levels of the Council hierarchy; the European Parliament and Economic and Social Committee are consulted for their views, and the final decision is taken by one of the sectoral Councils or the European Council. In a small but growing number of areas, the European Parliament acts as a co-legislator with the Council, and may even have a right of veto over the final decision. Decisions within the Council are normally taken on the basis of a specially formulated qualified majority, although they may also be taken by simple majority or unanimity, depending on the issue in question.

Figure 9.1: *The Council Hierarchy*

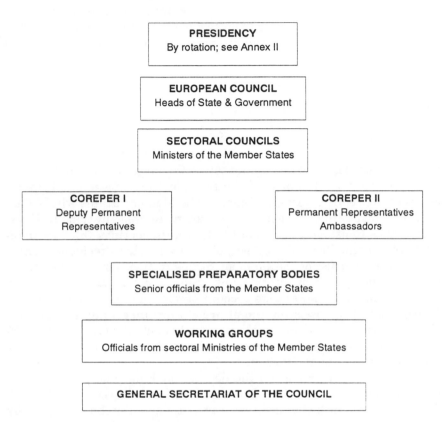

Three basic features of the Council's role in the decision-making process should be highlighted. The first and most obvious is the importance and input of each of the Member States at all levels of the hierarchy. Frequently, judging by the national media – and not just those of the less pro-European Member States – one could be excused for thinking that a body called 'Brussels' existed specifically in order to take the most unpopular decisions and impose them on the Member States! In fact, national representatives are engaged at all levels right from the beginning in a process of bargaining and negotiation on several fronts simultaneously – with the other members of the Council, with the Commission, with the European Parliament and Economic and Social Committee, and perhaps even with other members of their own government and administration.

The second noteworthy feature of the Council hierarchy is the importance of personal relations in the decision-making process. Engaged as they are in an on-going process of bargaining and negotiation – and this is particularly true of those officials attached to the national permanent representations in Brussels – the members of each of the different levels of the Council hierarchy are forced to spend large amounts of time in each other's company, hammering out agreements on often very technical issues. This enforced co-operation fosters a certain *esprit de corps*, giving participants an insight into and understanding of the attitudes and interests of other nationalities, which may prove decisive when compromises or allowances for different viewpoints are required in order to reach agreement at European level.

The third obvious feature of the Council system is the central role of the Presidency. It takes the full responsibility for Community/Union affairs over a period of six months, and the greater role attributed to it over the years has made it not only more prestigious but also more demanding. The fact that each Member State must take its turn at the Presidency makes them more aware of the inherent difficulties in getting and keeping everyone on board over a wide range of issues, and therefore more prepared to be conciliatory, where this is possible.

Relations between the Council and the other EC/EU institutions – specifically the Commission and the European Parliament – are predictably varied. Obliged to cooperage in order to achieve the policy outcomes by which they are judged by the citizens of the EU, they nevertheless engage in a certain amount of jockeying for position and mutual recrimination over the way in which they fulfil their respective roles in the process of European integration. The Council in particular has been subject to a large amount of criticism over the extent to which its organisation and operation comply with the notions of legitimacy and democracy. In examining these criticisms, this chapter will take the opportunity to describe the composition and functioning of the arguably most secretive and consequently least well-known and understood of the EC/EU's institutions.

LEGITIMACY AND THE COUNCIL: REPRESENTATION

At the European level, the Council fulfils the basic representation criterion by being composed of governmental representatives of each of the Member States, who articulate and defend the interests of their countries in negotiations with each other, with the Commission and with the European Parliament. The only exception is in the case of Luxembourg which, given the limited number of its personnel, occasionally arranges to be represented by one of the other Benelux countries in working groups where their interests coincide. Officials from the Commission and the Council Secretariat also attend meetings at all levels of the Council hierarchy, in order to represent the views of the independent Commission (which has normally drafted the chief documents under discussion) and to ensure that the ensuing discussion and decisions are properly recorded and documented.

Input from the European Parliament at most meetings within the Council hierarchy is normally in the form of documents. Alternatively or additionally, the Parliament's views may have been transmitted orally to the Commission or Council during the latter's attendance at a plenary session of the Parliament or by a delegation of MEPs who are responsible for the issue in question. MEPs may be invited to attend Council meetings to put their point of view, though this is still an unusual occurrence. The exception to this general rule concerns the attendance of the President of the European Parliament at the opening session of the European Council, at which he is expected to articulate the point of view of the Parliament on the issues on the agenda.

The voting system within the Council also reflects the notion of representativity. Despite a move towards a greater use of majority voting over the years, unanimity is still retained for a number of areas, including those most fundamental to the Union, such as enlargement and amendment of the Treaties. Under the system of unanimous voting, each Member State is viewed as equal, having a single vote, and efforts are made to accommodate the wishes of Member States who cannot accept what is being proposed. While the smaller Member States frequently express concern about their position vis-à-vis those with greater economic power and larger populations, the emphasis here is on genuine difficulties rather than the size of the Member State in question.

The varying size of the Member States is reflected in the system of qualified majority voting, which is now in widespread use. Under this system, the Member States have weighted votes, the intention being that the number of votes attributed to each Member State should approximately reflect the size of its population. However, the position of the smaller Member States has been protected by weighting the votes disproportionately in their favour. This has led to some unavoidable distortions. For example, Germany, with a population more than 80 times greater than that of Luxembourg has only five times as many votes, while the United Kingdom has double the votes of Belgium, although its population is ten times greater.

To what extent are the views of ordinary citizens of the Union capable of being represented directly in the work of the Council, as opposed to indirectly through its individual members? With the Europeanisation of problems which were previously viewed and dealt with on a national level, interest groups are increasingly being created and operating at European level and attempting to introduce their views into the policy-making process. Individual members of the Council are open to lobbying at national level by national, regional and local interest groups, while the Council as a whole is targeted for lobbying by pan-European interest groups.

Members of the Commission and European Parliament may also attempt to influence the members of the Council, individually or as a body, to support their views or proposed amendments on particular issues. The Ministers, however, are only the most visible level of the Council; much actual decision-making takes place at the sub-ministerial (i.e. COREPER or Working Group) level by unelected officials, acting on the instructions of and ultimately answerable to their governments. The Council Working Groups are composed of technical experts in the relevant fields from each of the Member States. They can be contacted and lobbied individually or as a whole by national and international interest groups, in an attempt to ensure that the interests and concerns of the lobbyists are taken into account when the Working Group is drafting what may well become the final piece of legislation. The committed lobbyist identifies and targets these officials in addition to their ministerial masters.

As mentioned above, the Council has frequently been criticised for its dealings with the other institutions, in particular the European Parliament. Relations with the Commission are close, if not always cordial. The two institutions are in constant contact and are mutually dependent – the Council needs the Commission to table legislative proposals and the Commission needs the Council to agree to them before they become law. The meeting of these two bodies provides the forum where the Community and national interests clash most spectacularly, but enforced co-operation over the years has resulted in an efficient working relationship with periods of inevitable acrimony.

Relations with the European Parliament have been less co-operative, partly as a result of the EP's original incarnation as a toothless assembly, courtesy of the member governments. Treated with benign neglect by the Council in the early years, the European Parliament fought for and gradually gained greater powers in the legislative process. Judicious use of such powers as well as frequent appeals to the

European Court of Justice against the Council have gradually made the EP a force to be reckoned with. Together with its more natural ally, the Commission, the European Parliament has increasingly engaged as an equal in legislative combat with the Council in the budgetary field, as well as by means of the Co-operation and Assent Procedures in the areas to which they apply. In order to do so, it has had to amend and improve many of its internal working methods, earning it the grudging if infrequently articulated respect of the Council. As with the early days of the Co-operation Procedure, initial teething problems can be expected with the new Co-decision Procedure, as the Parliament tests the limits of its new powers vis-à-vis the Council.

Another cause of friction between the two bodies is the apparent lack of accountability of the Council before the Parliament. Efforts have been made to improve this situation, by means of increased contacts at all levels. The President of the EP attends and addresses the opening session of each European Council meeting; Presidency ministers address the EP at the beginning and end as well as during their six months in office and after each European Council; many ministerial and official contacts take place at committee level; a Conciliation Committee allows for direct relations between the EP and the Council in the event of conflict over certain types of proposed legislation. All of these contacts fall short of the more direct accountability which exists between national parliaments and cabinets, but they are a distinct improvement on the earlier situation.

Some members of the EP are still concerned at the extent to which so-called Council decisions are actually taken at working group and COREPER level and adopted by the ministers in Council without discussion. However, it has on the whole been accepted that, given the non-permanent nature of the Council and the number of decisions to be taken, the ministers must concentrate on the most important and most contentious matters while delegating the rest of its work, however informally, to its preparatory bodies. Such delegation is subject to strict guidelines and the decisions taken at the preparatory level are always subject to ministerial agreement.

What should and does concern the European Parliament even more about its relations with the Council is the spirit with which the latter approaches them. The originally weak position of the EP in the institutional set-up of the Community was the direct result of the national governments' desire to retain as much sovereignty as possible. Having ceded authority to the then High Authority, they were reluctant to give the new European Assembly any substantial powers. Since the 1950s, the Parliament has been pushing against a door guarded by a Council which is wary of what its prisoner will do if released on all but the tightest rein. The Parliament has steadily managed to gain a partial entry into the Council's presence but is still regarded with great suspicion. It is an attitude which will change only slowly.

LEGITIMACY AND THE COUNCIL: EFFICIENCY

The Council produces policy outcomes in the form of Regulations, Directives and Decisions, which are implemented by the Member States and the Commission, and rigorously enforced and interpreted by the Court, thereby ensuring the stability of the system. The body of laws and regulations produced by the Council over the years now fills an impressive and rapidly growing number of volumes, which bear at least partial witness to the efficiency of the Council. When it is borne in mind that the Council is not a permanent body, but convened at intervals in order to debate and take final decisions, this prodigious output is all the more notable. Clearly, it can only be achieved by means of a rigourous organisation of its work, including detailed preparation of its agendas which may include a delegation of decision-making for all but the most important issues.

The Council and its preparatory bodies have long been accused of a lack of transparency in their working methods. Meeting as they do *in camera*, and only making available to the public the text of the final decision, it is difficult for those not directly involved to know how the decision-making process really operates and to monitor the progress of particular pieces of legislation. Publications produced by such bodies as the remarkably well-informed *Agence Europe* have proved invaluable for interested persons both inside and outside the process, but the Council has long resisted pressure to make its working methods more transparent, pleading the need for privacy during negotiations.

However, public concern with these opaque working methods, so different to those of accountable legislative bodies in the Member States, was highlighted in the various national processes of ratification of the Maastricht Treaty. In particular, the refusal of the Danish people to ratify the Treaty in June 1992, and the doubts expressed by the British as to whether they could sign up to this new phase in European integration, resulted in a number of measures being introduced in an effort to increase the wider public's confidence in the administration, and specifically to help Denmark and the UK reconsider without recourse to redrafting (and therefore requiring a complete renegotiation of) the Treaty.

The Maastricht Treaty itself had recognised the need for greater transparency and contained a 'Declaration on the Right of Access to Information' which read:

> The Conference considers that transparency of the decision-making process strengthens the democratic nature of the institutions and the public's confidence in the administration. The Conference accordingly recommends that the Commission submit to the Council no later than 1993 a report on measures designed to improve public access to the information available to the institutions.

The Conclusions of the Lisbon European Council of 26–27 June 1992 included a section entitled 'A Union Close to Citizens', which stressed the need for a greater degree of transparency in the decision-making process. The extraordinary European Council held in Birmingham on 16 October 1992 reinforced this initiative by declaring that the Member States were 'determined to respond to the concerns raised in the recent public debate'. Meanwhile, detailed work on specific measures was going on in the background, the results of which were made public at the end of the Edinburgh European Council of 11–12 December 1992, and in a number of other documents thereafter.

The Conclusions of the Edinburgh European Council outlined a number of measures designed to increase the transparency and openness of the decision-making process, which were reiterated and expanded in a Code of Conduct approved by the Council and Commission on 6 December 1993 concerning public access to their documents. It was announced that:

– subject to a unanimous vote, some meetings or parts of meetings of the Council would be held in public (i.e. televised);
– the voting records of the Member States would be published, when a formal vote was taken in the Council;
– press briefings and information material would be improved;
– the Council Secretariat had been instructed to improve the drafting of legislation, in order to make it simpler and clearer;
– members of the public were to be allowed to make written applications for specific Council and Commission documents.

This was clearly a start, although there were criticisms that the proposed measures merely paid lip-service to the notion of transparency, and would do little to increase openness in practice. For example, the European Parliament had proposed that Council meetings be open above all when legislation was being adopted (i.e. when the members were voting), whereas the Member State governments decided that the cameras should be allowed in only when orientation debates on work programmes or major new legislative proposals were being discussed.

Similarly, the publication of votes is a major advance on previous practice, and should make the members of the Council more accountable, if only through the media. However, a formal vote is not always taken, in the sense that the President may merely note that a qualified majority in favour of the measure exists, without having recourse to a show of hands. In such cases, it is frequently difficult to know exactly who is actually in favour of or against the measure in question.

The improvement of public access to Council and Commission documents should, in theory, make the task of researchers and monitors easier. However, the Preamble to the relevant Council Decision (of 20 December 1993) stated that such access 'must be subject to exceptions, particularly as regards protection of the public interest, the individual and privacy'. In addition, the onus is entirely on the applicant – failure on the part of the Council to reply to an application within one month of its submission is deemed to be a refusal, and it is up to the applicant to pursue the matter by making a confirmatory application and as a last resort referring the matter to the Ombudsman or the Court of Justice.

The problem of the simplicity and clarity of legislation was addressed by a Council Resolution of 8 June 1993 on the quality of drafting of Community legislation, known colloquially as the 'Ten Commandments'. It consisted of ten guidelines for the drafting of EC/EU legislation in order to make it more accessible, covering such issues as simplicity of wording, clarity of definitions, consistency and lay-out. These guidelines, though neither binding nor exhaustive, were intended to contain criteria against which the quality of drafting of Community legislation would have to be checked. Such guidelines, and the time it must have taken to draft and agree them, provide ample ammunition for critics of the Community.

Finally, the Council's rules of procedure were also amended in order to take account of the decisions announced at Edinburgh to improve transparency. Thus, for example, it was laid down that certain of the Council's policy debates would be televised (Article 6), the record of certain votes taken in Council would be made public (Article 7), and common positions adopted under the Co-operation Procedure, and the reasons underlying their adoption would be published in the Official

Journal (Article 15).

The overall efficiency of the Council will be tested by enlargement, and grave concern is already being expressed about its ability to maintain the present level of output with greater numbers. The enlargement process will probably be used as an opportunity to refine some of the Council's working methods, making them more efficient and even parliamentary in style. Some changes which have been mooted with varying possibilities of acceptance include: abolishing the time-consuming practice of the *tour de table* in favour of group spokesmen, thereby increasing the need for and amount of coalition-formation in advance of meetings; lengthening the period for which the larger Member States at least hold the Presidency; utilising the written procedure instead of meetings at the level of preparatory groups to speed-up the process; and introducing a double qualification for achieving a qualified majority, to include a majority of votes and a majority of population. The vexed question of the setting of new thresholds for the attainment of qualified majorities and blocking minorities necessitated by increased membership has been rather unsatisfactorily settled for the present in advance of the next wave of enlargement, and is due to be discussed in some depth in the context of the 1996 Intergovernmental Conference, along with other aspects of the Council's efficiency.

DEMOCRACY AND THE COUNCIL: POPULAR SOVEREIGNTY

At the time of the creation of the European Communities in the 1950s, the most prevalent political system in Western Europe was the parliamentary democracy, with the parliament as the central political institution. However, when it came to creating a representative democratic system at supranational level, a number of checks and balances were built-in, since the governments of the relatively newly-created and liberated nation states were nervous of handing over their sovereignty to an untried superstate. They therefore attempted to retain control of the new entity by according strong powers to the Council and relatively weak ones to the European Parliament, although room for the growth and development of the latter's powers was built-in.

Today, the indirect link between the individual citizens of the Union and the final Council decisions have given rise to allegations of a democratic deficit at the very heart of the Union. Specifically, it is alleged that the members of the Council are accountable neither individually to their national parliaments nor as a group to the European Parliament, although various attempts have been made to improve this situation, as will be detailed below.

One of the consequences of the desire of the EC Member State governments to retain as much power as possible was that, although majority voting was provided for in most areas after a certain period of time, unanimity (or, in its absence, a lack of voting) became the rule in practice. The infamous Luxembourg Compromise (which was never recognised by the Commission and did not have the force of law in the Community), coupled with successive enlargements admitting new members with differing priorities and preoccupations, served to prolong the search for unanimity within the Council. This gave rise to a number of working habits which, once established, proved difficult to break. Today, majority voting is more commonplace although problems remain, as will be discussed below.

Growing resentment against what was seen as excessive centralisation by 'Brussels' has been a common feature in most Member States for the last two decades. This resentment, coupled with a general feeling of impotence on the part of individual citizens vis-à-vis the Union and those people who were supposed to be representing their views and interests there – i.e. the national governments – finally and most directly manifested itself in opposition to the Maastricht Treaty and its ratification. The extent of the opposition took most governments by surprise, and forced them to assess such fundamental notions as popular sovereignty and the democratic nature of the Union, its policies and institutions.

Given the huge policy output of the Council and the direct effect it has on the citizens of the Union, some countries have felt it necessary to set up national parliamentary committees to monitor the course of Community (now Union) legislation. The most rigorous is the Danish Parliament's Market Relations Committee (*Markedsutvalget*), which debates and votes on the proposed position of Danish Ministers in advance of Council meetings. Less binding are the British and Irish committees, which tend to monitor the situation *ex post facto*. The Germans, in the course of their national debate on the ratification of the Maastricht Treaty, decided to establish a committee to monitor EU legislation, and during the Dutch debate, the Lubbers government pledged not to take any decisions under the third pillar (Justice and Home Affairs) without prior referral to its parliament.

The renewed interest in such committees comes in the wake of criticisms of the indirect control exerted not only by the members of national parliaments but also by individuals and groups of citizens over their governments in Union affairs. Ordinary citizens who are dissatisfied with the way in which they are being represented by government ministers and officials have limited options for expressing their displeasure. They can try to lobby their national representatives in advance of Union decisions or, as a last resort, attempt to vote them out in national elections to be replaced by others who share the citizens' views. Neither of these approaches is completely satisfactory, and many citizens are left with a deep-seated feeling of impotence vis-à-vis the Union which, it is felt, is depriving the Member States of any residual national sovereignty they have so far managed to retain. National Parliament-based monitoring and mandatory committees give a semblance of control, but are not very popular at European level because of the inevitable delay they introduce into the decision-making process.

Another attempt to bring the decision-making process closer to the citizens involved the introduction of the notion of subsidiarity, a federal concept which helps to define who does what in multi-level systems. The basic idea is that decisions should only be taken at the level of the Union when they cannot be more effectively taken at the level of individual states or regions. This definition was emphasised in the wake of the Danish people's refusal to ratify the Maastricht Treaty, and was interpreted by some Member States as a safeguard for national sovereignty. The concept of subsidiarity has been notoriously difficult to define and explain, and successive attempts have resulted in pages of political and technical analysis which do little or nothing to elucidate matters. In spite of these difficulties, subsidiarity has become a political buzz-word while the practical effects of its application are still awaited.

DEMOCRACY AND THE COUNCIL: MAJORITY RULE

As in most democracies, consensus has formed the basis of the EC/EU's working methods to date, according to the sound principle that governments are more likely to enforce and abide by rules they agree with and/or have been instrumental in creating. In the context of the EC/EU's decision-making rules, consensus has taken the form of unanimity and a qualified form of majority voting which attributes weighted votes to Member States in rough proportion to the size of their population. The Luxembourg Compromise of 1965 ensured the effective continuation of unanimous voting beyond the deadline laid down in the Treaties of Rome for the introduction of qualified majority voting in certain areas. The ensuing slow-down in EC decision-making, caused by the need to bring all Council members on board before a decision of any importance could be adopted, coincided with an extended period of economic decline when swift, hard-hitting decisions were most vital. It was clear that fundamental changes were required if the EC decision-making process and the entire system of European integration were not to grind to a halt.

By 1985, a consensus had been reached that a majority rather than unanimity would suffice for reaching an agreement in certain areas, and the Single European Act provided the means of introducing the new regime. In some areas, this merely entailed implementing original Treaty articles which had in the meantime been subject to the Luxembourg Compromise; in others, the Single European Act introduced new articles on areas which had previously been reserved for unanimity. After an uncertain start, the Council quickly adapted to the new method of decision-making and there was little or no opposition to the further extension of the use of qualified majority voting by the Maastricht Treaty.

The use of qualified majority voting has had the effect of speeding-up EC decision-making (Sloot and Verschuren 1990) and has given rise to a system of coalition-building and package-deals which now characterise the process. The question of whether the Luxembourg Compromise could still be invoked was deliberately fudged. Some Member States have been very publicly and painfully over-ruled when attempting to use it, with the result that individual Member States cannot afford to be in a minority of one on an issue of importance to them which can be reached by majority voting. The search for coalition partners has heightened the importance of the work of the preparatory groups and also that of the Presidency, which frequently initiates or is closely involved in any compromises required to reach agreement. While a large number of decisions are now taken by qualified majority, the importance still attributed to consensus ensures that voting does not always take place in practice. Instead, coalitions are formed to push certain points of view, and package-deals and negotiated trade-offs are utilised to head-off the possibility of Member States opposing the proposed piece of legislation.

While the principle of qualified majority voting in most areas, apart from the most fundamental ones (i.e. enlargement, appointments to Community institutions and amendment of the Treaties), is now accepted almost without question, the principles underlying the mechanics of the process are another matter. The original system provided for in the Treaties was designed to protect the position of the smaller Member States by ensuring that the larger states alone could not impose their wishes on their smaller partners. The majority required for adoption of a proposal was set at about 70 percent in 1957, and subsequent alterations to the system necessitated by enlargement have not substantially affected this level (see Annex II).

The question of how many votes to attribute to acceding members has always been a delicate political consideration, and much time has been spent pondering the mathematics of the system. The most recent enlargement to admit Sweden, Austria and Finland (and originally Norway as well) has proved no exception, with attention being focused on the number of votes which will in future constitute a blocking minority – i.e. the number of votes required in order to prevent a qualified majority being achieved.

In the course of the accession negotiations which began in 1993, the allocation of four votes each to Austria and Sweden and three votes each to Finland and Norway effectively confirmed their status as prospective smaller Member States of the Union. The ensuing necessary adjustments to the voting system, while maintaining the status quo, required a raising of the number of votes on a pro rata basis for a qualified majority in a Community of Sixteen to 64 votes out of a total of 90, and a consequent raising of the number of votes for a blocking minority to 27 votes. The most important effects of these changes were a decrease in the relative power of the five largest states working together – their votes would now represent 53 percent of the total as compared to 63 percent in the Community of Twelve – and an increase in the power of the smaller states, eight of whom could now form a blocking minority without the assistance of a larger Member State.

The UK and Spain launched a major offensive to retain the number of votes required for a blocking minority at 23, arguing that the original disproportionate weighting of votes in favour of the smaller Member States would now mean that a grouping of small states representing a minority of the Union's population would be able to block and wishes of the rest, who represented the majority. However, the other Member States countered these attacks on the undemocratic nature of the system and calls for a stricter correlation between votes and population by citing the twin needs to preserve the interests of the smaller Member States and to prevent one or two large states from dominating the process.

In the event, a stalemate was avoided by the adoption of a lightened version of the Luxembourg Compromise, agreed in Ioannina in northern Greece in March 1994. The compromise, adopted in the form of a Council Decision lays down that:

> If Members of the Council representing a total of 23 to 26 votes indicate their intention to oppose the adoption by the Council of a decision by qualified majority, the Council will do all in its power to

reach, within a reasonable time and without prejudicing obligatory
time limits laid down by the Treaties and by secondary law ... a
satisfactory solution that could be adopted by at least 68 votes.

The Council Secretariat had suggested including an obligation along
the above lines in the Council's Rules of Procedure, thereby giving it a
measure of legality, but this suggestion was rejected in favour of a gen-
tleman's agreement. The effect of the Ioannina Compromise, like that
of the Luxembourg Compromise, will be the continuation of discussions
and the postponement of decisions for an (undefined) 'reasonable time'.
To this extent, the Ioannina agreement does not go as far as the Luxembourg Compromise, which called on the Member States to continue
discussions indefinitely in an effort to achieve unanimity.

In any event, the situation has now changed again following the
decision of the Norwegian people not to abide by the recommendation
of their government to join the EU. The total number of votes of the
fifteen Member States is now 87, and the level for a qualified majority
has been set at 62 votes (71.26 percent of the total) with the result that
26 votes are now required to constitute a blocking minority.

The whole question of the weighting of majority votes and the thresholds required for qualified majority decisions is due to be discussed in
any event at the 1996 Intergovernmental Conference. The heated debates on national sovereignty and relative power which took place in at
least some Member States in advance of the Corfu summit of June 1994
indicated the political importance attached to such issues, and the objections voiced over the retention of the status quo are a taste of things
to come.

CONCLUSIONS

The balance-sheet of the Council's score in terms of legitimacy and democracy has changed over time, and efforts are currently being made
to improve its performance in certain areas. In terms of legitimacy, the
Council scores quite well. It has been organised in such a way as to
ensure that each of the Member States is represented at all levels, and
has arguably over-emphasised the role of the smaller states in an effort
to prevent their being dominated completely by the larger ones. Efficiency criteria are difficult to apply, but criticisms as regards transparency have been taken seriously and measures have been introduced to
improve openness, although doubts have been expressed as to the utility of such measures; in any event, it has been acknowledged that a
completely open system will never be possible.

As a democratic body, the assessment of the Council is less positive. The general perception of the Council is of an undemocratic, unaccountable institution, which has only grudgingly been prepared to share its decision-making powers with the European Parliament. Efforts have been made to make the Council more accountable to the Parliament, but these efforts fall short of what the supporters and Members of the European Parliament as well as many citizens would like to see.

The Commission and Council together have been accused of doing away with that most precious and elusive of national possessions, national sovereignty, although they would argue that it has merely been pooled rather than ceded to that mysterious bogeyman, 'Brussels'. The increased use of majority voting in Council decision-making is viewed as another sign of the demise of national sovereignty, and the undignified and ultimately unsuccessful efforts of some Member States to alter the basis of the system were merely an attempt to halt this process. Others view the system of majority voting as the sign of a mature, healthy and indeed highly democratic organisation.

The political and institutional system underlying the Union is already straining. The basic changes necessitated by the most recent enlargement to include Austria, Finland and Sweden have already magnified and drawn attention to existing problems, and the increased membership may even have the effect of creating yet more. Other applicant states are waiting in the wings and their integration into the system can be expected to throw up further problems. Fundamental issues must therefore be addressed as soon as possible, in an attempt to reconcile the requirements of democracy with those of efficiency and create a system which can accept new members with a minimum of disruption.

This will now be the difficult task of the 1996 Intergovernmental Conference, provided for in Article N(2) of the Treaty on European Union and originally intended to serve merely as a low-key occasion for a review of the implementation of the Treaty. It is now clear that it will instead and of necessity be a high-profile attempt to deal with the implications of deepening and widening, as well as those fundamental issues of democracy and efficiency highlighted by existing Member States during the present enlargement process.

The European Union as it exists and operates today is an amoeba, a spineless creature without limbs, which is constantly changing its shape. So Jacques Delors would have us believe, given his insistence that, by the time of the 1996 Intergovernmental Conference, the EU must have a backbone and arms (i.e. strong central institutions and a defence policy) if it is to cope with larger membership and the decisions and actions which will be required of it in the near future (*The Independent*, 19 May 1994).

Following the recent skirmish over voting rules, it is now clear that the 1996 Intergovernmental Conference will be a full-scale political battle between those who want to equip the Union with a proper spine and limbs and those who, horrified perhaps at their creation, would prefer to preserve it as it is, and even attempt to drain it of some of its life-blood. The Council, as one of its central and least democratic institutions, is an obvious target for both groups for different reasons.

Annex I : Rotation of the Presidency

1958–72 EC 6	1973–80 EC 9	1981–85 EC 10	1986–94 EC 12		1993–2003 EU 15
B	B	B	B	DK	F
D	DK	DK	DK	B	E
F	D	D	D	GR	I
I	F	GR	GR	D	IRL
LUX	IRL	F	E	F	NL
NL	I	IRL	F	E	LUX
	LUX	I	IRL	I	UK
	NL	LUX	I	IRL	A
	UK	NL	LUX	NL	D
		UK	NL	LUX	SF
			P	UK	P
			UK	P	F
					S
					B
					E
					DK
					GR

Until recently, the order of rotation of the Presidency was determined by the spelling of the name of each Member State in its official language or languages (see below). Two cycles were instituted in 1986, in order to ensure that individual Member States did not always exercise the Presidency in the same half of the year, an inevitable consequence of having an even number of Member States. In the second of these cycles, the normal pairing of Member States was inverted. Following the 1995 enlargement to include some of the EFTA states, the order was changed once again in an effort to ensure that the Troika (consisting of the present, preceding and following Presidencies) always includes at least one large Member State.

B	Belgium (Belgique/Belgie)
DK	Denmark (Danmark)
D	Germany (Deutschland)
GR	Greece (Ellas)
E	Spain (Espana)
F	France
IRL	Ireland
I	Italy (Italia)
LUX	Luxembourg
NL	Netherlands (Nederland)
A	Austria (Oesterreich)
P	Portugal
SF	Finland (Suomi)
S	Sweden
UK	United Kingdom

Annex II : Qualified Majority System

COUNTRY	EC 6	EC 9	EC 10	EC 12	EU 15
Belgium	2	5	5	5	5
Denmark	–	3	3	3	3
Germany	4	10	10	10	10
Greece	–	–	5	5	5
Spain	–	–	–	8	8
France	4	10	10	10	10
Ireland	–	3	3	3	3
Italy	4	10	10	10	10
Luxembourg	1	2	2	2	2
Netherlands	2	5	5	5	5
Austria	–	–	–	–	4
Portugal	–	–	–	5	5
Finland	–	–	–	–	3
Sweden	–	–	–	–	4
United Kingdom	–	10	10	10	10
Total votes	17	58	63	76	87
QM	12	41	45	54	62
% of total	70.59	70.69	71.43	71.05	71.26
BM	6	18	19	23	26

QM: Qualified Majority
BM: Blocking Minority

10
Voting Power Under the EU Constitution

Jan-Erik Lane, Reinert Mæland and Sven Berg

Looking at voting power in the EU is to examine an important aspect of democracy in the union. How much power can states and parties exercise in the Council and the Parliament? In any collective choice setting there has to be an identification of the members and the social choice rule aggregating preferences into outcomes. The European Union is no exception to this general statement about the relevance of institutions to group decision-making. What is critical in the EU's arrangements are:

1.   the assignment of votes to the players;
2.   the use of alternative rules for aggregating the votes of the members into a final decision.

In this chapter we will look at the EU institutions from a very special perspective, namely in terms of the voting power approach. It represents one way of looking democracy in the EU, especially with regard to two of its key political institutions, the European Commission and the European Parliament.

Much of the debate about constitutional issues in the European Union has focussed upon the subsidiarity principle and its interpretation in terms of decentralisation. This has overshadowed another key issue in the constitutional fabric of the European union, the question of how much influence the members can exercise over joint decision-making in the Council and the Parliament.

First we will analyse the rules that govern the composition of these two bodies, the Commission and the Parliament. Secondly we look at the voting power of the different members under the alternative choice rules.

COMPOSITION RULES

The constitution of the EU allocates votes in two ways. In the Council, each member state is given a specific number of votes that its representative may cast as a block vote. One critical question is the mechanism that distributes a differential number of votes to each state: Is it fair? The member states are very different in size: should size differences be reflected in the number of votes each state may cast? If so, what formula should be used?

In the Parliament each representative may cast only one vote – the principle of one man/woman, one vote is upheld. But each Member State sends a different number of delegates. However, even though this may mean that each state can control a block vote of a certain size, the representatives need not vote as a single Member State collective.

MEPs may vote on party lines, so that representatives from the same country may vote differently. Despite this, it is still important how many delegates in total each Member State may send to the Parliament. If the size of the population of the country is taken into account, then what mechanism relates the number of seats to a Member State's population? The EU employs a rule that transforms the differences in votes (Council) and seats (Parliament) allocated to Member States in accordance with the differences in their population sizes. The Council allocates a number of votes (V) to each Member State while the Parliament allocates a number of seats (S) to the States proportional to the n_cth root respectively the n_pth root of population (P).

Describing these differences by ratios, the seat ratio of two states is proportional to the n_pth root of the corresponding population ratio, i.e.,

$$\frac{S_i}{S_k} = \left(\frac{P_i}{P_k}\right)^{\frac{1}{n_p}} \tag{10.1}$$

for two states i and k. A similar relationship is valid for Council votes with n_p replaced by n_c, and S by V.

Table 10.1: *Allocation mechanism**

	1958	1973	1979	1981	1986	1987	1994	1995
Council, n_c	2.25	2.15	–	2.20	2.25	–	–	2.36
Parliament, n_p			1.50	1.51		1.51	1.48	1.47

* The allocation mechanism is estimated at enlargement years (Council), and election years (Parliament).

What the Union has to decide are the parameters n_c (Council) and n_p (Parliament) respectively. The closer the parameters n_p or n_c are to 1, the more the allocation of seats or votes is proportional to a country's population. The larger these parameters are, the smaller the number of seats and votes for the larger states, relatively speaking, and consequently the more the seats and votes for the smaller states.

Until now the Union has allocated votes (Council) and seats (Parliament) in a manner that leads to the parameters, n_p and n_c, being estimated using simple regression with the extreme case of Luxembourg excluded Table 10.1).

The allocation of votes to States in the Council has changed along with the enlargement of the union with new Member States. Table 10.2 shows how the number of votes has increased as well as how the distribution of votes has changed since 1958.

One may distinguish two extreme allocation rules. On the one hand, there is the confederal mechanism in which each state casts one vote independently of the size of the country, thus also giving it the ability to have a veto. On the other hand, there is the opposite rule under which the number of votes a state has directly reflects the size of the country, measured in terms of its population. Such a proportional rule provides the larger member states of the EU with a great many more votes than the smaller ones.

The actual allocation of votes in the EU Council (Table 10.2) involves a compromise between these two extremes, where n_c varies between 2.35 and 2.15. The number of votes differs between the states, but these differences are far from being strictly proportional to the differences in populations. Instead of strict proportionality, the EU uses a version of the square root law, according to which the differences, described as ratios, in the country votes are proportional to the square root (n_c=2) or the cube root (n_c=3) of the differences of the country populations (cf.

Table 10.2: *Composition of the EU Council: votes*

Country	Population*	1958	1973	1981	1986	1995
France	56.6	4	10	10	10	10
Germany	79.1	4	10	10	10	10
Italy	57.7	4	10	10	10	10
Belgium	9.9	2	5	5	5	5
Netherlands	15.0	2	5	5	5	5
Luxembourg	0.4	1	2	2	2	2
Denmark	5.2	–	3	3	3	3
Ireland	3.5	–	3	3	3	3
United Kingdom	57.4	–	10	10	10	10
Greece	10.3	–	–	5	5	5
Portugal	10.4	–	–	–	5	5
Spain	38.4	–	–	–	8	8
Austria	7.8	–	–	–	–	4
Finland	5.0	–	–	–	–	3
Sweden	8.8	–	–	–	–	4
Total	365.5	17	58	63	76	87
n_c**		2.35	2.15	2.20	2.25	2.26

* 1995
** The allocation mechanism, n_c, is an estimate of the actual parameter employed.

Equation 10.1, where n_p is replaced with n_c and S replaced with V. Such a mechanism admits of some proportionality, (n_c=1)). The sovereignty principle of 'one state, one vote' still has some influence on decisions made in the EU Council.

A similar analysis of the European Parliament (Table 10.3) shows the distributions of seats allocated to each member state as well as the empirical allocation mechanisms, n_p, that result in a somewhat different distributions of seats.

As can be seen in Table 10.3, the allocation mechanism n_p, with an actual value of 1.47, is far lower for the composition of the Parliament than for the Council. This means that the differences in population size are better reflected in the Parliament: the allocation of seats to the EU Parliament is closer to the democratic principle, giving equal voting power to each EU citizen.

Table 10.3: *Composition of the EU Parliament: seats*

Country	1979	1984	1989	1994	1995
France	81	81	81	87	87
Germany	81	81	81	99	99
Italy	81	81	81	87	87
Belgium	24	24	24	25	25
Netherlands	25	25	25	31	31
Luxembourg	6	6	6	6	6
Denmark	16	16	16	16	16
Ireland	15	15	15	15	15
United Kingdom	81	81	81	87	87
Greece	–	24	24	25	25
Portugal	–	–	24	25	25
Spain	–	–	60	64	64
Austria	–	–	–	–	21
Finland	–	–	–	–	16
Sweden	–	–	–	–	22
Total	410	434	518	567	626
n_p*	1.50	1.51	1.51	1.48	1.47

* The allocation mechanism, n_p, is an estimate of the actual parameter employed

DEVELOPMENT OF VOTING POWER

The EU Council

The development of the EU decision rules may be analysed by means of the power index method. In Tables 10.4–10.6 we reproduce the power index scores for the different member states under alternative decision rules. The power index employed is the normalised Banzhaf index which has a straightforward interpretation as the percentage of swings a state may make within a coalition that either says YES or NO.

Four decision rules are feasible in the context of the EEC/EC and the EU: (1) unanimity or veto power; (2) qualified majority: (3) qualified majority with the additional qualification that two-thirds of the member states are in the coalition; and (4) simple majority voting. Voting in the former EEC/EC and the present EU is based upon quantita-

Table 10.4: *Voting Power* under Qualified Majority and Two-thirds of the Members*

Country	1958	1973	1981	1986	1995
France	.238	.167	.158	.129	.112
Germany	.238	.167	.158	.129	.112
Italy	.238	.167	.158	.129	.112
Belgium	.143	.091	.082	.067	.059
Netherlands	.143	.091	.082	.067	.059
Luxembourg	.000	.016	.041	.018	.023
Denmark	−	.066	.041	.046	.036
Ireland	−	.066	.041	.046	.036
United Kingdom	−	.167	.158	.129	.112
Greece	−	−	.082	.067	.059
Portugal	−	−	−	.067	.059
Spain	−	−	−	.109	.092
Austria	−	−	−	−	.048
Finland	−	−	−	−	.036
Sweden	−	−	−	−	.048

* Normalized Banzhaf power indices.

tive voting, i.e. a member state casts several votes. The exact number of votes each state casts may change with enlargement of the EU since the EU allocates of votes to a member state approximately in proportion to the square root of its population (Tables 10.1 and 10.2).

The unanimity rule creates little difficulties in terms of calculating the power indices, as each state will have the same power index measure. The crucial question in relation to unanimity is its existence, given the trend not to employ it except for major matter such as constitutional revisions. However, the derivation of the power index scores for the other decisions rules (Tables 10.4–10.6) shows a few interesting results.

First, in general, the more countries that are members of the union, the less the voting power of each single member. The exception to this trend, called the paradox of new members, is that very small members, e.g. Luxembourg, may actually gain influence after enlargement by new member states. However, this effect is negligible compared to the overall trend of reduced influence. In the 1958 EEC, the large states of Germany, France and Italy had more than 20 percent of the voting power, which now is down to 10 percent in the 1995 framework (see Table 10.4), and would decline to less than 10 percent in a future super EU

Table 10.5: *Voting Power* under Qualified Majority*

Country	1958	1973	1981	1986	1995
Germany	.214	.154	.134	.121	.101
France	.214	.154	.134	.121	.101
Italy	.214	.154	.134	.121	.101
Belgium	.167	.103	.091	.070	.061
Netherlands	.167	.103	.091	.070	. 061
Luxembourg	.024	.026	.064	.025	.031
Denmark	–	.077	.064	.053	.043
Ireland	–	.077	.064	.053	.043
United Kingdom	–	.154	.134	.121	.101
Greece	–	–	.091	.070	.061
Portugal	–	–	–	.070	.061
Spain	–	–	–	.104	.085
Austria	–	–	–	–	.052
Finland	–	–	–	–	.043
Sweden	–	–	–	–	.052

* Normalised Banzhaf power indices.

(Table 10.10). Power will become highly diffused in the European Union.

Secondly, the special decision rule of the EU, in the form of qualified majority voting with the additional requirement that at least two-thirds of the members, support a motion is no longer of any practical significance (Table 10.5). With 15 members in the 1995 EU this special qualified majority voting rule has the same effect as unanimity.

Thirdly, the difference between the power index scores derived from simple majority voting (Table 10.6) and the power measures arrived at by means of qualified majority voting are becoming less and less pronounced. Comparing the figures for the present EU, the difference for the major members under the two schemes is only 3 per cent and even less for some of the minor players. The conclusion is that the EU could move to adopt one decision method only – the simple majority rule – except when special matters are at stake, for which unanimity may still be required.

The EU Parliament

Power scores for the EU Parliament it may be calculated in two ways: either by treating the state as the collective player, with a unanimous vote cast by all its representatives, or by treating the party family as

Table 10.6: *Voting Power* under Simple Majority*

Country	1958	1973	1981	1986	1995
France	.233	.174	.162	.134	.117
Germany	.233	.174	.162	.134	.117
Italy	.233	.174	.162	.134	.117
Belgium	.100	.087	.079	.064	.056
Netherlands	.100	.087	.079	.064	.056
Luxembourg	.100	.043	.038	.024	.022
Denmark	–	.043	.038	.040	.033
Ireland	–	.043	.038	.040	.033
United Kingdom	–	.174	.162	.134	.117
Greece	–	–	.079	.064	.056
Portugal	–	–	–	.064	.056
Spain	–	–	–	.107	.091
Austria	–	–	–	–	.047
Finland	–	–	–	–	.033
Sweden	–	–	–	–	.047

* Normalised Banzhaf power indices.

Table 10.7: *Voting Power* in the Parliament: States*

Country	1979	1981	1987	1994	1995
France	.174	.170	.166	.161	.144
Germany	.174	.170	.166	.178	.166
Italy	.174	.170	.166	.161	.144
Belgium	.087	.064	.037	.037	.037
Netherlands	.087	.074	.037	.045	.044
Luxembourg	.043	.011	.004	.010	.009
Denmark	.043	.053	.027	.024	.024
Ireland	.043	.053	.025	.024	.022
United Kingdom	.171	.170	.166	.161	.144
Greece	–	.064	.037	.037	.037
Portugal	–	–	.037	.037	.037
Spain	–	–	.134	.126	.106
Austria	–	–	–	–	.031
Finland	–	–	–	–	.024
Sweden	–	–	–	–	.032

* Normalised Banzhaf power indices.

Table 10.8: *The EU Parliament: seats of party families*

Party Family	1979	1981	1984	1989	1994
COM-LEFT	45	50	44	46	45
SOC	113	123	132	180	183
GREEN	–	–	9	26	21
CHR DEMO	98	98	92	93	86
LIB	28	28	22	37	50
CONS	108	116	108	92	96
FAR RIGHT	1	5	16	21	25
REG-NAT	6	6	5	15	15
OTHER	8	8	6	8	46
Total	206	434	434	518	567

the collective player, with each member voting according to party ideology along the left–right scale. In reality, one may expect that members will sometimes vote according to state preferences and, at other times, according to party ideology, assuming that there is no ideosyncratic voting. The power scores for the states are given in Table 10.7.

Table 10.7 indicates that the larger states have more power, in relation to the small states, in the Parliament than they have in the Council. In this case, the enlargement of the EU has not brought about any substantial reduction in the power of the larger states: Germany, for instance, has almost the same power score in 1995 as in 1981.

Let us look now at the power measures when the members are treated as party families. Table 10.8 indicates the composition of the party families, which has been done by aggregating election outcomes using conventional criteria for how close various political parties are on the left–right continuum.

The largest block is clearly the set of socialist parties. The set of Christian-Democratic and the set of Conservative parties were almost as large back in the early 1980s, but are now only half the size of the set of socialist parties. The Green family has increased considerably, which is also true of the far-right and the regional-national parties. The power scores for the party families are presented in Table 10.9.

There is one dominant member in the EU, the set of socialist parties. It holds 41 percent of the voting power. There is no similar group on the right, as the Conservatives and the Christian Democrats reach only 14 percent each of the voting power. It seems as if the voting power

Table 10.9: *Voting Power* in the Parliament: Party Families*

Party Family	1979	1981	1984	1989	1994
COM-LEFT	,000	.010	.038	.088	.070
SOC	,333	.330	.340	.438	.409
GREEN	–	–	.009	.041	.035
CHR. DEMO	,333	.310	.264	.152	.139
LIB	,000	.010	.038	.060	.070
CONS	,333	.310	.264	.152	.139
FAR RIGHT	,000	.010	.028	.032	.035
REG-NAT.	,000	.010	.009	.023	.035
OTHER	,000	.010	.009	.014	.070

* Normalised Banzhaf power indices.

of the left has increased at the expense of the voting power of the right, which may explain the increased attention of the EU to social issues and questions about rights.

VOTING POWER AND FUTURE ENLARGEMENT

Looking at a super EU (Table 10.10), the critical question is whether the power differentials between the large members and the small members are substantial enough, considering the immense differences in resources and population. If one employs the square root principle strictly, then Germany should have 12 votes with the other major members retaining 10 votes each. However, in a future extended EU with 26 members, none of the major members will be able to secure 10 percent of the voting power under any scheme. The power differentials between the major and the minor members will be reduced considerably. This reduction in the power of the major members must be a source of concern, especially if, for instance, the level of EU taxation were to be increased. Is it really possible in such circumstances to uphold the principle of allocating votes proportionately in accordance with the square root rule?

Here, we see that the mechanism for the allocation of votes to Council members implies a further weakening of the voting power of the large states. The same is to be found with regard to an extended EU Parliament, but not in such a dramatic form, as Table 10.11 shows.

Table 10.10: *Voting Power* in a Super EU: the Council*

Country	Votes**	Qualified Majority	Simple Majority
Germany	12	.085	.097
Italy	10	.075	.079
United Kingdom	10	.075	.079
France	10	.075	.079
Spain	9	.068	.070
Poland	9	.068	.070
Romania	7	.055	.054
Netherlands	5	.040	.038
Portugal	4	.032	.030
Hungary	4	.032	.030
Czech Rep	4	.032	.030
Belgium	4	.032	.030
Greece	4	.032	.030
Bulgaria	4	.032	.030
Sweden	4	.032	.030
Austria	4	.032	.030
Slovakia	3	.024	.023
Denmark	3	.024	.023
Finland	3	.024	.023
Norway	3	.024	.023
Ireland	3	.024	.023
Lithuania	3	.024	.023
Latvia	2	.016	.015
Slovenia	2	.016	.015
Estonia	2	.016	.015
Luxembourg	1	.008	.008

* Normalised Banzhaf power indices.
** The number of votes have been allocated proportionately to the square root of the country population.

Thus far, we have spoken about the voting power of each member acting separately either on a state or party family basis. Now, we discuss whether voting power can be increased by strategic behaviour.

Table 10.11: *Voting Power* in a Super EU: the Parliament*

Country	Votes **	Simple Majority
Germany	99	.116
Italy	87	.100
United Kingdom	87	.100
France	87	.100
Spain	64	.072
Poland	64	.072
Romania	46	.051
Netherlands	31	.034
Portugal	25	.027
Hungary	25	.027
Czhech Rep	25	.027
Belgium	25	.027
Greece	25	.027
Bulgaria	22	.024
Sweden	22	.024
Austria	21	.023
Slovakia	17	.019
Denmark	16	.018
Finland	16	.018
Norway	16	.018
Ireland	15	.016
Lithuania	15	.016
Latvia	12	.013
Slovenia	11	.012
Estonia	10	.011
Luxembourg	6	.007

* Normalised Banzhaf power indices.
** The number of seats have been allocated by simple interpolation in the actual Parliament (1995).

COALITION BUILDING

The Council

The transformation of the EU power structure with a larger number of members sharing power will call for coalition building. Given the employment of the qualified majority institution, it is clearly in each player's interest to enter coalitions in order to either get a motion accepted

Table 10.12: *Coalition Power Measures, the EU Council, 1995*

Members	Votes	Normalised Banzhaf Indices						
Mediterranean—4								
Italy ⎤ Spain ⎟ Portugal ⎟ Greece ⎦	28	0.247	0.264	0.288	0.321	0.342	0.412	0.500
Germany	10	0.131	0.125	0.118	0.099	0.089	0.059	–
France	10	0.131	0.125	0.118	0.099	0.089	0.059	0.000
United Kingdom	10	0.131	0.125	0.118	0.099	0.089	0.059	0.000
Netherlands	5	0.062	0.058	–	–	–	–	–
Belgium	5	0.062	0.058	0.053	–	–	–	–
Austria	4	0.052	0.058	0.053	0.074	0.063	–	–
Sweden	4	0.052	–	–	–	–	–	–
Finland	3	0.037	–	–	–	–	–	–
Denmark	3	0.037	–	–	–	–	–	–
Ireland	3	0.037	0.031	0.029	0.025	0.038	0.000	0.000
Luxembourg	2	0.024	0.031	0.029	0.025	–	–	–
Coalitions Index	–	–	0.125	0.194	0.259	0.291	0.412	0.500
Votes	–	–	10	15	20	22	26	36
Members	–	–	Nordic	Nordic Netherlands	Nordic Belgium Netherlands	Nordic Benelux	Nordic Benelux Austria	Nordic Benelux Austria Germany

Table 10.13: Coalition Power Measures, the EU Council, 1995

Members	Votes	Normalised Banzhaf Indices/Qualified Majority						
EU Core States — France, Germany, Belgium, Netherlands	32	0.276	0.289	0.354	0.387	0.387	0.441	0.500
Italy	10	0.139	0.126	0.098	0.067	0.067	0.029	–
United Kingdom	10	0.139	0.126	–	–	–	–	–
Spain	8	0.107	0.111	0.085	0.067	0.067	0.029	0.000
Greece	5	0.066	0.063	0.049	0.040	0.040	0.029	0.000
Portugal	5	0.066	0.063	0.049	0.040	0.040	0.029	0.000
Austria	4	0.050	0.047	0.037	0.040	0.040	–	–
Sweden	4	0.050	–	–	–	–	–	–
Finland	3	0.036	–	–	–	–	–	–
Denmark	3	0.036	–	–	–	–	–	–
Ireland	3	0.036	0.047	0.037	–	0.040	–	–
Coalitions Index		–	0.126	0.293	0.360	0.360	0.441	0.500
Votes		–	10	20	24	23	27	37
Members		–	Nordic	Nordic UK	Nordic UK Austria	Nordic UK Ireland	Nordic UK Ireland Austria	Nordic UK Ireland Austria Italy

or to block a motion. The same holds, of course, if the simple majority is used. A member who does not engage in coalition building may effectively reduce its power significantly.

Here, we will give two examples of possible regional of coalitions in the extended EU of 1995, employing the qualified majority voting institution without any additional requirements. Table 10.12 contains the power index scores for a coalition process initiated by the forming of a coalition of the four Mediterranean states of Italy, Greece, Portugal and Spain.

Such a coalition would capture 25 percent of the total voting power. Another possible regional coalition would be the three Nordic countries, which together would seize 13 percent of the voting power. If such a Nordic coalition were extended to include the Benelux countries, Germany and Austria, it would capture 50 percent of the voting power. The paradox is that the process of forming such a larger coalition would also drive up the power measure for the Mediterranean coalition to .500, resulting in an effective loss of power for the members outside the two coalitions, i.e. France, the United Kingdom and Ireland.

Such a paradoxical outcome may be reached from another equally possible coalition process, shown in Table 10.13.

Here, we start from a coalition of the four core EU states. A counter-coalition of the three Nordic countries is again formed to which other members are added, including the United Kingdom, Ireland, Austria and Italy. Such a process would place Spain, Portugal and Greece in a powerless position.

Interestingly, it is not possible to generate such a paradox under majority voting in the EU, where it usually pays for a large member to commit itself as late as possible (see Table 10.14). The paradox reflects the fact that, under the EU qualified majority institution, a blocking coalition needs only 26 votes out of the 87 votes.

Generally speaking, the number of coalitions that can form is very high, but there will be situational factors that constrain the coalition possibilities. Probably each issue area will see its own specific coalition pattern. Enquiring into how coalitions are made in the new EU is an urgent task for research. The only way to shape the amorphous power structure of the new EU will be to create stable coalitions based upon the interests in various policy areas of the member states. It would further make decision-making more transparent and coalition building less paradoxical, if the EU adopted only one institution, the simple majority scheme.

Table 10.14: *Coalition Power Measures, the EU Council, 1995*

Members	Votes	Normalised Banzhaf Indices/Simple Majority						
EU Core States								
France ⌐ Germany Belgium Netherlands ⌐	32	0.607	0.571	0.463	0.393	0.418	0.357	0.231
Italy	10	0.065	0.071	0.111	0.143	0.127	0.143	–
United Kingdom	10	0.065	0.071	–	–	–	–	–
Spain	8	0.057	0.061	0.093	0.107	0.127	0.143	0.231
Greece	5	0.041	0.041	0.056	0.071	0.055	0.071	0.077
Portugal	5	0.041	0.041	0.056	0.071	0.055	0.071	0.077
Austria	4	0.033	0.041	0.056	–	0.055	–	–
Sweden	4	0.033	–	–	–	–	–	–
Finland	3	0.020	–	–	–	–	–	–
Denmark	3	0.020	–	–	–	–	–	–
Ireland	3	0.020	0.031	0.037	0.036	–	–	–
Coalitions — Index	–	–	0.071	0.130	0.179	0.164	0.214	0.385
Coalitions — Votes	–	–	10	20	24	23	27	37
Coalitions — Members	–	–	Nordic	Nordic UK	Nordic UK Austria	Nordic UK Ireland	Nordic UK Ireland Austria	Nordic UK Ireland Austria Italy

Table 10.15: *Coalition Power Measures, the European Parliament, 1995.*

Members	Votes	Normalised Banzhaf Indices						
EU Core States								
France								
Germany								
Belgium ⎤	248	0.591	0.606	0.485	0.456	0.462	0.423	0.231
Netherlands								
Luxembourg ⎦								
Italy	87	0.076	0.084	0.142	0.165	0.154	0.192	–
United Kingdom	87	0.076	0.084	–	–	–	–	–
Spain	64	0.074	0.073	0.123	0.126	0.115	0.115	0.231
Greece	25	0.033	0.024	0.034	0.029	0.038	0.038	0.077
Portugal	25	0.033	0.024	0.034	0.029	0.038	0.038	0.077
Austria	21	0.027	0.019	0.025	–	0.038	–	–
Sweden	22	0.027	–	–	–	–	–	–
Finland	16	0.021	–	–	–	–	–	–
Denmark	16	0.021	–	–	–	–	–	–
Ireland	16	0.020	0.013	0.015	0.029	–	–	–
Coalitions	Index	–	0.073	0.142	0.165	0.154	0.192	0.385
	Votes	–	54	141	162	156	177	264
	Members	–	Nordic	Nordic UK	Nordic UK Austria	Nordic UK Ireland	Nordic UK Ireland Austria	Nordic UK Ireland Austria Italy

Table 10.16: *Coalition Power Measures, the European Parliament, 1995.*

Members	Votes	Normalised Banzhaf Indices						
Mediterranean–4								
Italy ⌉								
Spain	201	0.445	0.421	0.393	0.364	0.368	0.321	0.167
Portugal								
Greece ⌋								
Germany	99	0.142	0.136	0.134	0.144	0.158	0.179	—
France	87	0.132	0.121	0.104	0.093	0.088	0.107	0.167
United Kingdom	87	0.132	0.121	0.104	0.093	0.088	0.107	0.167
Netherlands	31	0.027	0.045	—	—	—	—	—
Belgium	25	0.026	0.039	0.066	—	—	—	—
Austria	21	0.022	0.032	0.053	0.076	0.053	—	—
Sweden	22	0.022	—	—	—	—	—	—
Finland	16	0.016	—	—	—	—	—	—
Denmark	16	0.016	—	—	—	—	—	—
Ireland	15	0.015	0.021	0.032	0.042	0.053	0.036	0.000
Luxembourg	6	0.007	0.010	0.019	0.025	—	—	—
Coalitions Index		—	0.054	0.096	0.161	0.193	0.250	0.500
Votes		—	54	85	110	116	137	236
Members		—	Nordic	Nordic Netherlands	Nordic Belgium Netherlands	Nordic Benelux	Nordic Benelux Austria	Nordic Benelux Austria Germany

The Parliament

Strategic behaviour in the EU Parliament may relate either to states co-ordinating their voting on issues of mutual concern, or to party families voting in a similar fashion on certain questions. Starting with various states voting in coalitions, Tables 10.15 and 10.16 show what would happen to the power scores if states join together in a few plausible coalitions. We see that it pays to join a coalition.

Table 10.17 takes up the question of whether blocks of parties can enhance their power by coalition behaviour. We divide the party families into four major blocks: (1) Left (SOC + COM/LEFT); (2) Centre (CHR-DEMO + LIB); (3) Right (CONS + FAR-RIGHT + REG-NAT); and (4) Other.

Interestingly, the advance of the Left group shows up in a very high combined power index score of 1/2. The increase in power for the Left has meant that the Centre and the Right no longer matches the Left. It has also resulted in a situation where the set of other parties has become an influential player.

If the union is extended to include the former Communist countries in a Super EU, then the combined power score of the entire left will probably go over 1/2 on the Banzhaf scale. The members of such a Parliament would rationally expect a different trade-off between efficiency and equity in EU policy-making on allocative and redistributive issues than that implied by the distribution of voting power when the Parliament was first set up in the late 1970s and 1980s.

In the EU Parliament the parties form groupings with special labels. Table 10.18 presents the groupings in the extended 1995 Parliament.

Table 10.17: *Voting Power* of Party Blocks in Parliament 1979–1994*

PARTY BLOCK	1979/1981/1984	1989/1994
LEFT	1/3	1/2
CENTRE	1/3	1/6
RIGHT	1/3	1/6
OTHER	0	1/6

* Normalised Banzhaf power indices.

Table 10.18: *EU Parliament: Party Groups, 1995.*

Party Groups	Seats	Voting Power*
Left Unity group (LU)	31	.044
Greens	25	.044
Rainbow group (RBW)	19	.044
European Socialist Party (PES)	221	.377
Independents	79	.167
Liberal Democratic and Reformist group (LDR)	52	.096
European People's Party (EPP)	173	.184
European Democratic Alliance (EDA)	26	.044

* Normalised Banzhaf power indices.

The strongest group is the PES with power share of 38 percent. There is a sizeable group of independents with 17 percent of the voting power. The LDR have almost 10 percent whereas the other groups hardly score 5 percent.

The more the EU develops into a real Union, the stronger the role of the Parliament will be. The importance of the Parliament will reduce the democratic deficit of the Union, especially if the huge population differences across the Member States are reflected in the voting power scores.

CONCLUSION

Voting power in the EU is an important aspect of democracy in the Union. How much power can states and parties exercise in the Council and the Parliament? The answer depends primarily upon two things: (a) the allocation of votes and seats in relation to country size; (b) the adoption of various rules for aggregating votes. Secondarily, power reflects the capacity to enter winning or blocking coalitions.

We have shown that the decision rules in the Council of Ministers need to be revised to reflect fully the effects of the extensive enlargements that have taken place since 1958. Arguably, unless unanimity is required, there is only one decision rule that makes sense after the 1995 enlargements and in view of a coming future super EU, namely the simple majority rule. The qualified majority rule no longer results in outcomes that are different from unanimity.

The EU may need to take a closer look at the allocation mechanism of relating votes or seats to population size differences. The EU Council sets the parameter n_c greater than the parameter n_p used by the Parliament (Equation 10.1), with the result that the larger states have relatively more power in the EU Council than in the EU Parliament. Which parameter value of n_c and/or n_p is the most democratic one? Should the differences in country population be better reflected in the votes and seats allocated to each state, meaning that the value of n_c and n_p should be closer to 1?

Finally, we have shown that the set of socialist parties have a unique position in the EU Parliament, scoring a high 41 percent power index measure. The Left at present could be balanced by the Right and the Centre in a coalition, though this may be considered unlikely due to the problem of collaborating with the Far-Right parties.

In general, coalition behaviour pays off under the EU constitution. In the EU Council coalitions are a must, since changes require large coalitions forming qualified majorities at the same time as small minorities may form blocking coalitions.

11
The European Parliament
Juliet Lodge

Democratic legitimacy in the EC has traditionally been seen in limited terms as a problem of securing the election of the European Parliament by direct, universal suffrage. The issue is more complex and multi-faceted. Legitimacy is contested. It is conditional and evolutionary. It is expressed through the dispute over the appropriate balance of power and exercise of authority among the key supranational decision-making institutions and the argument over the issue of decision-making appropriateness, efficiency, transparency and accountability. The continuing problem of democratic legitimacy is inherent in the EU's crisis of political authority and identity. The new provisions introduced through the Maastricht process may de-legitimise rather than reinforce legitimacy: they are essential but not sufficient preconditions to remedying the democratic deficit and democratic legitimacy.

BACKGROUND: EURO-ELECTIONS, THE DEMOCRATIC DEFICIT AND DEMOCRATIC LEGITIMACY

Conceptual confusion persists over the term 'democracy' when applied in the EC context. Arguably, until the first Euro-elections in 1979, democracy was conflated firstly with the quest to secure parliamentary oversight of the EC's newly acquired own resources in the mid–1960s, and secondly, and more importantly, with the holding of elections to the European Parliament. Inadequate parliamentary control over the Commission and especially the Council coupled with the absence of direct elections were seen to make up a *'democratic deficit'* in the EC. By the time of the Edinburgh European Council in December 1992 it had also come to be associated with the idea that the Commission was insufficiently transparent and democratic. In addition, and increasingly in the 1990s, the democratic deficit was seen in terms of an incremental and continuing erosion of national parliaments' powers over EC legislation on a zero sum basis to the advantage of the European Parliament.

What was and remains ill-understood is the degree to which the European Parliament has not won powers forfeited to national governments by national parliaments: neither can exercise effective control over either what national governments do in the EU or what the EU executive does. National governments were responsible for this situation and deliberately engineered a situation whereby national parliaments were denied effective controls over national executives. This made it easier for national governments, working within the Council, to escape national as well as European parliamentary scrutiny and control. Thus, allegations that the European Parliament was engaged in an exercise to increase its powers at national parliaments' expense were based on a false premise: national governments, not the European Parliament, were the beneficiaries of parliamentary weakness at both national and EU level. National parliaments failed to engineer an effective scrutiny, monitoring or control role for themselves *vis-à-vis* national Ministers and governments. They also failed, until 1990, to engage in constructive dialogue – and more importantly, in continuing, regular, communication – with the European Parliament. Given that European Parliamentary scrutiny and control were negligible and deficient, the overall result was to increase the democratic deficit. For a long time, however, electoral preoccupations meant that it was assumed that the democratic deficit would be erased merely by the fact of the EP having been directly elected.

The failure to disaggregate the concept of democracy led to confusion between one aspect of the democratic conduct of politics (the holding of periodic elections in which citizens elect candidates from a variety of parties to represent them in a parliament) with another – that of democratic legitimacy. Moreover, the tendency to equate the holding of direct elections with the EC's transition to a federal polity rather than as a means of enhancing democratic legitimacy muddied the picture still further. Argument raged over the likely impact of direct elections over the longer term on EP–Council relations and on the balance of power between them. It was presumed that ultimately a bicameral legislature would be created in which the Council would represent the states (rather than performing its incompatible dual function as the EC's legislature and the advocate of national interests). In a bicameral system, the EP would become the lower house. Instead of such a development being reviled as federal, it would have been more helpful to recall that bicameral arrangements were far from alien. They were typical of member states' existing polities. They were therefore recognisable features of contemporary political cultures. This might have helped to reinforce a public sense of the EC's growing democratic legitimacy.

Yet democratic legitimacy implies also that government is lawful and that its authority is accepted: something that could not be deduced merely from Euro-elections. The confusion was compounded by the fact that notions of representativeness and accountability are also associated with the conduct of democratic politics in the member states and have been implicitly subsumed in the ways in which the terms democracy, democratic deficit and democratic practice have been applied in the EU setting.

Leo Tindemans was right, up to a point, when he claimed in 1975 that:

> Direct elections... will give this Assembly a new political authority [and] reinforce the democratic legitimacy of the whole European institutional apparatus.

Euro-elections were expected to perform a dual function. Firstly, to alter the basis of the EC's legitimacy from it being derived to direct; and secondly, to augment the democratic nature of the EC by providing for public participation (albeit indirectly) in decision-making. It was assumed that by participating in Euro-elections, citizens would assent to the EU's authority structure and so confer direct legitimacy on it. The acquisition of direct legitimacy was seen as important in justifying how political power was exercised, particularly by the EP, and in empowering citizens' representatives to play more than a 'supervisory and advisory' role in the EC. While the elections augmented aspects of democracy in the EC, they did not necessarily lead to concomitant increases in legitimacy (Lodge 1993a). The contrary occurred. Widespread ignorance about the EP and the EC meant that then, as now, voters did not necessarily acquiesce in or actively assent to what MEPs envisaged. Nor is it evident that socialisation, familiarisation and education processes were at work which instilled in voters a belief in the EC's democratic legitimacy.

The EC's institutions were not, and are not, visible, tangible and intelligible to voters. The one institution traditionally seen as capable of engendering popular belief in its own and the EC/EU's democratic legitimacy, the European Parliament, suffered from the outset from being a marginal player in the system. The mere fact of it having been directly elected was not and is not enough to generate the democratic consent needed to give EC authority structures legitimacy. Yet, legitimacy rests on the capacity to engender and maintain belief in the appropriateness and effectiveness of existing political institutions.

Many observers and practitioners felt that EC institutions were not appropriate in the sense that the exercise of power by certain institutions did not correspond to an ideal type of democracy. The executive and legislature did not function in the same way as they did in the member states: parliament did not determine either the composition or the duration in office of the Commission or of the Council. Nor did the Council (in many ways the EC's actual legislature) operate accountably or publicly at the supranational level. Such failings compromised the vision of the EC engaging popular opinion and support and providing an example of peaceful co-operation worthy of emulation by states around the world.

Internally, the hierarchical ordering of 'direct legitimacy' over 'derived legitimacy' challenged the authority and relative positions of the European Parliament and the Council of Ministers respectively. The Euro-elections were seen to confer 'direct legitimacy' based on the people's sovereignty on both the EP and the EC. This was seen as preferable and superior to the derived legitimacy conferred by member governments' consent: superior because it conferred independence on the European Parliament as a source of political authority. The idea of democratic legitimacy inhering in the one institution that can lay claim to the superior legitimacy has since been superseded by the concept of a dual legitimacy: that expressed through the directly elected and popularly accountable EP, and that expressed through the Council of Ministers whose members may have been directly elected in national elections or who will have been appointed by a government elected by the voters in a member state.

While it is easy to see why the ideas of representativeness, accountability and democracy have become intertwined in the democratic legitimacy debate, Euro-elections have neither closed the democratic deficit completely nor have they caused the Council of Ministers to become daily accountable on a collective basis to any other EU institution. Its accountability is contingent upon the legal base of legislation: only the co-operation and co-decision procedures provide for a form of accountability to the European Parliament. Council members also elude effective and consistent democratic control at national levels. The effect, while unintentional, is to create a double bind: a *double* democratic deficit which inhibits the consolidation of EU claims to democratic legitimacy.

As the scope of EU competence has grown, so has the democratic deficit at supranational and national level. Thus, Euro-elections have not justified the manner in which political power is exercised: they have justified repeated challenges to both the distribution and exercise of political authority in the EC. MEPs sought to rectify failings by asserting their democratic and legitimate claims to exercise genuine influence (bolstered by entrenched expanded legislative competencies). They have constantly had to contest how power is distributed since the inception of the Common Assembly and have confronted in often highly innovative ways the problem of altering the distribution of legislative power in particular among the Commission, Parliament and Council.

Contrary to accepted wisdom which cautioned against a frontal assault on institutional and constitutional affairs, it was only when the European Parliament adopted a bolder stance on these matters that real progress began to be made. This coincided with a new institutional/ constitutional building phase exemplified by the attempt to set out the parameters of a constitution for European Union from the mid–1980s onwards. However, it is important to note that while the reforms in inter-institutional relations introduced by the Single European Act began to close the democratic deficit through the operation of the co-operation procedure (Lodge 1986, 1989), improvements at the supranational level had the unforeseen and paradoxical effect of re-opening the issue of the EC's and Parliament's democratic legitimacy.

Two factors help to account for this. First, because the European Parliament, through the co-operation procedure, was seen to be able to affect the content of EC legislation in a direct way that national parliaments could not, there were renewed allegations that it was usurping the role of national parliaments to the exercise of rightful control, scrutiny and influencing roles. They were largely excluded from playing such roles in monitoring EC legislation. That their own national governments had, with their concurrence, connived at their exclusion or at providing them with but a minimal role, upon ratification of the Treaty of Rome, was conveniently overlooked. Second, the ratification of the Single Act led to referendum, for instance in Ireland, which contested the very legitimacy of EC processes and the expansion of the scope of the EC's competence into new areas.

THE DEMOCRATIC DEFICIT AND SUBSIDIARITY

The democratic deficit is not simply a problem of the horizontal distribution of power among EC-level institutions. The vertical dimension is important and varies significantly from state to state. More recently, concern over the precise meaning of 'subsidiarity' has obfuscated this vertical democratic gap. But if subsidiarity implies that power should be devolved to the most appropriate lowest levels of government, the potency of the vertical deficit is bound to increase. National MPs were remarkably slow in recognising this. Preoccupied with the alleged (but in actual fact negligible) threat to national parliaments' powers from the EP, they have only recently appreciated how unaccountable national governments have eroded national sovereignty and how, in practice, subsidiarity could further marginalise them. This arises not just because Maastricht envisages the establishment of a consultative Committee of the Regions, but because of the direct links that regional, municipal and local governments have set up with EC bodies – and often in conjunction with the assistance of the relevant MEPs.

Democratic legitimacy and the question of redressing the EC's democratic deficit became part of the debate about the European Union during the Intergovernmental Conference on European Political Union. The IGC was entrusted with a review of the functioning, efficiency, accountability and democratic nature of the EC's institutions. An underlying assumption was that political action should comply with the rule of law. By the end of December 1991 when the Maastricht Treaty on European Union (TEU) was agreed, it was apparent that the institutional reforms agreed did not match the exponential change in the demands facing the EC with the opening of the Single Market. Not only were additional states clamouring for membership, but the very question of what 'democracy' meant to the EC was being defined and outlined in the treaty. This definition was derived from contemporary liberal democratic practices and assumptions in the member states. It rested on notions of parliamentary pluralism and open, representative government. But its function was not to set out an ideal-type of political system to be realised at supranational level. Rather, the crude attempts at definition both symbolised core, shared political values and sent a signal to applicant states, notably in Central and Eastern Europe, as to what the EC meant when it set 'political maturity' as a precondition of EC membership, and when it subsequently argued that enlargement could only proceed if it did not dilute the acquis communautaire and if the Community itself was ready for it. This led both to a reappraisal of the question of democratic legitimacy in the EC context and to a reassessment of the question of the durability of existing, and even newly reformed, legislative practices and institutional arrangements.

Originally, the realisation of democratic legitimacy in the EC rested on the attainment of two key objectives: first, expansion of the European Parliament's decision-making powers to enable it to approximate the role traditionally associated with legislatures in Western European democracies; and second, ensuring that the way in which its members were chosen and exercised their powers conformed to accepted democratic practices. More recently, with the progressive and continuing attainment of earlier goals, the European Parliament has launched into a far broader debate about the *raison d'être* of the EC and its transformation into a European Union.

THE EP AND DEMOCRATIC LEGITIMACY: A SHARED AND DIVIDED LEGITIMACY?

The European Parliament has been centrally concerned with democratic legitimacy since before the merger of the three Communities (ECS, EEC and Euratom) in 1967. While democratic legitimacy was largely seen in parliamentary terms and therefore as the EP's preserve, more recently – indeed as recently as 1989–90, the EC's democratic legitimacy has been conceptualised as divided between the European Parliament, on the one hand, and the member governments, on the other. However, three developments were important in changing the dimensions of the debate. During the first phase attention focused on the question of what powers the European Parliament should exercise over the EC's 'own resources' (an argument in the mid–1960s which led to de Gaulle's empty chair policy for France) (Camps 1966). In phase two the concern over powers was supplemented by more vociferous arguments over the 'no taxation without representation' principle. Inspiration was drawn from the earlier constitutional debacle during the failure of the European Defence and European Political Communities in 1954, from the Parliament's own Dehousse report, and from the practice of liberal democratic, representative forms of federal government. Concern over transforming the 'Assembly' into a 'Parliament' shifted to electoral issues and MEPs (then the dual-mandated appointees from national parliaments) sought to realise Article 138 of the Rome Treaty. This prescribes the election of the European Parliament by direct, universal suffrage.

Throughout the early 1970s, the desirability of holding elections to a relatively impotent 'Assembly' was repeatedly contested. It was argued that there was no point in trying to mobilise the electorate to vote for a poorly known institution devoid of power but having parliamentary and legislative pretensions; and that a low turnout would seriously damage the 'Assembly's' claim to democratic legitimacy. It was on this claim that its demand for greater powers rested. The vicious circle of whether or not its powers should be increased before or after direct elections was breached with the first enlargement. It was assumed that the UK (the 'mother of parliaments') would have a beneficial impact on the 'Assembly's' development and prospects.

Democratisation became a leit-motif. But democratisation had two faces. On the one hand, it referred to the holding of direct elections, and on the other to making the Council of Ministers accountable to the European Parliament. Both rested on the member governments' unanimous approval: treaty reforms could not enter into force unless ratified in accordance with national provisions. The fact that any such increases would necessarily curb the autonomy of the Council of Ministers (and hence of member governments) did not augur well for MEPs' ambitions. Nevertheless, small advances were made using the financial and budgetary control levers in 1970–73. These paved the way for agreement in 1976 to hold direct elections, first scheduled for 1978 but postponed until 1979 pending the adoption of the necessary enabling legislation in each of the member states. The differing national provisions inevitably meant that the Treaty provision for a uniform electoral procedure would be ignored and that discrepancies would occur in the conduct of the elections. This was seen as a price worth paying in order to get governments to accept direct elections (Lodge and Herman 1982).

During the third phase, the non-elected MEPs' insistence that direct elections would not induce the elected Parliament to seek greater power, notably at the Council's expense, bedevilled elected MEPs' efforts to transform the European Parliament's authority and to alter its supervisory and advisory functions and transform it into genuine legislative authority. Shortly after the first elections, tension developed between MEPs seeking treaty amendments to meet Parliament's desires and those intent on allaying some governments' anxiety lest an inter-institutional confrontation occur by adopting a strategy of using procedural changes to gradually increase Parliament's influence by exploiting fully existing Treaty provisions. The tension was to prove constructive and productive as MEPs developed a dual-pronged strategy to advance on both fronts simultaneously (Louis 1985).

This was based on exploiting the minimalist *petits pas* approach advocated by those adept at capitalising on existing treaty provisions and at revising in an innovative way Parliament's own Rules of Procedure. It owed much to the idea that anything that was not explicitly prohibited by the Treaty was implicitly permissible. This strategy was supplemented by the maximalist approach inspired by Altiero Spinelli and the Crocodile Club (Jacque 1983; Spinelli 1983, 1983a) of letting political elites and parliaments devise a vision of the future in constitutional terms (Bieber and Schwarze 1984; Lodge 1982, 1984) This dual-pronged strategy significantly influenced the evolution of Parliament's position throughout the 1980s. It left its imprint on the history of European integration. Although it is easily encapsulated in the phrase 'the quest for democratic legitimacy', this strategy proved to be a vital legacy to MEPs for the 1990s. Moreover, the deroulement of the IGC on Political Union and the ensuing problems over the ratification of the Maastricht Treaty on European Union showed how essential it remains to learn from and heed its lessons. This strategy needs to be purposefully pursued if democratic legitimacy is to become a reality. It is a necessary but not a sufficient condition of success. But as the Maastricht deliberations showed, without a continual, high profile input from the European Parliament, direction is lost and the fragility of existing democratic legitimacy and equally importantly a sense of common identity and purpose are challenged and shaken. The resultant indecision erodes rather than strengthens democratic legitimacy.

The phrase 'democratic legitimacy' has long been associated with the European Parliament alone. But as the European Parliament has developed, it has become clear that there is a need to inject some clarity into the meaning and application of the concept of democratic legitimacy at EU level. Equally, since the 1991 IGC, a more expansive interpretation of democratic legitimacy has evolved. It has been essentially derived from the obstructiveness and opposition of member governments to remedying the democratic deficit through the expansion of supranational legislative power and authority for the European Parliament. The member governments switched attention to the Commission, arguing – somewhat disingenuously – that the democratic deficit could only be remedied if the allegedly closed and secretive nature of Commission deliberations were made more open and 'transparent': this, from the practitioners of closed and secret decision-making in the Council, the EU's legislature (Lodge 1994: 343–68)

The European Parliament clearly has played and does play a role in redressing the democratic deficit and addressing the democratic legitimacy problems. Traditionally it has attacked the issue from the vantage point of:

(i)   changing inter-institutional relations, and notably the legislative imbalance between itself and the Council of Ministers. To that end, it engaged on a process of continually
revising its own internal organisation to enhance its potential effectiveness, bolster incipient coherence and reform
its formal powers.

(ii)   changing and adapting decision-rules and processes to enable it enhance its ability to exercise its treaty given powers effectively and to enable it to acquire genuine legislative authority. To that end, it has developed its budgetary,
assent and legislative powers (through the conciliation, co-
operation and co-decision procedures), its direct legislative
initiative abilities (Art. 138b TEU) and indirect legislative
initiatives. The latter include own initiative reports, joint
declarations (for example, on fundamental rights (1977),
the budgetary procedure (1982), racism and Xenophobia
(1986), budgetary discipline (1988 and 1993) and on democracy, transparency and subsidiarity (1993). These allow new
procedures, not provided for in the treaties to be implemented. They entail legally binding obligations. Any subsequent legal measures that violate them can be ruled void
by the Court of Justice.

Indirect influence is also exercised via the annual legislative programmes prepared by the Commission and submitted to the EP and calling for one-off actions, preparatory
studies and so on which opened the door for new items and
programmes – such as the food aid programme within the
EU's development policy) and its supervisory powers vis-à-
vis the appointment of the Commission).

(iii) changing its participation in Euro-elections. To that end, it
started in 1978 with a very modest 'information provision'
role vis-à-vis the national parties that comprised its party
groups and through them to the public. This was followed
by more overt funding of electoral activities and continued
pressure for the implementation of a common electoral procedure.

The problem is that these steps have not been sufficient to
render the EU's claims to democratic legitimacy sufficiently
credible in the eyes of national elites and publics to obviate
challenges to them of such magnitude that throw the whole
European integration exercise into doubt and by themselves
further erode the EU's image of legitimacy.

The democratic legitimacy crisis is most manifest when considering the role of the elected chambers purporting to represent the people and guard them from the abuse of executive power. It is tempting to see in the extent of the democratic legitimacy crisis at EU level, little more than a catalogue of failures. The attempts to rectify the democratic deficit and to enhance democratic legitimacy have addressed a range of related issues which, when listed together, easily lend themselves to being described as a catalogue of failures. They include:

failure to reconcile horizontal institutional rivalry
- imperfect bicameralism;
- imperfect parliamentary supervision and control over Ministers;
- imperfect co-operation among the institutions;
- different interpretations of the decision rules that inhibit efficient decision-making and co-operation by the legislative arms;
- imperfect access to information that is essential to optimising legislative performance by the various institutions.

failure to overcome vertical institutional rivalry
- differential electoral systems;
- weak EP parties;
- failure to establish effective co-operation between national and European parliamentary and representative institutions.

failure of mutual accommodation to enhance the common good
- contradictions in operationalising the ideal of open government at EU and national levels;
- contradictions in reconciling democratic practice with efficient government;
- failure to advance a European constitution.

failure of mobilisation
- failure to mobilise the electorate and promote positive attitudinal change;
- failure on the part of the elected national political elites and leaders themselves to accept and internalise the legitimacy and authority of the system they both construct and work in.

failure of effectivity
- partial failure to deliver policies/programmes of direct relevance and clearly visible to the electorate;
- imperfect development of parliamentary oversight of and influence on the EMU (from the Central Bank to the EMI and influencing EU economic policy);
- failure to develop a constitutional role with the ECJ.

FAILURE TO RECONCILE HORIZONTAL INSTITUTIONAL RIVALRY

Arguably, until the advent of the Single Act and the introduction of the co-operation procedure, inter-institutional competition between the two arms of the EC's legislature – the European Parliament and the Council of Ministers – persisted in part because there was little formal or legal need for them to cooperate. The Council could, and did, ignore the European Parliament, thereby asserting its supremacy in the legislative process. The co-operation and later the co-decision procedures altered this situation. This change occurred for a number of reasons. First, the European Parliament and the Commission stimulated effective legislative planning and co-ordination, partly through computerisation of the various stages and introducing inter-institutional opaqueness and openness into their internal management of the progress of the legislative programme. Second, the European Parliament successfully challenged the Council over amendments to controversial environmental legislation. Third, the European Parliament used the assent procedure to assert its views against those of the Council and Commission. Fourth, the European Parliament continued to interpret its own Rules of Procedure imaginatively to facilitate an expansion of its role vis-à-vis the Council of Ministers and the Commission. Such interpretations paved the way in the 1980s for its augmented legislative influence and the co-operation procedure and in the 1990s for its currently enhanced position, for example, in respect of the selection and appointment of the incoming Commission. How? First through the vote of investiture (subsequently incorporated into the TEU Art. 158: 2) and making the terms of office of the Commission and the European Parliament concurrent, and second through its decision to cross-examine those appointed by the member governments prior to their formal assumption of office, and even though MEPs still lack the right to censure individual Commissioners. Will this help enhance democratic legitimacy? Possibly, if it is felt that voters trust MEPs sufficiently to endorse the quasi-leaders of the EU. The absence of effective and meaningful links between the 'government' of the EU and its parliament do imperil the EU's democratic legitimacy given that the publics identify with and more or less trust national leaders more than they do supranational actors.

The overall result has been a procedural reduction in but not the elimination of horizontal institutional rivalry. Commission – European Parliament co-operation has steadily improved: Commission officials attend EP committee and Commissioners often attend part sessions. The amelioration has been less pronounced and more tortuous in respect of the Council and the European Parliament. This is partly because some Council activities take place outside the EC framework altogether: notably those concerning the second and third pillars on the common foreign and security policy and co-operation in justice and home affairs. While symbolic improvements have been made – Ministers from the Presidency usually attend EP committees in their sphere of responsibility at least twice per Presidency, and plenaries – accountability remains weak. The European Parliament continues to work towards the ideal of co-equal legislative power-sharing between itself and the Council: imperfect bicameralism exists; the inter-institutional imbalance to the European Parliament's disadvantage remains; and the onus remains on MEPs to seek, justify and secure changes to the imbalance. The problem in doing so resides partly in the persistence of vertical institutional rivalry and suspicion among national parliaments (see below).

If imperfect bicameralism exists, it follows that parliamentary supervision and control of Ministers neither matches an ideal nor meets the requirements of effective democratic checks on the potential abuse of legislative authority by the Council. It is still the case that the Council may pass legislative proposals that have neither been endorsed by MEPs or by national MPs. The 'A' points procedure in COREPER, for example, while arguably efficient does not conform to democratic ideals of participation and supervision by the elected representatives of those subject to the resultant law. There has been some improvement in respect of Council secrecy. The Council secretariat press releases may specify the voting (majority or unanimity) on a decision and indicate which member states abstained or opposed the proposal on which it was based. Reasons for voting, however, have to be elicited by MEPs and immediacy and spontaneity is lost at a critical juncture. Some Council sessions are now televised (17 had been by late 1994). MEPs have participated at some Council meetings – a procedure introduced on the initiative of the Kangaroo group of MEPs during the deliberations on the realisation of the Single Market in the 1980s. This is neither the norm nor is it accepted as the most appropriate way of engineering supranational parliamentary control over Ministers, all of whom – necessarily – escape rigorous parliamentary supervision at national level. But this is not sufficient to obscure the fact that Council secrecy has not been eradicated. The absence of a public gallery in the Council's new building suggests that public scrutiny is not wanted.

In short, co-operation between the EU's legislative institutions is imperfect. It develops in an ad hoc fashion according to pragmatic principles rather than in line with a known and shared vision of what kind of division of authority among them would be appropriate. This is partly because of continuing uncertainty as to the end-goal. The EU is a polity. It does have a system of governance. But the polity does not yet conform to any existing model of liberal democratic, representative government. It is merely assumed that democratic principles should guide it. Even then, this was not formally entrenched until the TEU.

The picture of incoherence and horizontal inter-institutional rivalry may, of course, be magnified by further inter-institutional rivalries – for example, those between the European Council and the Commission, and those resulting from the introduction of cosmetology procedures which curtail both the European Parliament's and the Commission's influence and enable the Council to exercise executive powers through management and consultative committees.

This is also exacerbated by the different interpretations of decision rules by the main institutions which may inhibit efficient decision-taking and co-operation among them. This is not to subscribe to notions of a conspiracy theory to explain failings. It is, however, to highlight that both inadvertent and sometimes deliberate differences in the way in which procedures and policy ideas are interpreted and processed may aggravate failings in inter-institutional co-operation. It is, of course, quite usual for the Commission to exercise particular care in the selection of the legal base for legislative proposals. Indeed, the legal base may prescribe or exclude a legislative role for the European Parliament. Exclusion is not compatible with the realisation of democratic legislative procedures. But it may better suit the requirement of efficiency, for maintaining the imbalance in power to the Council's advantage over the European Parliament and for highlighting the continuing inferior position of the latter as supplicant.

The European Parliament's inferior position can also be underscored by denying it access to essential information, or by making it difficult for it to acquire current information that may inform its deliberations, possibly to the detriment of Council consensus. The problems are even more acute in respect of the second and third pillars where the European Parliament is either denied any effective oversight, scrutiny or supervisory roles (as in the case of Justice and Home Affairs) or given very limited functions (as in the case of the Common Foreign and Security policy). Under Title VI of the TEU, the European Parliament is to be kept informed and consulted (Art. 6). Again, while the Commission is usually co-operative, the Council is less so. When David Martin, MEP, submitted a written Parliamentary question on the publication of the Council's decision, under the cfsp on the lifting of EU sanctions on South Africa, he was told that such 'decisions' did not have to be published and if they were, it was a 'courtesy' only. (Question no. 95 (H–1082/91)) Moreover, the European Parliament has had to ask the Council to use a legal base to ensure that MEPs may give their views, such as Art 228a. (PE 1994) Beyond that, it may use – and exploit – its budgetary muscle in these two pillars as the administrative and a part of the operational expenditure of both are a charge on the EU budget. Otherwise, the European Parliament must try and influence policies when they are communitized (possibly through the application of Art 100c as in the case of visa policy) or realised through the EU framework.

FAILURE TO SURMOUNT VERTICAL INSTITUTIONAL RIVALRY

The weaknesses in democratic legitimacy are not just a product of unsatisfactory allocation of competence between the EU's legislative bodies. They also inhere in the exclusion of national parliaments from the decision-making processes relating to things EU at the national level as well as the supranational level. While the Single European Act began to close the democratic deficit through the operation of the co-operation procedure (Lodge 1986, 1989), improvements at supranational level had the unforeseen and paradoxical effect of re-opening the issue of the EC's and Parliament's democratic legitimacy.

Two factors help to account for this. First, because the European Parliament, through the co-operation procedure, was seen to be able to affect the content of EC legislation in a direct way that national parliaments could not, there were renewed allegations that it was usurping the role of national parliaments to the exercise of rightful control, scrutiny and influencing roles. They were largely excluded from playing such roles in monitoring EC legislation. That their own national governments had, with their concurrence, connived at their exclusion or at providing them with but a minimal role, upon ratification of the Treaty of Rome, was conveniently overlooked. Second, the ratification of the Single Act led to referendums, for instance in Ireland and Denmark, which contested the very legitimacy of EC processes and the expansion of the scope of the EC's competence into new areas.

The problems caused by imperfect/sub-optimal access to information also inhibit the ability of national parliaments to play a role in influencing the EU's legislative process. Excluded from this role largely by their own governments at the point of accession to the EC, national parliaments have differed widely in their willingness to liaise with MEPs. Too many, for too long, have subscribed to the fatuous view that the European Parliament was their rival and the direct beneficiary of any reduction in their own powers when they should have appreciated the need for parliaments to work together.

National parliamentary parties have often spurned and excluded MEPs though practice varies across the EU. For example, until 1991, when the Labour constitution was amended, Labour MPs failed to use the Euro-expertise of Labour MEPs effectively. Now, five MEPs sit on Labour's policy forum, the National Executive Committee must consult the MEPs over the Euro-manifesto, and MEPs can elect one of their members to regional party executives. (Constitutional Amendments, Labour Party 1991). Corbett has shown that elsewhere, in eight of ten socialist parties, MEPs participate ex-officio with speaking rights in the party congress; in seven of ten MEPs are represented ex-officio in their party executive or bureau; in five, MEPs attend and speak as of rights in national parliamentary party group meetings; in four, a liaison committee exists of the group in the national parliament and MEP (including the leaders of Landtag party groups in Germany)(Corbett 1994). MEPs can also informally influence national parties. But again, this is not always well-appreciated or publicised.

Too often MPs have seen MEPs as rivals for public loyalty and for legislative power. By failing to capitalise on the information and expertise available in the European Parliament, national parliaments have undermined their own ability to supervise their national governments and ministers in the EC. National parliaments have excluded MEPs from relevant deliberations (and even physically from their buildings, as in the case of the House of Commons). The overall effect has been to weaken parliamentary possibilities for holding the EC's executive arms accountable.

National parliamentarians have failed to assist as well as they might in the development of mutually useful links between their parliamentary parties and their respective components in the European Parliament. Again, communication links have often been sub-optimal. This may well have served the MEPs' interests in the exercise of their individual mandate and allowed the supranational party groups to develop their own identities and policies in a relatively unfettered way. However, it had the unintended and unanticipated effect of underlining the sense of vertical institutional competition between the two levels of parliamentary work. Working together, they might have been a good deal more effective in asserting the democratic principles and practices of holding ministers accountable for their actions in the EC and even in influencing policy in ideological directions (inevitably representing a centre-ground compromise).

National parliaments might also have assumed a stronger role in arguing for the introduction of a common electoral procedure for Euro-elections: vested national interests inhibit a few even today from doing this. Yet, the ramifications affect the ideological composition of the European Parliament, undermine the extent to which it can claim to be genuinely representative of the spread of public opinion, and affect citizens and residents in the exercise of a political right (by making it contingent on national rather than European electoral provisions).

National parliaments might also have been more objective in their assessment of the impact of integration on their own oversight powers vis-à-vis national governments. As integration as expanded so has the scope of governmental authority which eludes parliamentary oversight. The European Parliament has not recouped such losses. Indeed, following the adoption of the Single European Act, MEPs investigated again the institutional costs of 'non-Europe' (Catherwood 1988) which informed the Herman report (OJ C 190 20 July 1987: 71) on its strategy for European Union (EP Resolution A3–0123/92: 7 April 1992). Particular attention was paid to the democratic deficit (Official Journal C 187 18 July 1988: 229).

Vertical institutional rivalry has not just been apparent among parliaments. Rather, it is even more pronounced where governments are concerned. This inheres in part in persisting confusion over the presumed impact of European integration on national sovereignty, where integration has been seen as having a zero sum outcome for national sovereignty. It is also clear in governments' reluctance either to accept Commission President Jacques Delors' claim in 1988 that the Single Market's realisation would mean that around eight percent of all legislation enacted in the member states originated at EU level, or take an objective view of the functioning of the EU.

The TEU's pillar approach represented an ad hoc and politically expedient response to the need to contemplate further integration as a logical corollary to the removal of internal frontiers in the wake of the creation of the Single Market. But many governments feared that this would lead to further co-operation among national/regional authorities which would further erode their supremacy in practice. By shouting 'foul' and describing new developments as encroachments on national sovereignty to be resisted, they lost an opportunity to clarify the system, preferring instead the resort to the principle of subsidiarity (Commission 1994; Endo 1994, Kapteyn 1991; EPA3–163/90; A3–0267/90). However, vertical institutional rivalry within the member states – for instance among national, regional, local and municipal government, where these exist – may re-appear at supranational level as the Committee of the Regions gains a voice and, as a body of elected representatives, seeks a position alongside the European Parliament.

There is belated recognition that parliaments must work together to reassert democratic controls over executives at *national* and supranational levels. Because both are popularly elected, both can lay claim to direct legitimacy. Both have a role in lending legitimacy to the exercise of authority. Working together, and with regional bodies, both could serve to justify, legitimise and reinforce the democratic legitimacy of the European Union's authority structures.

FAILURE OF MUTUAL ACCOMMODATION TO ENHANCE THE COMMON GOOD

Contradictions in operationalising the ideal of open government at the EU level have revealed weaknesses at the national levels. The TEU provided for the creation of the post of ombudsman (Casini, Forte and Preto 1994; Millar 1994), someone to be appointed on the recommendation of the Petitions Committee by the European Parliament and to be responsible for investigating claims of administrative failure by EU institutions. Not only was this post highly controversial but it became linked with two developments exemplifying the problems of vertical and horizontal institutional rivalry. First, the European Parliament's attempt to expand its right of legislative scrutiny and supervision into the judicial and home affairs and common foreign and security policy pillars of the TEU met with a good deal of resistance. This was understandable in terms of the probable sensitive nature of much of the work in that area but was not entirely acceptable in terms of the exercise of democratic principles regarding government/executive accountability. Second, governments tried to evade augmenting the Council of Ministers' (and hence their own) accountability to the European Parliament by insisting that a problem of opacity and a lack of openness existed not within their own ranks, nor in respect of the inter-institutional balance between the European Parliament and the Council of Ministers but instead resided within the ranks of the Commission.

The Birmingham and Edinburgh European Councils sought to enhance 'transparency' in the EU. Attention focused on the allegedly closed nature of Commission decision-making. Rules and guidelines were set out governing the release of documentation to the public, the introduction of green and white consultative papers, processes of consultation with interest groups, lobby bodies and others with a legitimate interest in upcoming Commission legislative proposals. What this exercise revealed was not only that the Commission was probably the most open of all the civil services operating in the EU of Twelve but that several governments operated very restrictive practices and were far from open. Contradictions between the rhetoric and reality became apparent (Lodge 1994).

Transparency became a vehicle for containing openness. This was clear both in the letter of the guidelines (which prescribed conditions under which the release of information might be refused because prejudicial or because of its financial sensitivity) and in the arguments over the operation of transparency. The Dutch and Swedish parliaments objected that they would not follow the guidelines which conflicted with existing national rules on openness. The ability of the ombudsman to treat objections by citizens of the member states equally (as required by the Rome treaty) was also challenged since they would not necessarily be equally entitled to information, nor would national Ministers or MPs.

The transparency argument magnified the contradictions in reconciling efficient government with democratic government. It is undoubtedly true that secrecy is sometimes essential to the success of negotiations and bargains. But it is less obvious that information open to the public in one member state should be refused to that in another. It is also probable that efficiency gains can be made if parliamentary scrutiny/interference and oversight in policy and decision-making are minimised. Indeed, technocrats might happily dispense with politicians; verbal face-to-face discourse might also be dispensed with on the grounds that efficiency gains and cost savings can be made by communicating as interactive citizens teleconference fashion on the information super-highway (DGXIII 94); and efficiency might also be enhanced if consultation were reduced or eliminated.

While these are extreme examples of the efficiency versus democratic practice dilemma, attention does need to be paid to an appropriate trade-off between the two. More efficient government does not necessarily imply better or even good government. What the pressure to realise greater efficiency does, is to underline the competition for financial resources among policy sectors and their concomitant policy communities which may, of course, include the EU's institutions. As yet, efficient government has to be defined. How would it be recognised? At the very least, it is clear that efficiency gains could be made at the EU level in terms of time-saving, if legislative procedures, practices and inter-institutional interactions were better co-ordinated and streamlined in pursuit of a common goal.

Such change might be achieved through the elaboration of a document that was recognised and accepted as the constitution of the European Union. The series of treaties and treaty amendments, coupled with the ever-changing territorial boundaries of the European Union create an impression of unfinished business. This in turn gives succour to those wishing to inhibit integration, a change in inter-institutional relations and the division and exercise of power and authority in the EU. It also allows the destructive whine of those intent upon measuring every alleged integrative 'gain' against some fanciful ideal of a complete (but illusory) national sovereignty under attack. Once again, the European Parliament – notably since the time of the Crocodile Club – has been instrumental in trying to put a written constitution on the agenda (Martin 1991).

A FAILURE OF MOBILISATION?

Arguably, a written constitution setting out the parameters of the EU and the powers, responsibilities and obligations of its institutions, might stem public uncertainty as to the purpose and scope of the EU and its institutions whose authority is not satisfactorily accepted or regarded as legitimate. In the short term, however, it might have the opposite result and highlight a grass roots challenge to the EU. In short, the public fails to differentiate between the various components of the EU and to dissociate EU institutions from one another. Consequently, any failing in any sphere or institution may easily redound to the disadvantage of the EU as a whole casting doubt on its overall legitimacy. This example illustrates a further aspect of the crisis in the EU's democratic legitimacy and its democratic deficit: the European Parliament may see itself as the conscience of the EU, as the voice of its people, as their 'grand forum'. But the people themselves do not identify with it, with its outputs, its parties or its MEPs. The reasons for this are legion. They owe much to:

- the youth of the European Parliament;
- the struggle it has had in securing recognition for itself and in justifying a legislative role for itself through which it could influence the content of policies;
- the fact that the Council has the final word on legislation, the fact that even where MEPs have influenced the shape of legislation that influence may be invisible or masked by subsequent bargaining within the Council of European Council;
- the innumerable problems associated with the Euro-elections and mobilising the electorate to turn out and vote; and
- the absence of a consolidated socio-psychological community to underpin the European Union.

The European Parliament has tried to foster a sense of common purpose and endeavour in the elaboration of a European constitution by involving closely national parliaments in the exercise. The 1990 Rome 'Assizes' were an attempt both to overcome past weaknesses in collaboration between national MPs and MEPs, and to create consensus among the people's elected representatives as to the nature, scope and purpose of democratic institutions for the EU.

The decline in positive attitudinal change towards European integration has many causes outside the scope of this chapter. It reflects a failure of cognition and a failure to mobilise the public, an associated feature of the democratic legitimacy crisis. Just as the democratic deficit could not be entirely remedied merely by the providing for the election of the European Parliament by direct, universal suffrage so the democratic legitimacy crisis cannot be overcome merely by changing the role of the European Parliament in the legislative process and vis-à-vis the public. The member governments have aggravated the crisis themselves. They have failed to internalise the legitimacy and authority of the very system of which they are part and which they are creating simultaneously.

The Maastricht treaty referendums revealed governments reneging on and denying agreements they had endorsed at the IGC. Indeed, the processes by which the decisions of the IGCs have been ratified have, to some extent, de-legitimised the reforms and exacerbated the crisis of democratic legitimacy. Whether the European Parliament can redress the situation, through improved links with national parliaments to give its own work greater legitimacy, through more public hearings (which rose from an average of two to twenty a year between 1974–79 and

1980–89 respectively (Corbett 1994: 178)), through continued imaginative or and obstructive exercise – via Chapter 100 entries, for example
– of its budgetary rights and authority to grant or withhold discharge
of the budget, or through the elaboration of a draft constitution enjoying their support, or through supporting the Euro-ombudsman and the
development of EU citizenship remains to be seen (Meehan 1993).

The creation of a European citizenship will not necessarily remedy
deficiencies in democratic legitimacy if steps to realise it are miscon-
strued in a zero sum way as representing a commensurate loss of national citizenship. While the concept of European citizenship might in
itself be seen as a corrective to negative ideas as to the EU's relevance
to 'the ordinary person', its elaboration in terms of an ill-understood
and discriminatory set of rights might unintentionally undermine rather
than support affective identification with the EU and so widen rather
than narrow one aspect of the democratic deficit.

It would be wrong to suppose that the issue of citizenship had not
been addressed by the EC before Maastricht (Lodge and Herman 1977).
The Treaty of Rome contained the range of measures that have become
entrenched in the TEU as citizen rights. These included:

–   prohibition of discrimination on grounds of nationality (Art.
    7);
–   freedom of movement for workers within the EC (Art. 48);
–   adoption of social security measures necessary to ensure
    the free movement of workers (Art. 51);
–   freedom of establishment for the nationals of one member
    state in the territory of another (Arts 52–56);
–   the right of citizens of one member state freely to provide
    services in another member state (Arts 59–66);
–   the requirement for equal pay for male and female workers
    (Art. 119).

The October 1972 EC summit (forerunner of the European Councils)
on declaring 'European Union' to be an EC goal instigated a debate as
to the status of citizens within a European Union. In Copenhagen in
December 1973, the nine Heads of State and Government adopted a
declaration on European identity that stated their determination to
'defend the principles of representative democracy, of the rule of law, of
social justice – which is the ultimate goal of economic progress – and of
respect for human rights'. These were seen as 'fundamental elements
of the European identity' which the Nine felt corresponded with 'the
deepest aspirations of their peoples' whom they called on to participate

in its realisation 'particularly through their elected representatives'.

In July 1975, the European Parliament called for the establishment of a 'Charter of the Rights of the Peoples of the European Community'. In November 1977, it invited the Commission to make proposals o special reciprocal rights. It also listed the kind of civil, political, economic and social rights which it felt should be included. The 1983 Stuttgart Declaration on European Union called for the harmonisation of laws to facilitate closer relationships among nationals of the EC's member states.

In 1984, the European Parliament's Draft Treaty establishing the European Union defined Citizenship of the Union as:

> The citizens of the member states shall, ipso facto, be citizens of the Union. Citizenship of the Union shall be dependent upon citizenship of a Member State and nay not be independently acquired or forfeited. Citizens of the Union shall take part in the political life of the Union in the forms laid down in this Treaty, shall enjoy the rights granted to them by the legal system of the Union and be subject to its laws. (Art. 3)

In June 1984, the Fontainebleau European Council stated that it was essential for the EC 'to adopt measures ... to strengthen and promote the identity of the Community and its image in the minds of its citizens and in the world as a whole'. It set up the Adonnino Committee on *A People's Europe* whose report and recommendations were approved by the Milan European Council in June 1985. This was followed by the Single European Act and by important reports in the European Parliament by David Martin and Emilio Colombo which outlining the European Parliament's views on citizenship in the European Union. The Martin Report of October 1990 accentuated the need for a declaration on Fundamental Rights and Freedoms and on their protection as well as on democracy. The Colombo Report of November 1990 on the Constitutional Basic of European Union included several articles on citizenship which drew on all the preceding ideas. Finally, the TEU entrenched EU citizenship:

1. Every person holding the nationality of a Member State shall be a citizen of the Union.
2. Citizens of the Union shall enjoy the rights conferred by this Treaty and shall be subject to the duties imposed thereby.

The TEU also includes a commitment to respect 'fundamental rights, as guaranteed by the European Convention for the Protection of Human Rights and Fundamental Freedoms signed in Rome on 4 November 1950 and as they result from the constitutional traditions common to the Member States, as general principles of Community Law'.

The crisis in democratic legitimacy is often laid at the door of the European Parliament. But this is not altogether appropriate since it obscures a wider crisis of public confidence in the systems of governance encountered at supranational, national and regional level.

The European Parliament may, however, have a special responsibility for challenging and checking the basis of the evolving democracy in the EU. The EU, if it applied to join itself, might find its own democratic credentials a little short of its ideals. However, if public power is derived from the people who invest a directly elected institution with representing their interests, then it follows that the European Parliament must ensure that the other institutions are accountable to it: the European Parliament gives expression not only to the political relationship between citizens (the governed) and the Union (the 'government') but is the vehicle through which democratic legitimacy is conferred on EU laws drafted by authorities who are seen to exercise power in a lawful way. The problem for the EU is not that it acts in an unlawful way, nor even that its interventions are disproportionate in relation to the goals, but that the way in which it acts and the effectiveness of its policies and programmes are either ill-understood, invisible or unconvincing.

A FAILURE OF EFFECTIVITY?

There has been a partial failure on the European Parliament's part to meet the requirement of effectivity by delivering policies and programmes that are both visible and directly relevant to the electorate. This is a partial failure only because it is primarily one of visibility rather than of competence or commitment. The co-operation procedure augmented the effectiveness of EP influence through the system of two readings whereby the European Parliament's amendments could only be overturned by unanimity in the Council at second reading, and whereby the Council had to adopt its common position by majority rather than unanimity. As a result, 50 percent of Parliament's amendments were adopted by the Commission and 25 percent by the Council. This is still too small a proportion but represents progress compared to the situation under the traditional consultation procedure. The relative invisibility of the EP's amendments and the EP's success in securing their adoption means that it is difficult to argue that they have enhanced either public perceptions of the EP's effectivity or democratic legitimacy.

It is also early to judge the effectiveness of the European Parliament in exercising its powers of co-decision, notably in the five new spheres of competence in which it has the last word: education, culture, health protection, consumer protection and trans-European networks for transport, telecommunications and energy. According to Commission estimates, these areas – broadly speaking – are likely to account for around half of the future legislative programme of the EU.

It is arguable that the relative invisibility and/or uncertainty as to the origin and identity of the disbursement of EU 'public goods' reduces the possibility for an instrumentally-driven affective link and identification to develop between the EU and the public. The European Parliament has pretensions to being the intermediary between the EU governing bodies and the public. In seeking to redress the democratic deficit by suggesting that the EU is indeed an effective MEPs are limited by several factors: the competing claims of member governments; the public's identification with traditional territorial authorities; the circumscriptions on the European Parliament's powers and ability to deliver high-profile socio-economic packages that might encourage people to identify the EU as the source of 'goodies' and also to identify themselves with the common good they supposedly embody; and the European Parliament's limited impact on expenditure decisions.

The European Parliament has, over the years, managed to alter the distribution of available resources in EU expenditure and redirect a greater proportion to socio-economic welfare programmes by insisting on a cut in expenditure on the CAP. The impact and amounts available vary across the member states and are easily masked in national public expenditure programmes except where boards are erected specifically to highlight that a programme (such as industrial renewal of infrastructures) is supported by the EU structural funds.

In addition, there has been an exponential growth in the lobbying of the European Parliament by private sector and private sector interests which attests to their view of the increasing *importance* of MEPs in the legislative and policy-making processes (European Parliament, Galle report, 16.03.92, doc. PE.200.405). MEPs are useful sources of information and conduits of views as the work progresses in the various committees during the co-operation and co-decision procedures. While the European Parliament's budgetary authority is restricted to non-compulsory spending, since Maastricht, an inter-institutional agreement allows it to scrutinise every line of the budget and, in effect, to challenge the legal base of expenditure and assess whether specific lines should follow under headings which make it subject to EP intervention. It has limited powers to amend the draft budget and the final word on the budget overall.

Unless the European Parliament uses opportunities to highlight publicly (or to embarrass) governments over spending plans or failures – as in the case of national governments' apparent acquiescence in agricultural fraud – its activities remain invisible to the public eye. The same is true, except in highly publicised cases, of its use of its assent power. The TEU expanded the right given to it by the Single European Act to give its assent to international agreements, including accession treaties and association agreements. It intervened politically on human rights grounds and refused to vote financial protocols attached to their Association agreements with the EC.

More visible perhaps has been the newly elected European Parliament's attempt to vote against the appointment of Jacques Santer over Jean Luc Dehaene as Commission President. But it is doubtful that this act, which very nearly succeeded, reinforced its democratic credentials and legitimacy in the public mind. The mere exercise of its new rights in respect of the appointment of the Commission are the logical counterpart to its right to dismiss the Commission en bloc. Its intended cross-examination of individual Commissioners prior to their taking up office in January 1995 must be exploited to the full if MEPs genuinely are to influence the content, priorities and orientation new Commission's legislative programme. MEPs expect the Commission – as a result of the appointment process – to be more mindful of EP views than previous Commissions. This has yet to be tested.

The final arena in which the European Parliament's effectiveness vis-à-vis the public has been tested concerns citizens. Apart from its powers to call the other institutions to account (in committee, in plenary session, by written and oral questions, and through the various stages of the co-operation and co-decision procedures) it can claim to represent voters' interests. It investigates petitions received from them on matters under EU competence; may appoint committees of enquiry to investigate matters of EU concern; appoints the Euro-ombudsman and sets out the rules regarding his/her staff, budget and remit. In short, it has a watchdog and guardian roles to perform where citizens are concerned. Again, it is doubtful that the public is either aware of this or appreciates its significance. Consequently, while the preparatory groundwork for an accretion in democratic legitimacy has been done, the democratic deficit remains. Nor has the new Committee of the Regions as yet done anything to assist in cutting it.

One way of assessing the public's view of the effectivity of the European Parliament might be to examine election turnout figures. Turnout can only be one extremely crude measure of democratic legitimacy. But it has been the one indicator which has been used to support or deny the justifiability of the European Parliament's quest for greater power. The lack of correlation between the outcome of the competitive election and the colour of the 'Euro-government' has been used to explain modest turnout figures and the failure, in several states, to mobilise latent support. The overall decline in turnout since 1979 might be interpreted as symptomatic of dissatisfaction with the effectivity of the European Parliament.

However, it is difficult to disaggregate this from both negative impressions of the EP (whether couched in terms of its peripatetic nature and attendant costliness, the stature of its candidates and outgoing MEPs or its powers) and poor general awareness of what the European Parliament does, or is capable of doing, compared with national parliaments (whose outputs are readily conflated with those of national governments). It is also hard to separate this from the overall problems of increasing turnout which may be attributed to failure of party mobilisation, failure of campaigns, weaknesses of national and transnational party organisation, perceived absence of candidate and/or party differentials as well as to programmatic failure signalling dissatisfaction with the EU's legislative output and even a lack of conviction that the European Parliament can do much to influence and determine legislative outcomes. If the electorate is not convinced of the utility of voting, improving their awareness of electoral campaigns and opportunities will not significantly increase turnout.

Overall, the unintentional effect of Euro-elections perhaps has been indirectly to heighten scepticism about the EU's democratic legitimacy, effectiveness and the appropriateness of its institutional arrangements. The EP's dynamic role in advancing a European Union endowed with appropriate, democratic institutions and policy-making and legislative procedures has not been sufficiently visible or appreciated by the public to enable it to justify its claim for greater power with reference to its heightened public esteem. Until this happens, it will be difficult for MEPs to redress the democratic deficit in the way originally foreseen. Moreover, if voters are ignorant about or disinterested in European integration, do not distinguish the particular role of the European Parliament in the EU and are at odds with the position that their national governments take on further integration, the legitimacy of the existing EU is likely to be queried. This means that the multifaceted nature of the democratic legitimacy problem has to be addressed from a variety of perspectives. The problem for the EU, however, is deciding how to achieve this and whether there is enough time to do this when new applicants wish to accede to the EU before fundamental difficulties have been overcome. Their competing claims on the EU and their inevitable dissatisfaction and disappointment with EU performance and EU ability to deliver economic goodies as swiftly as might be hoped could seriously further erode the incipient democratic

Furthermore, in an era when the frontiers of political life are no longer contained within the territorial boundaries of the old nation states and when non-elected, non-parliamentary actors, including a range of technocratic and private sector bodies, play an instrumental role in setting, adjusting and influencing the legislative agenda, the issue of defining and rectifying the EU's democratic deficit by reference to the socio-political norms of a bygone age may no longer be entirely appropriate. This observation does not justify abandonment of the exercise. It merely alerts one to the need to take a more imaginative approach to identifying the problem, strategies to ameliorate the situation and approaches to rectifying the democratic deficit in its many guises.

CONCLUSION

Legitimacy rests on the capacity to engender and maintain belief in the appropriateness and justness of existing political institutions. The European Parliament is still in the position of having to challenge interinstitutional arrangements. It does so both to justify its own quest for greater legislative power and to check the potential abuse of power by the chamber which should share power with it and assume an equal, but not superior, voice to it. Gaining public appreciation of the myriad difficulties involved is hard and protracted. However, the European Parliament must continue giving voice to constitutional and policy concerns if it is to be seen as a legitimate player and if citizens are to internalise the EU's legitimacy, identify in some way with it and become active rather than passive subjects in the emergent polity.

Part IV
The Future of EU Democracy

12
The European Union: 1996 and Beyond – a Personal View from the Side-line

Rolf Gustavsson

The European Union has not yet fully recovered from the deep crisis of confidence which followed the ratification and the application of the Maastricht Treaty. Nevertheless it already faces a new set of extremely important external and internal challenges which will require even more sophisticated intellectual and political skills to master than have been displayed so far.

There are more Maastrichts to come, each with more difficult, controversial choices. No quick fix and no easy solutions are available to the problems which lie ahead of EU. It becomes increasingly urgent to clarify the central existential questions – the *raison d'être* – of the EU. Continued ambiguities and unanswered questions about the aims and the means of the European integration will only produce more unrealistic expectations or more unfounded fears among the European citizens.

The fundamental issue at stake is nothing more and nothing less than the future of the unique post-war venture to create a peaceful and prosperous Europe by means of a progressive process of economic and political integration. There is today an emerging awareness of the danger that the European Union might fail and be subjected to a kind of *paralysie générale*. In such an event, the EU would become just another case of an impotent pan-European talking shop; another combination of letters in the European *Alphabetensalat*.

The task is simple and overwhelming. Two giant historical processes have to be synchronised and geared into a positive dialectic. There is pressure to pursue the process of economic and political integration in order to strengthen Western Europe, which means a deepening of the integration within the EU. This would benefit the EU and also the rest of Europe, because only a strong Western Europe will have the power to rescue the countries in the post-communist Eastern and Central Europe; nobody else is in a position to help. The countries of Eastern and Central Europe can only achieve their reform programmes if there is a positive spiral in which three components interact: growing economic prosperity, social stability and political legitimacy. Western Europe can in many ways make decisive contributions to such a positive development. All three factors must be successful more or less simultaneously, or they will all fail in the long run, to the detriment to the whole of Europe.

The new dramatic European *Schicksalsgemeinschaft* or *Communauté de destin* implies that the destinies of the different parts of Europe are more intimately linked than ever before and that the task of creating a new, stable and prosperous Europe must be a common endeavour.

The linkages between the process of integration inside the EU and its enlargement to the countries of Eastern and Central Europe create a basic dialectic which is often overlooked in the current discussion. The on-going debate about the conditions and time-tables for the transition to the third and last stage of the Economic and Monetary Union (EMU) is good example. We are daily given detailed analysis of the important and complicated technicalities of the transition to a single currency, but only on a very few occasions are the fundamental political considerations taken into account. These are of course directly connected with the future destiny of Germany in Europe. The decisive political dimension of EMU and the single currency is the simple fact that it creates an irreversible guarantee against any future German *Sonderweg* or *Alleingang*. Germany will be permanently anchored in Western Europe and in the EU, which has been the basic political objective of both Chancellor Helmut Kohl and of President Francois Mitterrand (and any future French president). But such a step will probably be seen and presented as a German concession to France (and the rest of the EU) and therefore connected with German requests to its partners – as *contre-partie*. You can already guess that one part of these requests will come in the field of the *Ostpolitik* of the EU. Germany will be anchored in the West and the Western European countries will have to accompany Germany in opening its doors to East and Central Europe. In this way the EMU can be one very important part not only of the future EU but also of a general pan-European dialectic.

Alleingang is not an option for Germany, and the governing CDU/CSU have rejected it because, in relation to the external challenges facing it, Europe has only comparatively small and weak nation states. Even the strongest regional power is too weak. Yet much of the discussion in Europe continues to be about the concept of the nation state and the division of Western and Eastern Europe. Any serious approach to the future must start from the post-Cold War realities.

The new departure must be on two tracks: both the process of integration in Western Europe and the reform process in Eastern and Central Europe will have to succeed and to reinforce each other to achieve a new satisfactory European order. The benefits of a successful outcome are enormous for the whole of Europe. This is purely political common sense and the biggest long-term European business opportunity at hand.

Failure in one of the two processes will inevitably influence the outcome of the other one and may have incalculable consequences. In the worst case, we will witness repeats of the disasters of the past.

The present and the future problems of the European Union have to be understood in this historical context. A paralysed EU would be highly damaging for the whole of Europe because it is – for all its weaknesses – the only European organisation with any prospect of acting as a catalyst in the creation of a new European order. The EU is the most important European instrument at hand.

The next reforms of the EU will be discussed in a difficult political context where a lot of distrust and confusion prevail in many member countries in a mixture of genuine concern and populist neo-nationalism. There is a huge comprehension deficit concerning both the achievements of the European integration and the way the EU functions. The achievements are normally taken for granted without any considerations about the alternatives. Public confusion about the functioning of the EU is an almost natural state of mind given the complexities of the organisation. Even the experts are often confused. Therefore simplification and clarity have become the slogans *à la mode* in the preparations of the next reform conference.

CHALLENGES OF 1996

However, the basic challenge for the inter-governmental conference (IGC), which will formally start the review of the Maastricht Treaty on European Union in 1996, comes from the next enlargement of the EU. The task of the IGC should be to propose a new design for the EU which is compatible with the enlargement. The main perspective for an assessment of the future results of the IGC should therefore be to analyse to what extent it has addressed the problems emerging from an extension of the EU from 15 to around 30 member states.

The problems in the present EU have been clearly identified and indicated in the famous CDU/CSU reflexion paper (Bonn 1 Sept 1994):

- Over-extension of the EU's institutions, originally set up for six member countries;
- A growing differentiation of interests fuelled by differences in the level of socio-economic development;
- Different perceptions of internal and, above all, external priorities;
- A process of profound structural economic change;
- An increase in 'regressive nationalism' in almost all member countries;
- Fears and anxiety tempt people to seek refuge in a return to the nation-state;
- Enormous demands placed on national governments and parliaments.

The French socialist member of the European Parliament, Elisabeth Guigou, seems broadly to be in agreement with this analysis of the present state of the EU and warns for the future of the EU (in her Reflexion document to her parliamentary group 31 January 1995):

> The European Union has its back to the wall: it must choose between a reform of its working methods or its dilution into a large free-trade area.

And she concludes:

> Enlargement without a general reform of the common policies and institutions would lead to stagnation and dilution.

The danger of paralysis is the most obvious future problem and it is already visible today. It is present in discussions of 'consolidation' which often appears to entail a slowing or halting of development. It is also present in arguments about the need for more 'efficiency', especially in the decision making process.

The problems of efficiency differ, of course, between the different EU institutions. The most serious danger lies in the decision making process in the legislative body, the Council of Ministers, where further enlargement connected with a simple arithmetic adjustment of the present voting system might lead to paralysis. It might be too easy to form blocking minorities. In the Commission a similar simple arithmetic adjustment to enlargement would create a body with around 30 commissioners on the top, despite the fact that there are serious portfolios available for only around half that number.

The European Parliament would also increase its numbers to the point of absurdity. Even if there are good political reasons for all member states to have a commissioner as well as a reasonable number of MEPs, a new balance will have to be found.

As soon as you address the problem of increased efficiency, you immediately face opposing arguments about improving 'legitimacy', which after the Maastricht experience is an unresolved and increasingly important political problem. The future EU cannot be built without the positive consent of its citizens. The present distrust endangers the entire project.

The key to success is thus to find a solution which reconciles the perspective of enlargement with the reinforcement of the efficiency and democratic legitimacy of the EU. The textbooks do not provide any prepared solution because the EU is a complex *'sui generis'* construction operating on unexplored territory. Until now and probably for the foreseeable future, in my opinion, only more or less imperfect solutions are available.

There are evidently linkages between the problems of more efficiency and increased democratic legitimacy. One strong source of legitimation for European integration is its capacity and efficiency in delivering what the citizens expect from the EU. It has generally been a major contributor to peace and prosperity in Europe. But, as indicated above, the results are often taken for granted and overshadowed in the Maastricht debate by the problems. In the worst case analysis, the EU can be seen as having created expectations of peace and prosperity which are in vain when the citizens see the political paralysis in relation to the civil war in Bosnia, to growing mass unemployment and to the currency turmoil!

Consequently, to improve the legitimacy of the project, the EU must deliver the goods and explain what realistically can be expected. If the EU is unable to do this because it becomes a victim of a general paralysis, then its legitimacy would of course be destroyed.

LEGITIMACY, SOVEREIGNTY AND SUPRANATIONAL AUTHORITY

The legitimacy problems differ between the institutions. The European Parliament in itself does not have any problem. It is elected in democratic and direct elections.

The main source of democratic legitimacy for the legislative body of the EU – the Council of Ministers – is indirect and originates formally from the member states and their democratically elected and controlled national governments. They are the masters of the EU so long as they are the only law makers and so long as they are the masters of the treaty possessing the monopoly of the '*Kompetenz-Kompetenz*'.

One important transfer of sovereignty which is often overlooked is the law-making power given from the national parliaments to the national governments. They exercise collectively their powers in the Council of Ministers, behind closed doors and often without a proper democratic accountability and control at national or European levels. The Council of Ministers constitutes the legislative body of the EU but it deliberates and decides in secret as if it were a government or a cabinet. I am personally convinced that the way the Council of Ministers operates creates a lot of confusion and distrust among citizens. Why could not the EU Council of Ministers be as open as the German *Bundesrat* ?

To fill this democratic gap the European Parliament is seeking a general co-decision procedure in all those matters of European legislation which, in the Council of Ministers, are decided with qualified majority. It is also seeking a general '*avis conforme*' in all decisions taken with unanimity. These are two of most important proposals from the European Parliament to the IGC of 1996. If achieved, they might contribute in overcoming the problem of the democratic deficit. Arrangements where national parliaments are given an increased role in the process of national democratic control of community affairs might also increase the legitimacy of the EU.

In the public debate more attention has been paid to the supranational aspects of the EU, notably to the role of the European Commission and to the European Court of Justice. The members of these institutions correspond to the vulgar public perception of faceless Eurocrats who are thought to run Europe without a political mandate and outside democratic control. The truth is much more prosaic because the Commission in some respects works as any other civil service. The civil servants are strong when the political leadership is weak and confused. The commissioners themselves are the political leaders of the Commission. They are appointed by the governments and collectively scrutinised by the European Parliament. The scrutiny could of course be increased but if the Commission were to loose its independence in relation to national governments and national interest groups the whole project would be in jeopardy.

The fundamental idea behind the Commission is different from a national civil service. It has the responsibility for making proposals for Community measures in the common interest taking into account as far as possible the needs of all the member states. Its aim is to protect and develop the common interest – not to look for the smallest common denominator among the member governments.

Much more important than increasing the supervision of the Commission would be to invent a new working method for the EU. It must simply abandon the traditional Monnet–Hallstein method of the 'benign conspiracy'. According to this method the EU operates with a process of small, gradual, technical adaptations without publicly clarifying the long term political objectives. Economic integration has been seen as the main instrument for the achievement of political integration and discussion of the political unification of Europe has been deliberately avoided.

The absence of a clear, explicit political discussion in the traditional Monnet–Hallstein method was advantageous because the deliberate ambivalence made it much easier to obtain consensus – *'dans le flou artistque'*. Some political leaders in the member states were afraid to discuss *'les finalités politiques'* of the EU, as they feared adverse domestic public opinion. Others simply felt that no explanation was necessary because the political aims for Europe were considered self-evident. This absence of a political debate has now become a serious handicap, especially in those member states where the political leaders did not want to recognise what kind of a organisation they were in.

In the post-Cold War context the direct external threat to Western Europe has disappeared, and the whole of Europe is now involved in a democratic renaissance. In this context the old 'benign conspiracy' is not only inadequate but directly counter-productive, especially in regard to issues which are heavily laden with national emotions, such as currencies, foreign policy, defence and police. Insiders know that in the present post-sovereignty period the emotions are out of touch with the realities, and that this is exploited by some politicians not only to preserve national interests but above all to preserve their personal interest in staying in power. Nevertheless, the national emotions are political facts, *'Politicum'*, and have to be taken into account when the EU tries to regain popular support.

In order to make the EU more acceptable to its citizens it has become common wisdom to state the need for a radical reform which clarifies the complex division of competencies between different levels and institutions, simplifies the decision-making process in the jungle of procedures and spells out the aims and means of the shared sovereignty in European integration.

The real problems will arise when these general principles are to be applied in the new treaty. Then the representatives of the governments in the IGC will face the dilemma of choosing between consensus or clarity. It is unlikely that they will be able to achieve both.

If they choose consensus, then radical reform will be postponed and the most that the IGC will achieve is some fine-tuning of the present system, a *'reformette'*. As a consequence the ambitions of a rapid enlargement of the EU to include the countries of Eastern and Central Europe will also be postponed.

If clarity prevails, which is seldom the case in such situations, they will discover what they already know: that there are quite different, incompatible aims among the participants. The more or less implicit political ambivalence of the previous period will become explicit.

We can broadly distinguish two different views of the future EU. The first one could be called *'Maastricht Plus'*, and its objective is to pursue the path of European integration from the Maastricht treaty onward. It corresponds to a common idea that enlargement and deepening go hand in hand. More members require stronger integration; otherwise the enlargement would weaken the EU.

The other concept, which we call *'EU Light'*, would be a deliberate process of diluting the present EU, as advocated by John Major. The next enlargement would reduce the EU to a common market – a free trade area – combined with some kind of security regime in connection with Nato. It would be a loose club without the obligation of a unique legal and institutional framework. It would be a *'Europe à la carte'* where you can pick and choose according to your taste.

The key concept of 'Maastricht Plus' is integration within a unitary legal framework of community law and within an institutional framework of supranational bodies with well-defined powers. Inside the single legal and institutional framework, it would of course be possible to allow for transitional arrangements and different speeds, but not a *Europe à la carte*. As the old dreams of a 'United States of Europe' have been proved obsolete the main present political ideal is presented – *faute de mieux* – as a 'federation of nation states' or 'supranational union of sovereign nations'.

The idea of the 'federal approach' has been summarised by Jacques Delors in the following way:

> Je dirai que des nations souveraines décident, dans un traité international, la possibilité d' agir ensemble, chaques fois qu'elles ont un intérêt commun à défendre ou à promuvoir. Les domaines d'actions communes sont rigoureusement définies dans le Traité, ainsi que le processus de décision, c'est-à-dire la définition du nombre de voix-pondéré selon la taille de chaque nation – qu'il faut receuillir pour être en mesure d'agir en commun (la majorité qualifié). Tous les autres domaines relèvent de la seule souveraineté des nations. Ainsi chaque citoyen, chaque élu national, chaque élu du Parlement européen sauraient plus sûrement et plus clairement qui fait quoi, qui est responsable devant la souveraineté populaire. (Le Débat, janvier–février 1995)

The 'EU light' concept is based on the traditional ideal of inter-governmental co-operation between independent and sovereign nation states. It offers a lesser role for supranational bodies, such as the European Commission, the European Court of Justice or a future European Central Bank.

From the point of view of efficiency and legitimacy there is a clear distinction between the two options. 'Maastricht Plus' would probably be a quite efficient solution where supranational bodies prepare the proposals and where the Council of Ministers decides more matters with some kind of majority voting. The difficulty would be to reconcile this increased political integration with the requirements of a vitalised democratic legitimacy. As long as Europe is culturally pluralistic it will be more or less impossible to develop a real European democracy, because of the absence of the formal and informal structure of a 'European civil society' – or of a European *'Öffentlichkeit'*. The civil society in Europe is national and therefore the democratic legitimacy of the future EU must mainly be based on the democracy of the member states, as it is today.

On the other hand, an inter-governmental organisation in the shape of a 'EU light' would probably be considerably less efficient, as is usually the case when all member states can veto any proposal. The experiences not only of other classical inter-governmental bodies but also of the inter-governmental parts of the present EU are almost disasterous. What has been achieved in the CFSP? Daily improvisations and bureaucratic in-fighting are the main features. In the longer run the inter-governmental approach may weaken the economic integration and the political result may well be a return to the obsolete and dangerous European pattern of balance of powers.

CONCLUSION

As the inter-governmental approach is explicitly based on the existing nation states the problems of democratic legitimacy are easily solved, at least formally. But the picture gets more complicated if one goes behind this. The request for transparency is, for instance, less likely to be met in the inter-governmental context than inside the community system of the EU. Generally speaking, inter-governmental organisations are more secretive than the EU.

The main argument for the inter-governmental option is usually that all member countries are equal and they all have the right to veto any proposals. It is a safeguard for what is perceived as the national interest, though seen from a European perspective one might question its democratic value. If one small member states prevents the others from taking a particular decision you might well see it as an expression of *'la dictature des petits'*.

Some member governments may prefer the EU Light concept to Maastricht Plus. In such an event the idea of *'Kern Europa'* can emerge not only as a provocative threat but as a necessary step for some other member states. If and when it would occur depends in the last instance on domestic political developments inside Germany and France. There will be no *'Kern Europa'* without Germany, and it is an open question whether there would be a domestic political consensus inside Germany to fulfil the responsibilities and obligations of such a project.

While it is urgent to clarify the future of the EU and to reconcile the future enlargement with the need for more efficiency and better democratic legitimacy, there is this fundamental dilemma: a choice between a quasi-federalist option which probably provides more efficiency but weaker formal democratic legitimacy and a confederalist option with less efficiency but stronger formal legitimacy.

It remains to be seen if this is a real dilemma or if it reflects a debate about the next century intellectually bound by the concepts from the last century.

13

The European Union and the Erosion of Parliamentary Democracy: A Study of Post-parliamentary Governance

Svein S. Andersen and Tom R. Burns

This chapter argues that the EU is an instance of *post-parliamentary governance*, where the direct 'influence of the people' through formal representative democracy has a marginal place. Along these lines, Schmitter (1995b: 7) stresses that individual citizens voting in free, equal, fair and competitive Euro-elections cannot influence the composition of Euro-authorities, much less bring about a rotation of those in office. For instance, a majority vote generated by the European electorate at large cannot be translated into an effective and predictable change in government or policy. In general, the EU is not a political system in which rulers are held accountable for their policies and actions in the public realm by citizens, and where competing elites offer alternative programmes and vie for popular support at the European level – and in this sense, it is not a modern political democracy (Schmitter 1995b:7) The EU is characterised by the principles of *national representation*, *interest representation*, and *representation of expertise*. These complex, representational processes are central in constituting the specialised discourses, negotiations, conflict resolution, and policy-making processes in the EU. At the same time, EU policy-making is vulnerable to criticism and challenge because of the marginal role of representative democracy. Hence, the polemics about the 'democratic deficit' and political legitimisation in the context of European political culture. One asks where are 'the people', where is parliamentary overview and sanction?

Although parliamentary institutions are the core of Western political systems, they are undergoing systematic erosion. Modern governance is increasingly divided into semi-autonomous, specialised segments or sectors; that is, it is multi-polar with the interpenetration of state agencies and agents of civil society. In everyday policy-making, there is no single centre. The complex differentiation of society is reflected in the differentiation and complexity of governance, the differentiation of representation, the differentiation of systems of knowledge and expertise, and the spectrum of values and lifestyles of ordinary citizens. One can distinguish between *government* based on representative democracy and *governance* based on a variety of different regulative, representative and authority processes (see Hirst and Thompson 1995).

This characterisation does not claim that parliamentary democracy has become largely meaningless, or has no future role to play. It still remains the major basis for legitimising political authority and government in modern, Western societies. Parliament is defined and understood as the symbol and agent of the nation, as ultimately responsible to 'the people' for policy-making and policy implementation. At the core of our political culture is the expectation that parliament and popular democracy should play a leading role in legislation and policy-making. However, as we argue in this chapter, the opportunities for popular representatives and their institutions to play their 'proper roles' are very limited, if not becoming largely infeasible.

The common denominator in the institutional arrangements and ongoing restructuring of modern political systems is the introduction and engagement of private and semi-private actors in 'public' policy-making, that is the reconquest of political authority by societal actors. At the same time, new non-parliamentary and non-governmental forms of 'legislative' function and regulation are increasingly common and penetrate most areas of modern society. (1) On the macro-level, neo-corporatist structures ('iron triangles') of interest mediation have been important in a number of European societies (Schmitter and Lehmbruch 1979). (2) On the sectoral level, one finds various stable policy networks or sub-governments involving interest groups engaged in particular policy issues or problems.

While studies of neo-corporatism and policy subgovernment capture several major features of modern governance, our research stresses two other developments where policy negotiations and decisions transcend the parliamentary framework. The various sectors of governance which are interdependent with one another (and also with the larger world) are subject to frequent, even permanent restructuring by the agents involved in various subgovernments, policy networks and social movements.

One of the main reasons that parliamentary systems are increasingly marginalized in modern politics and governance is that Western societies have become highly differentiated and far too complex for a parliament or its government to monitor, acquire sufficient knowledge and competence, and to deliberate on. Today manifold discourses, negotiations, policy-making and implementation take place in thousands of specialised policy settings or sub-governments. Each specific policy area requires specialised technical and often scientific expertise and engage multiple interests and groups with special concern or interest in the particular, specialised policy matter. They represent themselves, *self-representation*. Such patterns contrast sharply with the territorial representation of citizens in parliamentary democracy.

In these specialised policy settings, the democracy of individual citizens tends to be replaced by a *de facto* democracy of organised interests, lobbies and representatives of organisations (and movements) that engage themselves in policy areas and issues that are of particular concern to them. In other words, *the system of post-parliamentary governance tends increasingly to be one of organisations, by organisations and for organisations. Expert sovereignty tends to prevail over popular sovereignty or parliamentary sovereignty* (the principle of applying expert knowledge in policy-making and implementation is widely diffused in the world as part of a global 'rationalisation process' (Thomas, et al. 1987). It is generally expected that, in policy-making, systematic technical and scientific knowledge will be mobilised and applied. Policies and regulations are legitimised by – but also shaped and influenced by – expert knowledge (as opposed to popular, common-sensical, everyday knowledge).

Part of our argument here entails pointing out that the legitimacy criteria – the organising principles of modern democracy – are, in a certain sense, contradictory. The notion of government by, for and of the people (where the latter are constituted and participate as individual 'citizens') is not fully consistent with the principle of a democracy of organisations (interest mediation, interest groups, etc.). Nor is it fully consistent with the key role given to – and expected of – experts. These contradictions have become more serious as (1) policy-making has entailed greater application of expertise and increased role of systematic knowledge representatives; (2) there has been an expanded use of the strategy of interest group formation and engagement; and (3) the increased complexity, differentiation and rate of change of modern society has made more and more obvious the inability of politicians and parliamentary bodies to maintain the myth of their capability of monitoring, assuming responsibility, being accountable, and exercising political authority.

One further development which challenges and erodes parliamentary democracy is the expansion of governance to global levels where the logic of 'people's democracy' seems less appropriate or viable (and where other types of 'representation' seem more appropriate or legitimate). It is difficult or infeasible to realise or embody the idea institutionally. At least, one sees no immediate formation or embodiment of the idea. In the particular case of the EU, we find cognitive, institutional, and political problems in connection with the principle of 'democracy of the people'. For instance, who are 'the people' – where is the polity? Other 'principles of democracy' make more sense, or are easier to realise:

- 'national representation' implies that the people back home are represented by their heads of states with cadres of advisors;
- there is self-representation of interest groups and social movements, that is, the principle of direct participation and 'direct democracy' of affected interests in specialised policy arenas;
- in the context of a stress on 'rationality' and effectiveness, expert representation is a central feature and can be combined readily with national and interest group forms of representation indicated above.

This chapter examines our general thesis about the emergence and increased prominence of post-parliamentary forms of governance in the context of the European Community. The development of EU governance lends support to and illustrates some of our main arguments, in particular the central role of interest groups and organisations as well as experts in modern law- and policy-making – and the marginality of parliamentary representational forms in many important instances of policy-making. The 'democracy of organisations' tends to replace the democracy of citizens and their territorial representatives, and expertise is strategically engaged in policy processes often at the expense of elected officials and government leadership.

We should stress that the concept of parliament or the institutions of parliamentary democracy continue to be paid homage. They are expected to play their proper role in monitoring, critically examining and regulating. Thus, even in the case of EU, there is the principle that all treaty revisions are to be ratified in national parliaments, giving them a type of veto-power.

This analysis is based, in part, on an argument that the new forms of governance are more technically effective and flexible than the forms of representative democracy, and that they tend to replace and crowd out the latter (Burns and Andersen 1992; Burns 1994). The new forms also enjoy considerable legitimacy in democratic culture, the legitimacy of direct interest representation (although this is not the core feature of popular or citizen democracy). These forms have arisen and been reinforced and elaborated in the context of a highly differentiated, complex society. Agenda-setting and decision-making authority are increasingly diffused downward into the society and upward into international networks and institutions.

THE EUROPEAN COMMUNITY AND POST-PARLIAMENTARY GOVERNANCE

The central EU institutions are the European Commission and the Council of Ministers (Brussels), the European Court of Justice (Luxembourg) and the European Parliament plenary sessions (Strasbourg). Questions regarding the European system of governance and administration typically refer to the European Commission, that is the daily executive of the EU, where many policies are initiated (Toonen 1992). Attention is also focused on the Council of Ministers, which is effectively the formal EU *legislator* and is composed of departmental or sectoral ministers of the 15 member states. The European Council, which is composed of the government leaders of the member states, is of course highly visible.

Community legislation is the result of a complex and often *lengthy process of consultation and negotiation*. Under the treaties, the Commission has the exclusive right to propose new legislation. Where the Council of Ministers wants action taken, it may request the Commission to undertake studies and submit appropriate proposals (Andersen and Eliassen 1991: 179). The starting point for attempts to influence EU policy is, then, the Commission.

The EU is not a state in the traditional European or even contemporary international sense. It is a new form of super-national authority. The EU is based on strong *national systems* which have surrendered – or are surrendering – degrees and types of national sovereignty in a wide spectrum of policy areas.

The Commission plays the key role with the exclusive right to initiate legislation. When final decisions are made, the Council is the major actor. Parliament is politically weak, with very little initiative or positive influence.

The Commission has strengthened its position through coalition building with European interest associations. More than 200 'Euroquangos', advisory and consultative bodies with representatives of both interest organisations and Community institutions, have been established. Most of these bodies have only an advisory status. More generally, there are in the EU elaborate networks of contact between societal interests and EU institutions. Indeed, *governance networks with the involvement of 'public' and private actors are the real core of the political system*. Of course, there continues to be a 'representative authority' in the system. Formal decisions are taken by the Council of Ministers (with representatives of the member states, or more precisely their national parliamentary system). The European parliament has some influence but no final decision-making authority.

Lobbying in Europe appears to have exploded since 1987. The interest groups on the EU scene today include, of course, associations representing industries and agriculture as well as many other sectors of society. There are numerous professional lobbyists (including accounting firms, legal advisors) and representatives of companies, countries, counties, and cities. Interest organisations from such sectors of society as education, culture, social services, trade unions and environment numbered 126 in 1980, 29 percent of all Euro-groups, and now constitute the major proportion of organised interests represented in Brussels (that is, more than a thousand). Particularly interesting is the emergence of new types of interest organisations such as consumer interests and individual firms as well as municipalities that have established themselves as lobbyists (and this to a much greater extent than in national politics). About 40 percent of the interest associations recognised by the Community in 1980 represented industrial employer interests and one-third were from the food and agricultural sectors (more than 70 percent of the total). By 1985–86 only 55 percent of the European organisations were from industry and agriculture; the proportion of associations representing industry, labour and agriculture was dramatically reduced during the late 1980s. As of 1991, it is estimated that *only about 30 percent of the interest groups lobbying in Brussels in 1990 represent industry and agriculture* (Andersen and Eliasson 1991).

Individual business firms have established offices whose task is to influence Community policies. All major European firms and also several American and Japanese multinationals are present in Brussels. Some industrial sectors such as the car industry have established their own interest organisation. But for the most part, the experience of these businesses is such that *Commissioners prefer to be in contact with manu-*

facturers themselves or their direct representatives. Federations or associations are further away from the 'ballgame'. (The 'ballgame' in this field being technical regulations, notably those relating to safety or the environment (Andersen and Eliasson 1992: 177)).

The key institutional development that set off the exponential growth in lobbying and the emergence of entirely new types of lobbying groups was the passage of the Single European Act. This made *EU policy-making an important political arena.* The stage was set for profound and vital decision-making processes in Brussels. Before 1987, lobbying of the main EU institutions was mostly done by representatives of national organisations, who often also presented the views of special interests within the country involved. The major channel of influence was through national representation of the Council (Andersen and Eliassen 1991).

In sum, the Commission (but also the Council of Ministers and the Parliament) have increasingly been approached directly by – and interact with – a wide range of actors including individual firms, regional associations, professional lobbyists and national as well as global European interest associations. The Commission has developed a comprehensive network of contacts that cut across, and are independent of, member countries. Increasingly, it is necessary for lobbying to be based on broad alliances representing a more 'European' perspective.

Individual lobbyists, for example, lawyers and consulting firms, operate on behalf of associations, firms, regional or local councils in member countries and other institutions or individuals; increasing numbers of top civil servants in the Commission leave to take up positions as lobbyists for associations or industry. There are also representatives of various regional and local public councils – country councils, cities, regional development organisations and so on.

In general, we find a pattern where local and regional lobby organisations have typically chosen to establish offices in order to exert influence on matters such as the distribution of Community subsidies to regions and localities and the location of certain Community institutions and projects. In addition, representatives of non-EU nations are actively lobbying in Brussels. In 1990, more than 130 countries were represented by ambassadors to the EU. Both the number of embassies and the total number of employees in these increased during the late 1980s.

Major EU institutions have developed complex webs of contacts independently of national representation (Andersen and Eliassen 1991: 178). At the same time, independent interests trying to influence EU decision-making have been forced to base themselves on broad cross-national alliances. There has also been a growth of complex, multi-level patterns of informal influence. The increasing importance of such patterns forces actors operating in the national channel of representation to engage in lobbying, regardless of their national tradition. *The EU system is now more lobbying-oriented than any national European system.*

The EU is, then, a mix between international co-operation with nation state representatives as key actors and particular forms of governance with elaborate, specialised sub-governments, policy networks and lobbying (member states and their sub-units may be involved in the lobbying and policy processes, in other words participation on several levels). Parliament is only marginally important even on the formal level.

The central institutions of the EU are the Commission and the Council of Ministers, not the Parliament. The Commission has executive power, but the Commissioners are not elected or responsible to any parliament. They are appointed by the Council of Ministers, that is by representatives of the member states. However, they can legislate – make rules and policies and support implementation – in many areas within more general existing legislation. The Council of Ministers acts as the formal legislative body, consisting of relevant national ministers responsible to national parliaments. The Council is the major source of transnational authority. Majority rule is accepted in defined areas. Otherwise, each member has the right to veto.

The European Parliament was, up to 1987, simply a 'hearing' institution. After 1987 it was given a consultative role; the Council of Ministers must utilise a unanimity principle in decision-making if the European Parliament is against a policy or law. Under the Maastrich Treaty, this power was increased, giving the European Parliament the right of veto. *This is not of course the same as legislative power.*

It has been a conscious policy of the European Commission to encourage direct contact with specialised affected interests and organisations and also those who mobilise expertise. This takes place above all in specialised policy networks and sub-governments. 'Public' authority is dispersed in these arrangements integrating public and private agents. There is not only the lack of a clear centre of authority, but very weak formal procedures regulating access to sub-governments and policy networks. When specific national interests are strong (e.g. agricultural and food issues), the process may take the form (or revert to) international bargaining among the member state representatives.

'Lobbying' in the EU works as follows: formal parliamentary arrangements and decision-making are replaced to a large extent by the principle that directly affected parties have the right to participate in and influence policy- and law-making. *This is the basis for self-representation and specialised representation in particular policy networks or sub-governments.* At the same time, expertise plays a central role in the discourse, negotiations, and decision-making. The technical – including legal technical – expertise disciplines the political bargaining in the specialised networks or sub-governments; it also provides a language and means of framing problems and their solutions, that is, to *structure the discourse of policy-making.* We would include here also those extremely broad issues such as the environment or women's position in society which cut across a number of specific policy issues. In sum, representation, participation and political influence are not primarily based or linked to EU citizenship. They are based on specialised, organised interests and the mobilisation of relevant expertise.

The reactions to the Maastricht Treaty, especially in Denmark but also in the United Kingdom and France, suggest continuing controversy around the question of national sovereignty/democracy and EU sovereignty. The EU system has a deep cleavage *between everyday organic democracy and traditional concepts of national parliamentary democracy.* This could be expected to result in conflicts and recurring mobilisations in opposition to the EU state, just as we find tensions and conflicts between formal parliamentary democracy and organic democracy within modern nation-states.

NEW FORMS OF GOVERNANCE: THE EVOLUTION OF WESTERN SOCIETIES AND GOVERNANCE PROCESSES

Modern society is characterised by manifold, interrelated but contradictory change processes: expansive capitalism and markets, expansive science and engineering, expansive professionalism, expansive governance and regulation, expansive representation and participation in governance. As argued in the previous section, the EU can be characterised in this way.

An underlying logic in the evolution of modern governance in advanced, Western societies is a particular duality: on the one hand, increasing monitoring and regulation of more and more areas of social life, and often greater systematic and rational regulation, and, on the other hand, the diffusion into civil society of governance powers or simply its appropriation by agents in civil society. *In a word, state government and society appear to interpenetrate – and to dissolve into – one another.* Administrative agencies penetrate into areas formerly free of state involvement, opening these areas up to regulation, bureaucratisation, professionalization and, in general, to discipline. We observe this in the cases of, for example, environmental and natural resource problems, technology, the relations of men and women, the treatment and education of children, child care, the social conditions and social life of the disabled, the use and treatment of animals, etc.

At the same time, governance involves numerous agents of civil society, and the governance processes are not controlled or dominated by government agents, although they are typically involved, playing the role of mediator or broker (Kohler-Koch 1995). Modern governance can no longer be arranged from a specific centre, simply territorially based, with a simple, territorial system of representation. This is not only a problem of levels (global, national, regional, local – for instance, the globalisation and localisation problematics). It is a matter of a profound differentiation and complexification of society that erodes and destabilises established institutions of government that may have been previously effective. The modern economy and its markets are highly differentiated and complex; public services consist of a vast array of activities; administration is substantially differentiated and complex; culture is differentiated in a world of growing diversity in values and lifestyles.

The profound differentiation and complexity of modern society is manifested in a number of different features that affect governance. The various processes relating to production, commerce, health, education, industries, service production, etc. are not overseeable. In sum, there is great societal complexity. There is administrative complexity; there is technical and scientific complexity; complexity of social values and life styles. The established, formal institutions of government cannot handle this complexity. There is an institutional gap or misfit between the relations or system of social regulation and the forces and practices of a dynamic, complex society. Government services alone consist of an array of different activities – with citizens and citizen groups demanding more varied and even personalised services, variation in part in connection with life style variation (Hirst 1995). Moreover, there is a continual cascading of problems: one tries to solve problem x, and may do so in a certain sense, but further problems y and z are generated. Hage and Hollingsworth (1993) point out that improved medical care and hygiene has increased longevity. In earlier times, few people lived to 80 but now many do. Now there is a whole new set of medical problems, costs, new types of medical facilities and programs to care for the elderly, the senile, and the (slowly) dying. We are confronted with questions such as what to do when almost a third or more of the population is retired; or whether we should use our available skills, techniques, facilities, and resources to maintain elderly people who would otherwise die.

Speaking on a more general level, this chapter (and our related work elsewhere) has identified *a new type of socio-political system*. We have referred to this as *post-parliamentary or organic governance* (Andersen and Burns 1992; Burns 1994). In several respects such a type of system can be considered democratic in character – at least in the sense of self-representation, direct participation, and the exercise of influence over (specialised) rule formation, institutional innovation and change, and determination of future scenarios. The system consists of particular institutional arrangements (not only the formal or legal ones), with their key types of actors. Of these actors, some who are prominent in democratic constitutions – such as citizens – may not play a prominent role at all; others such as experts who, although typically not defined or recognised in formal constitutions, nevertheless play strategic roles). This system has key organising principles and rules that differ substantially from territorial, parliamentary representation. Post-parliamentary governance is characterised in the following way, for instance, in the case of the EU.

(1) *Representation* is specialised, distributed and only to a limited extent territorial. There is a *representational complex*. (a) Nation-state representation: the political leadership that participates in or selects a subordinate to represent the country in the EU. (b) Specific national institutions are represented, such as energy or social welfare departments (there are, of course, various forms of delegation or authorisation, so that a minister designates his or her assistant to represent the department). (c) Interest and other group associations are involved in self-representation. (d) Parliaments represent their peoples, the various citizenries; (e) Those 'representatives' who *may speak for* the EU. (f) Finally representatives of expertise, science and systematic knowledge who are recruited to participate in discourses, negotiations and policy-making processes.

(2) *Sovereignty and authority* is specialised, distributed and to an important degree increasingly non-territorial (or it is very difficult to map to specific territories). Authority is distributed into civil society networks, subgovernments and movements (organic governance) and into international government bodies and networks.

Political authority (including agenda setting, legislative, participatory) authority is in large part highly differentiated, highly diffused. The diffusion of political authority outward and downward into society, and upward into international networks and institutions has a bearing on sovereignty. *Sovereignty is more and more differentiated and diffused (horizontally as well as vertically)*. We can see this in the EU with the complex set of rules where in some areas, EU is decisive, in other areas the member nation, and in some areas it is a matter of negotiation.

But if we look more closely at both of these cases we find that there is a *sovereignty complex* in European societies (as suggested in our research on modern, organic governance within nations). In written constitutions, the matter of sovereignty is relatively clearcut. But in actual practice – and in the developing *culture of authority and governance* – we discover a particular (re-) arrangement of sovereignty and authority which is in part, due to organic governance within societies and, in part, due to the globalisation and diffusion of authority and control into larger collectivities (EU and IGOs). Finally, central authority (parliament and government) is limited by the rule of law, a key element in European political culture. In sum, the hegemony of modern representative democracy in the West is perhaps more an illusion than a reality.

(3) *Responsibility* for 'lawmaking' and policy-making formally resides in the system of representative democracy. But in practice, as we have argued, other agents and their arrangements have assumed much of this responsibility. In other words, the institutions of representative democracy and its leader retain a high degree of responsibility – at least in the public mythology – but their practical authority – their possibilities of monitoring and governing – are minimal. The areas and problems for which parliament and the government are responsible has increased substantially, and continues to increase. Moreover, parliamentary bodies as well as governments have declining control: this is partly the result of a lack of technical resources and expertise (at least internal to the government); partly a result of limited resources; and partly the exponential growth of the problems, issues and questions which are to be dealt with.

At the same time, accountability is highly diffused. Most of those engaged in the complex policy-making and govern-ance of modern society are *not accountable to the larger public*, although they are accountable to themselves and to their specialised institutions and interests. These discrep-ancies or contradictions are the source of major misunder-standings, frustration and disillusionment of contemporary politicians and their publics.

(4) Even *'law' and public policy-making* is a differentiated and diffuse concept. Law is no longer simply the law of the na-tion state backed up, if necessary, by force. Rather, interna-tional, regional, local and sectoral agreements on rules and regulations are discussed, negotiated and determined in the *manifold forums and arenas of post-parliamentary govern-ance*. These are enforced through a complex of different social control processes that typically have little to do with coercion in any strict sense.

The effectiveness and, to some extent, the legitimacy of Western politi-cal arrangements – rule regimes – has rested in their capability to ad-dress policy questions openly and systematically, to organise discourses and negotiations, to resolve conflicts and to make and implement rules and rule changes. These institutional pillars are partially contradic-tory (Burns 1994). As pointed out earlier, the characteristic organising features of these arrangements are: (1) the prominent role of interest organisations or associations as opposed to individual citizens and their territorial representatives (and even in many respects, political par-ties), so that there is *de facto* a type of democracy of special issue and interest organisations; (2) experts play a central role; (3) the overall development consists of the displacement of rule- and policy-making from parliamentary bodies to informal groups and networks in society. Many of the most strategic forums/arenas of discourse, negotiation, conflict resolution and rule-making lie outside the parliamentary or representative democracy domain: for instance, banking, energy, new technology developments, globalisation, as well as many, many special-ised, focused policy processes.

The explanation of the new developments has to do with the ineffec-tiveness of the territorial, parliamentary system (and government) to deal with the highly differentiated, complex society of today. In order to solve problems, agents who are concerned and command resources – and have rights and privileges – shape and maintain the new forms. The differentiated, organic governance works in part because the agents who participate in governance are highly rational actors. They have access to and utilise expertise, they adhere to norms and procedures for rational discourse, negotiation and decision-making. These arrangements are generally effective for problem identification, negotiation, conflict resolution and policy-making. In general the many informal subgovernments and related forms of governance provides effective alternatives to territorial, parliamentary representation. Group mobilisation and specialised representation, mobilisation of specialised knowledge, engagement with key actors in the particular area are effective in governance and enjoy some democratic legitimacy.

In other words, *the robustness of these forms of governance is based in part on their effectiveness, but also on their democratic legitimacy* (this legitimacy is, however, weaker or more open to criticism than that of popular sovereignty/representation, which is part of the sacred core of the West (Burns 1994)).

Formal law-making conducted at the political centre with parliamentary government – that is, centralised, formalised law-making – is *technically inferior* to the organic forms of governance, in particular specialised policy networks and sub-governments having another basis of participation and representation (Burns 1994). *This is because the specialised forms bring together and organise agents with a particular interest in the policy area or issue; they also engage agents with specialised expertise essential to identifying problems and solving them in the area in question.* Relevant knowledge – and even knowledge production – can be brought to bear on the problems or issues. Through their collective activities, the actors involved in a particular policy network or subgovernment build up or develop specific norms and practices relevant to the governance processes. *These forms also realise, in a certain sense, general cultural notions of democracy, namely the right to form groups or organisations in order to advance or protect interests and the right to voice an opinion and to influence policies or laws that affect one's interests or values.*

In the case of any given policy issue or policy domain, there is often a spectrum of perspectives, values and interests which parliamentary representatives, 'generalists', cannot represent. Social reality is all too complex. Moreover, elected representatives find it impossible, or certainly very difficult, to know or to learn the minimal technical knowledge entailed in the variety of problem areas or issues with which they deal, or are expected to deal (see note 18). For any given issue, such as animal rights, bio-technology or telecommunications, the technical knowledge called for will vary, depending on which constituency – or constituencies – one takes into consideration: scientific, various animal rights movements, commercial interests, etc.

Parliamentary democratic forms based on *territorial and general representation* are inferior in *representing* the special interests, value groups or communities that are engaged in or concerned about *issue* X or *programme* Y. These agents want to be directly involved themselves – or if not directly involved themselves – to be represented by those with suitable orientations and with specialised or focused concerns and knowledge relevant to the problem or issue at hand.

The relevant issue or interest groups support specialised representation, representing themselves in the governance processes. These meet, negotiate and solve problems including the resolution of conflicts. Solutions are often forthcoming, in part, because subgovernments or actors in policy networks establish institutionalised strategies to resolve conflicts, but also because *issues are focused and circumscribed within these networks*.

Parliament and government do not encompass sufficient expertise or represent a broad enough spectrum of publics or interests to deal with many types of contemporary problems or issues. Decisions can still be made, of course, in the formal government structures, with inputs from expert advisors and interest groups. This is the form of parliamentary hearings and commissions. But the risks are great that without *negotiated* policies or settlements, public criticism and opposition may be forthcoming sooner or later; that is, there will emerge questioning, mobilised opposition and the possibility of unstable, escalating conflicts, derailing of projects and programmes. The legitimacy of laws or policies based only on parliamentary and ministerial discourses and negotiations is not sufficiently well-grounded in a complex differentiated society with important group interests and organisations and specialised expertise.

The specialised organic forms increase the likelihood that the multiple organising principles of modernity, which in part contradict one another, are integrated or realised in the same social space or setting and time-frame. Specialised representation and also direct self-representation is combined with relevant specialised expertise in *focused, organised discourse, negotiation and policy-making* – and this is accomplished in more flexible and systematic ways than is possible within parliamentary forms. Also, the policies and 'laws' agreed to are interpreted and implemented in large part through the established policy networks and sub-governments; this increases the likelihood of effective 'forward integration' linking policy-making to implementation in the organic forms (whereas law- and policy-making are separated in a parliamentary/administrative arrangement).

In general, the organic forms satisfy many of the technical imperatives of modern governance at the same time that they satisfy or realise certain principles of democracy (interpreted in terms of, for instance, interest group articulation and participation). *On a formal level, parliamentary organising principles do not readily bring together and organise – at least not on the basis of a formal mandate – relevant interests and expertise in specialised policy areas or sectors, in order to carry out discourse, negotiate, and formulate policy and laws.* If parliamentary leaders did draw these interests and experts into parliamentary discourses and negotiations, they would be giving over their responsibilities, indeed acting irresponsibly and even illegally in relation to their constituents.

Parliamentary representatives are insufficiently specialised to focus on each of many issues which must be dealt with in a modern society. Moreover, they do not necessarily represent the relevant interests – or the intensity of the interests – of those that are or would be concerned about the issue in question. Indeed, many representatives in a parliament may be unconcerned or have extraneous interests in a given policy issue or problem. Indeed, such representatives only complicate the decision setting: they may vote or arrange to trade their vote, but neither they nor their constituents have a genuine interest (or expertise) in the issue or problem in question.

In sum, the organic forms of democracy enable strategic, specialised actors in diverse sectors and domains of modern society to partially resolve contradictions within modernity, between democracy and bureaucracy, between democracy and expertise, in ways which parliamentary forms do not. Specialised sub-government forms draw together expertise, relevant interests able to deal technically with the specific, relevant problems – including those of participation and representation of relevant interests. The new forms of democracy have emerged and developed in the context of societal selection processes favouring them (Burns and Dietz 1992; 1995a; 1995b). There is a struggle between the old and the new forms of governance, but this takes place within a democratic culture – the different forms enjoy varying degrees of democratic legitimacy (in contrast to the historical struggles between democracy, oligarchy, monarchy and tyranny).

On a practical level the new structures successfully compete with and tend to supercede or crowd out the authoritative and formally legitimate forms of representative democracy.

They are favoured in the selection processes because: (1) They are not only compatible with several key modern principles or values of modernity (such as rationality and democracy) but they enable social actors to deal with key problems, solve conflicts, and address contradictions that are difficult (or very costly) to deal with within the framework of formal democratic arrangements. In this sense, *modern organic forms enable actors to directly and informally deal with contradictions between technocracy (expertise and bureaucracy) and democracy.* (2) Powerful actors, in particular interest groups, bureaucratic agents and professional experts, find the organic forms more effective, less constraining or costly than parliamentary forms and select them in order to address policy problems and conflicts, rather than rely on less effective, less dependable parliamentary forms. These agents of selection are not only those with economic power or with bureaucratic and professional power. They are also those interest groups and social movements that are motivated to effectively appeal to, and make use of, the normative principles of participatory democracy in protecting or advancing their interests. Their rights to participate and to exercise influence is a source of institutionalised power; it enables them to engage in concrete, highly relevant negotiations, governance and sub-government processes, rather than relying on parliamentary representatives to represent them and to decide on their behalf. The direct participation and self-representation of organic forms – together with the mobilisation of relevant specialised expertise – provide a relatively effective and reliable basis on which to exercise influence over modern policy-making and governance.

Our arguments suggest that the problem with representative territorial democracy are the institutional arrangements (formal rule regimes). They fail to provide the problem-solving capability for dealing with – at any level other than the sporadic at best or the symbolic at worst – the spectrum of contemporary governance problems. As a result, the institutional arrangements of organic governance effectively compete with and crowd out those of representative democracy. If this was only a matter of one form replacing another, in a purely technical or formal sense, there would be little else to the story. However, we are left with major discrepancies and a serious crisis of modern governance. Namely, *there is a frustrating and delegitimising gap between representative democracy's responsibility and its lack of structural capability and control. At the same time, there is a corresponding major gap between the actual control exercised by the agents and institutional arrangements of organic governance and their public accountability.*

CONCLUSION: THE EU AND THE FUTURE OF PARLIAMENTARY DEMOCRACY

Our analysis points up that the conventional idea of popular sovereignty vested in representative government has been and continues to be marginalised. Such government lacks the structural competence – its agents lack the time, energy and resources to make up the institutional gap – to deal with the myriad of differentiated processes and governance challenges of modern societies. It cannot monitor, hold accountable, engage in systematic public investigation and assure the effective overview and regulation of a vast array of governance processes for which it is, or might be, held responsible.

Parliamentary institutions and representatives remain accountable in everyday political culture as well as in normative theory; at the same time the complexity and difficulty of the problems and issues that governance needs to address expand exponentially. Unfortunately, parliament's position of responsibility has an open-ended character. Without an effective redefinition of representative democracy's role or function, its peripheralization is likely to continue. It will be increasingly difficult to maintain the public myth in the face of growing democratic deficits, the gap between responsibility and capability.

In spite of many indications of the developments discussed in this paper, it is still largely assumed in, for example, Europe, that the core of modern governance are – or should be – the parliamentary institutions and their representatives as well as the citizenry. All takes place within an established political mythology and set of cultural assumptions – relating to the symbolic centre of authority – *the place* for legislation and policy-making – grounded in representative democracy covering a particular territory. Democratic rituals and myths contribute to a certain sense that the parliamentary democracy 'functions': people elect a parliament, parliament seems to 'decide' a number of issues, the responsible government appears to govern, etc. In most Western democracies, if something goes wrong, parliamentary institutions are expected to intervene; and insist on transparency and on accountability.

Studies like ours suggest: (1) there is a growing divergence between the normative model of popular sovereignty and the actual practices of contemporary governance dominated by special issue and interest organisations. This is particularly evident in the case of the EU, which is in part related to the current issue of the 'democratic deficit' (and given the centrality of popular sovereignty in Western political culture, there are serious problems of legitimising governance forms whose principles of representation, technical character and low accountability deviate substantially from the concept of popular sovereignty); (2) the scientification and professionalization of policy-making also contributes to the divergence between normative theory and practice; indeed, this development is elaborated, even pushed by the experts involved and those elites making use of expertise in policy-making processes; (3) the multitude of interest groups and organisations (as well as experts) themselves develop the organic forms of governance – and contribute to the marginalization and erosion of parliamentary forms – in law-making and policy-making processes. Their interests and goals can be more readily, effectively and seriously realised through the organic forms; at the same time that these can also be legitimised in a certain sense as 'democratic'. This is the democracy of *direct participation* – a participation in policy processes of direct and immediate interest to them, and where at the same time their interests can be combined with suitable specialised expertise. This is well illustrated in the case of EU governance structures.

Contemporary 'politics' and governance is necessarily (at least if any concern with effectiveness is to be applied) highly specialised, differentiated and to a great extent already conducted outside the formal structures of representative government (not just its parliamentary bodies). The EU is an outstanding example of this. This form of governance – differentiated and distributed – is relatively effective and spreads, often in new elaborated forms. There is, in our view, little likelihood that *there will be a reversal or regression toward a classical ideal of effective representative democracy*.

Because modern regulation covers so extraordinarily much (Burns and Flam 1987), the feasibility of some parliamentary overview, not to speak of 'engagement', are very strictly limited. Systematic monitoring, overview, investigation, deliberation and decision-making are beyond the capacity of parliamentary bodies and their individual members. Only a very few issues can be seriously addressed under the very best of circumstances. Moreover, politicians lack, in general, the legal, technical and specialised knowledge and skills essential to the tasks at hand. Contemporary governance and regulation covers so much more, is so much more diverse and technically and procedurally more demanding than even the most professional of them can cope with. *Monitoring, overview, investigation, deliberation, decision-making is far beyond the capacity of a parliament (and its membership), no matter how large, how capable, how well organised, how specialised.* Of course, the hope, the trust, and the current myth is that at any time parliamentary bodies possess and are prepared to utilise their formal authority and political mandate to monitor, intervene and make an issue of any particular policy, program, agency or activity of government or governance. While this threat was also very limited in the past, it was still an important capability, *a potential threat* in relation to more modest, more limited problems of regulation and government. Today it is an illusion, an illusion regarding capability as well as accountability.

Having said this, we want to stress that there are, nonetheless, serious problems with post-parliamentary organic governance, in particular *legitimisation problems* and *problems of integration*. In this type of governance, economically well-endowed groups as well as highly organised groups and impassioned movements with focused interests can concentrate on specialised policy areas of particular concern to them. Large, unwieldy citizen populations and groups with broad collective interests are at an obvious disadvantage. This is especially the case in the many technical areas where specialised groups and organisations can mobilise essential expertise and participate effectively in the discourses, negotiations and policy-making for each particular policy area.

Although the post-parliamentary forms of governance tend to dominate and crowd out parliamentary influence in specialised areas of policy-making, particularly those involving the application of specialised expertise, they are not readily applied or effective in dealing with *overall or global legal and administrative regulation,* e.g. general legal and administrative functions as well as police functions (one important 'police function' is insuring that organisations and movements interested in subverting the system or carrying out a coup d'etat are apprehended or blocked). Nor are the specialised governance forms especially capable of dealing with the *fragmentation of policy-making, or the multitude of piecemeal developments whose interactions in the social or physical environment may lead – unintentionally or unexpectedly – to serious, even catastrophic economic, social, or ecological consequences.* A further weakening is that the specialised organic forms are not particularly effective at legitimising the system of modern governance. Typically, the formal democratic arrangements, in particular parliament, still remain essential in this respect.

One might note also that specialised subgovernments and policy networks cannot deal with certain types of ethnic or religions conflicts but then parliamentary bodies have not been particularly effective in theses areas either.

A revitalisation of democracy in Europe calls for a wide-ranging, highly participatory normative discourse. Who, or what agents, will take the initiative, assume responsibility, mobilise, and organise for this purpose? Failure to do this entails a genuine risk of eroding *the moral basis of democracy*. The *cynical society* might be near at hand.

The challenge is both a scientific and a normative or moral one (Burns and Ueberhorst 1987). Just when some leap with ectasy – and even declare the end of history – in that liberal democracy and liberal economy have 'triumphed'. They are long on proclamations and short on analysis. With ideological myopia they fail to see that modern democracies are not what the proclamations say, and that we are often blind to the risks and dangers of developments which we fail to grasp intellectually, normatively and practically.

Is there hope? We say yes, although with some reservations. On what basis can we make such a claim? First, there is in Europe a widely shared set of core democratic principles, a political culture as stressed earlier. There is also considerable social discipline (à la Norbert Elias), rationalised actors and governance processes – not garbage-can processes and chaos (Andersen and Burns 1992). Important here also is the diffuse network of concrete social controls that has a great deal to do with our being able to participate in modern experiments in some type of disciplined 'anarchy'. This *modern anarchy* seems to actually work. This is possible in the context of modern society since cultural integration – as well as many of our concrete means of social control – are based, at least in part, on the 'religion of modernity' (Burns 1994). We also have an advantage that, thusfar, many of the European institutions work more or less effectively; and also that, on some levels and in some areas they have considerable experience with, and developed, institutionalised arrangements (journalism, mass media, centres of research and investigation) for reflective processes such as identifying failings, traps, deadends, vicious circles and so forth. The arrangements are a very substantial asset and potentiality for the future of democratic development, even if they often engage in irrelevancies and superficialities and not least fail to address some of the problems and issues raised in this chapter. But they may be open to the challenge of our common futures.

On the level of a normative theory of governance, modern societies are faced with two major challenges, which are also essential in dealing with the democratic deficit such as that of the EU (but not limited to the EU): (1) to develop normative principles and guidelines that effectively regulate and hold accountable agents engaged in organic governance; (2) to reconsider and redefine the role of parliamentary bodies.

(1)   There is an obvious gap between the explicit normative theory of democracy (namely representative parliamentarism based on popular sovereignty) and the contem-

porary practice of organic governance. Many political leaders and citizens recognise that something is seriously wrong; there is a sense of institutional and normative crisis.

What sort of normative theory is required to define 'proper' agents, to regulate these differentiated governance processes? This would be a step toward securing greater legitimacy for the organic forms and their agents, for instance, their explicit authorisation by parliament.

We need to explicate the concept of a citizenship of organisations, an organisational constitution, defining the role of organisations in governance and providing explicit or public norms to regulate them. Similarly, the role of expertise including science must be defined and regulated (Burns and Ueberhorst 1987). This, of course, implies *formulating new constitutions for organic governance.*

Today constitutions do not explicitly regulate group interests and organisations, or for that matter the role of science and expertise in politics; That is, defining, controlling and legitimising post-parliamentary forms of governance. A new democratic philosophy and constitutional model would appear to be on the agenda. Such a philosophy – and constitutional frame – should be consistent with the larger society (economy, science, technology) which is envisioned as desirable; or vice versa, we may insist on principles of economics, science and technology that are compatible with the type of democracy we wish to establish and develop.

These considerations raise the question of the *architecture of a legitimate post-parliamentary political order*. An appropriate constitution should then not only refer to parliament, formal government, and citizens but to organisations, expertise, agents of civil society, etc. It would also articulate and legitimise *the organic forms of governance in terms of norms and values of democracy and define rights, limits and responsibilities*.

(2) Precisely what role, if any, can parliament play in the new order, a setting ironically enough characterised here as *post-parliamentary* governance? In a world of differentiated, diffused sovereignty, representation and rule-making, modern societies run the risk of increasing fragmentation, non-accountability and disorder. One potential role for parliament would be that of monitoring and holding accountable specialised governance systems, and possibly addressing

problems and issues of long-term global developments, the
tensions and contradictions between sectoral developments,
and overall social stabilisation. Is it feasible, for example
within the EU, to effectively combine specialised sub-government
systems and formal parliaments in a particular
division of responsibility and authority (a division of function)?

While it is true that we have argued that formal representative democracy
is not the dominant institutional arrangement for governance,
authority, and representation – although it continues to symbolise 'democracy'
for many, if not most – we do not mean that parliamentary
forms of democracy cannot be redirected to new responsibilities and
authority.

One feasible and strategic role for parliaments would be to address:
(1) 'constitutional' questions, to function as a permanent constitutional
congress appropriate for dynamic modernity; (2) the task of monitoring
and regulating the diffusion of sovereignty, representativity, and accountability
in contemporary governance structures.

(1) One strategic task confronting modern societies is that of addressing
in a systematic and continuing basis *constitutional questions*.
Constitution as a set of understandings, organising principles, norms,
and values) is interpreted here in a broader sense that the conventional,
formal constitutional idea: it concerns long-term, global developments
of social institutions and institutional arrangements, the material
and technological bases of society, environmental considerations,
etc..

National parliaments are institutional devices designed, among other
things, to represent the people of a given territory, typically having a
variety of differing interests, relationships and conditions. An essential
aspect of parliament's role should be an *integrative* one – one capable
of seeing beyond narrow issues and interests, developing an overview,
a long-term perspective, a *constitutional perspective*. There is a
clear and present need for a societal 'authority' or representative, such
as parliament, to address global, long-term societal problems. This is a
'constitutional task', entailing a new concept of constitution as not only
concerning governance, rights, and responsibilities, but also long-term
technological and environmental developments (Burns and Ueberhorst
1988). This suggests a special role for parliament, instead of the diffuse
role of the agent for all seasons and causes, which tries to – or is expected
to – monitor and engage in a multitude of policy-making and
governance processes, as exemplified by national efforts to try to moni-

tor and critically examine and regulate the engagements and decisions of their EU representatives. The idea behind such efforts is, of course, that parliaments establish review, special parliamentary bodies responsible for EU matters to approve and feed into EU processes. One may legitimately ask *why should this work in the case of the EU when it largely fails to work in the case of the regulation of national governance? One might counter that, for the sake of democracy, it is important to keep up this symbolic activity*. Certainly, there is some validity to the argument. Unfortunately, such symbolic activity gives a false sense of security: namely, that there is the capability of overview, that there is responsibility and accountability – *when in large part there is not*. This calls for action.

(2) Much of the public discourse on the development of the EU concerns the question of its formation as a confederation of states as opposed to a federal system. We have provided a somewhat different perspective, and suggested a different set of questions: namely, the EU as an instance of post-parliamentary governance. We have also suggested a different constitutional task than resolving the somewhat defunct issue of confederation versus federation, namely a reconceptualisation of the role of representative institutions, and in particular, parliaments in the context of organic governance. We propose:

(1)   Parliament's overall integrative function should be stressed – its role as representative of the people of a territory.

(2)   It should assume responsibility for questions of sovereignty by becoming a *meta-sovereign* – the generative source of sovereignty – in a complex, differentiated world with multiple, diffuse sovereignties. It could do this by constituting, legitimising, monitoring, and regulating the *agents of sovereignty* in the diverse forums and arenas of organic governance, both on the national level as well as on international levels. Parliament would delegate and charter.

(3)   It would provide general principles and guidelines for participation, for organising discourse, negotiation and accounting to the public; in a word, the ground rules for participating and playing a role in organic governance processes. In addition, there would rules about access and openness, about reporting and accountability (just as corporations and many voluntary organisations are required to give accounts of themselves).

(4)   It would hold participants in organic governance accountable – in part, in order to determine if they should be al-

lowed to continue to operate as sovereign agents (just as corporations and many voluntary organisations are required to give accounts of themselves; and if they break key rules, including those of accounting, they may be sanctioned or even dissolved as enterprises).

In sum, the essence of a new parliamentary role should be to address the issues and problems that relate to 'futures', for instance, the technologies that transform our lives (telecommunications, life sciences and genetic engineering, energy), environmental and natural resource developments; or the appropriate constitution for the agents and processes of organic governance; or the long-term and far-reaching changes in sovereignty, representativity and accountability that characterise organic governance.

14
Democracy: Traditional Concerns in New Institutional Settings

Svein S. Andersen and Kjell A. Eliassen

This book has discussed some major problems and issues of democracy which are ongoing concerns in every liberal western political system. For a long time these problems received little attention in the EU. This reflects the strong technocratic orientation and element of inter-governmental co-operation present in the EU until the late 1980s. The increased decision-making authority of the EU and the importance of EU decisions to member countries, combined with ambitions of building a political union, have gradually brought questions of democracy to the forefront of the debate. For obvious reasons the European parliament has been active in bringing these issues on to the agenda. After Maastricht, both public opinion and governments in several countries have taken a keener interest in issues of democracy. Further institutional elaboration and reforms in the EU have to find new ways of striking a balance between EU democracy and member state influence.

The point of departure for this book was that all political systems have shortcomings regarding the normative ideals of parliamentary democracy. In this regard it is hardly surprising the EU facing challenges as it gradually becomes a political system with a degree of autonomy from member countries. The question then is not whether the EU is democratic or not, but to what extent the EU can handle the traditional concerns of the democratic process while at the same time solving the effectiveness problems of the member states.

In this book we have approached the challenges of EU democracy in the context of the general experiences of Western democracies. Below we summarise and discuss the main perspectives and findings.

NUMERICAL DEMOCRACY AND LOBBYING IN EUROPEAN POLITICS

Part One of the book discussed the two major channels of articulation in the EU – political parties and lobbying. Parties constitute the core of all Western political systems, while corporatist interest articulation has been the dominant form of supplementary direct influence. There is an element of lobbying in all EU member states. In the EU itself, however, lobbying has become the most important form of direct interest representation. This is due to the weak role of parties at the EU level and the lack of an EU polity.

In Chapter 2, Mogens Pedersen argues that the European Parliament is on its way to becoming a genuine institution of representation, i.e. a real parliament. As a part of this process, a kind of party system is emerging at the European level. It can be argued that, in the long run, the new Euro-parties may constitute a challenge to national parties in general.

The political groups in the Parliament of January 1995 broadly reflect the traditional Left–Right cleavage but closer inspection reveals other political dimensions. In particular, the embryonic character of the new Euro-Party system can be discerned when we compare the 'fit' between the EU system of political groups and the national party systems. Although the political groups relate to the classical Left–Right dimension as well as to the newer and 'green' dimension, at least five important deviations from perfect congruence are observed. As a result, the 'fit' is far from perfect. The great variety of party systems in Western Europe preclude the formation of a relatively simple system of political groups in the European Parliament. The relative lack of powers of the EP also dampens the motivation among member states to change the present situation.

Pedersen maintains, however, that the linkage between the two levels is a problematic one. The problem for parties is that, in order to control the electorate, they have to be able to control all the electoral arenas in which citizens are active. This is becoming increasingly difficult and one of the factors which is making it so difficult is the European dimension. As soon as a party has decided to run EU candidates – and especially when it has gained seats in the European Parliament – it will also have to set up procedures for the co-ordination of the national and supra-national levels. If European topics are – or become – critically important for domestic politics, such co-ordination becomes a *must*.

Parties have to co-ordinate 'vertically' between the national and the supra-national parliamentary groups and also 'horizontally' co-ordinate within the European area. As a result, once a party decides to run candidates in the EU elections, it has to review its strategic thinking, because answers which are appropriate within the national party and in domestic politics, will no longer suffice. The problems faced by parties include that of interests articulation at the European level and choosing the type of individual who would function well as an MEP. In fact, recruitment patterns are undergoing relatively rapid change. So is the relationship between the European candidates and members and their parties.

Therefore, although European political groups in their composition remain extensions of national parties, the national parties themselves are facing a co-ordination problem in relation to the voters and to MEPs in Strasbourg. When co-ordination is defective, the parties find it difficult both to control the activities of the in MEPs and to persuade the electorate to follow along the integrationist route.

In any case, the European Parliament is not now and is unlikely in the foreseeable future to become the main source of authority and legitimacy in the EU. The European Parliament has only restricted powers in the day-to-day decision-making process and is very much on the sidelines in determining the large questions.

In Chapter 3, Andersen and Eliassen discuss lobbying in the EU in the context of the more general questions of democracy and legitimacy in the EU. Since the late 1980s and early 1990s, EU interest representation has differed from the pattern in national Western European systems in two important ways: (1) it is increasingly based on supranational authority (Europeification) and (2) the EU system, is less corporist and more lobbying-oriented than any national European systems. Whatever the national traditions are, everyone who wants to influence EU decisions, has to engage in lobbying. The importance of lobbying reflects special features of interest articulation in the Community institutional set-up and decision-making models.

Regarding democracy and legitimacy in the EU, Andersen and Eliassen point out a striking characteristic of EU lobbying: it takes place in a context of a weak party system and a weak parliament at the EU level. This means that direct influence replaces in many ways the parliamentary channel as the most important channel for influence, thereby leading to problems of democracy. On the other hand, there are many indirect ways in which parliamentary influence can be exercised at the EU level, the EU not being a state in the same sense as the member states. Nevertheless, this does not eliminate the problem of legitimacy raised by EU lobbying. However, even if EU lobbying is problematic in terms of democratic theory, it is widely recognised as a key factor contributing to the efficiency of EU policy making. As a result, the role of lobbying is likely to be a recurrent theme in the debate about further institutional changes in the years ahead.

The Europe outlined in the Maastricht Treaty has evoked an increasingly intensive debate about its legitimacy. This is a major topic in Chapter 4. There are two opposing views.

One view perceives the complexity of the Maastricht Treaty as a direct threat to democracy. In particular, the fact that, as there is no European people, no direct democratic legitimacy can be claimed by the Europeans bodies. As a result, the directly elected European Parliament does not dispose of an 'unfiltered' legitimacy similar to that of national parliaments. The transfer of competencies can only be limited and must always be linked to the real sources of legitimacy, i.e. national politicians and especially national parliaments. Moreover, the complexity of such arrangements has effects on democratic accountability, transparency and participation. The 'average citizen' looses any possibility of following the political process and of influencing its outputs. The bureaucracy in Brussels threatens the evolution of democracy.

The opposite view sees the Europeanization of many 'representatives' of the citizen. The actors within the EU system bring their respective legitimacy into the new polity. The fusion represents a new exercise in indirect democracy. The 'mixed polity' is not yet complete as some groups of actors, most notably the national parliaments, are not yet involved. The legitimacy gap is not to be taken lightly but is an unavoidable part of an evolution in which member states merge and pool their legal and budgetary means.

A wide range of alternative options regarding the future of the Maastricht Treaty and the European integration process as a whole are discussed as strategies of political orientation and action, directly affecting democracy and legitimacy.

Wessels takes the view that a new approach to the EU system is more necessary than ever. Since the institutional setting of the EU does not correspond entirely to national models and realities, it is unsurprising that democratic legitimacy is not to be found in familiar terms; but that does not mean that it does not exist at all. The 'polity' called the EU is not the ideal but it is highly practicable and thus – in terms of a realistic vision – 'optimal' form of government. It combines several levels of governance and a wide range of actors, thus creating a complex and highly differentiated entity which can be regarded as a solution to the problems of the modern Western European welfare and service states.

The EU as a developing phenomenon reflects a process of integration whose final features remain open and undefined. Depending on one's standpoint, this process can be seen as leading to the erosion of the nation state or to the shaping of a new kind of 'polity'. It represents either an opportunity or a risk at the same time. Discussions on the future of European integration are nowhere near a final resolution, nor have demands for an abandonment of the whole endeavour disappeared. As a result, the task of ensuring its democratisation and the reinforcement of its legitimacy will remain on the agenda for as long this process continues.

EU POLICY-MAKING AND NATIONAL INSTITUTIONS

Part Two includes a discussion of democracy as the key element in the linkage between the EU and the member states. To what extent the question of EU democracy is an important part of national debates on the Union varies considerably. We have focused on three countries where the relationship with the EU constitutes an important part of the national democracy debate. In France, the strong interest of the state and the state bureaucracy dominates relations with the EU. In Belgium a stronger EU is seen as a precondition for more regional self-government; while in Italy, EU membership represents a crucial stabilising factor in a parliamentary democracy threatened by serious internal crises.

In Chapter 5, Christian Lequesne discusses how the emergence of the Community political system confronted the French state with a gradual process of 'Europeanization'. Since the signing of the SEA and the Treaty of European Union, this process has been accelerated, thereby affecting the Jacobean principles of hierarchy and dependency on which the French state is based.

The widening of the Community agenda and the recent institutional changes have meant that the decision-making process has become more fragmented. As a result, the French government now has to face a situation in which the European unification process has imposed new ways of making decisions, based on horizontal and informal networking in contrast to the principle of vertical hierarchy on which its internal decision-making system was built. As a result, government co-ordination now involves monitoring various administrative autonomies, rather than exercising absolute control of the whole policy process from the centre.

Political processes, like the relations between the government and the parliament or the forms of mediation between the state and the interest groups, are all affected by this 'Europeanization', even when it has caused incremental adaptations rather than radical changes.

In terms of regional authorities, the 22 regions of France are still not in charge of the negotiations for the inter-regional distribution of Community credits under structural funds. It is the state that negotiates the targets of intervention and the criteria of eligibility. Despite this, however, direct representation of regions and departments in Brussels has increased noticeably following the SEA: several regions have set up offices in Brussels to conduct their own lobbying, aimed at both the Commission and the European Parliament.

With regard to the national parliament, its powers in relation to EU policies are advancing from simple information to control. In all members states, the growing interference of EU policies with domestic legislative activities has led national parliaments to seek powers of closer scrutiny of EU matters; the French parliament is no exception. The principle of reserves for parliamentary examination was for a long time unacceptable to French governments. It was regarded as contrary to their sphere of constitutional monopoly in the field of international negotiations. It has now been accepted, indicating that EU policies are no longer equated with foreign policy within the French government, – an illustration of how a domestic political process can itself be 'Europeanized'.

The neo-corporatist analysis has been applied to the case of France because institutionalised macro-negotiations between the state and the main social organisations have never established themselves there. Mediation of the sectoral corporatist type allowed for the coherence of public action. However, this kind of mediation has also been challenged by the European Community, especially since the launching of the internal market programme. By allowing national interest groups to use, in parallel, several channels of pressure, the EU has contributed to a change in the French model of sectoral corporatism, towards more pluralism. This pluralism in turn encourages competition and a fragmentation of interests which allows the French administration less easily to control the formulation and the implementation of policy.

From the time of the internal market debate, expertise on EU policies, formerly concentrated within the Secretariat general du Comite interministeral pour les Questions de Cooperation Economique Europeenne (SGCI), has diversified in France, though it remains within the state apparatus. One consequence of this has been the development of new mediating structures to determine priorities within the interest groups. Nevertheless, it cannot be concluded from this that decisions taken by the French government now effectively take into account the pressures of the interests groups. In fact, during the political negotiations leading to the Maastricht Treaty, expertise was the monopoly of the central state administration which pursued it in a situation of splendid isolation.

Cecilia Andersen, in Chapter 6, analyses the contribution which Belgium can make to more democratic decision making in the European Union. The current Belgian federal structure is unique and essential for the continued existence of Belgium as a Federal State. For the European Union, the ongoing process of federalisation in Belgium can be seen as an inspiration in overcoming the challenge posed by the democratic aspirations of regions at the European Union level. Some of the Belgian innovations can serve as examples for the future role of federated entities in Europe where subsidiarity should play a key role. For example, the Belgian federalisation process results in various 'governments' operating within the geographical context of Belgium and having the democratic right to be involved in the European Union developments.

The Belgian case, however, represents a complex and ongoing process, and its internal arrangements continue to be considered at EU level as an internal matter for Belgian constitutional law.

Despite this, Belgian is an interesting case in that it has been forced to find solutions to specific issues which inevitably come to the fore when a member state accords more power to its regions. This is important when considering the case for regional participation in EU decision-making as well as in the implementation application of EU legislation. The Belgian solution and its practical application provides valuable information on how to increase the democratic participation of regional entities in the ongoing integration process in Europe as a whole.

In Chapter 7, Federiga Mari Bindi shows how, in Italy, the EU system has long been perceived as the only means of bringing order to the national system. At times the EU system has been used by politicians as a means of justifying their actions or as a scapegoat for unpopular policies, though, Italy has one of the worse records for non-implementation of EU legislation.

In Italy, relations with the EU have mainly been handled by the Ministry of Foreign Affairs which is split into six directorates, each of which has an EU 'desk'. Both the Italian Parliament and the Regions have, on several occasions, expressed a wish to have a role in shaping Europolicies. When it comes to the role of the Italian regions in making EU law, it should be noted that the relationship between the central government and the regions has traditionally been uneasy one. The regions have not benefited fully from EU policies even in those areas where they have most power. They do not always make proper use of EU funds and fraud has been a problem. The central government argues that the regions are not able to exercise the power which they have, yet alone take on greater powers.

In this situation, Italian interest groups often by-pass national politics and directly represent their own demands at the EU level rather than at the national one. As a result, all big Italian industrial groups, both private and public, now have permanent representation in Brussels. Representatives of the major interest groups also sit on the Economic and Social Committee. In addition, Italian groups in Brussels contribute to the work of the European associations which they belong to. On the other hand, small interest groups are largely absent in Brussels and therefore have to rely on the limited amount of information supplied by local or national bodies.

Italy, in fact, plays little role in the shaping of EU law. Moreover, the Italian members of the experts' committees are often not sufficiently qualified nor interested in the work they are doing. Little progress has been made under Berlusconi, despite his claim that he would ensure that Italy would play a leading role in the framework of the EU.

Therefore, far from reducing the democratic deficit of the EU, Italy's internal contradiction serve to enhance it.

THE EUROPEAN UNION: LEGITIMACY AND DEMOCRACY

Part Three focuses on the democratic aspects of key EU institutions. A characteristic element of the EU is that the roles and functions of its central institutions are defined somewhat differently than in member states. This is particularly the case with the Commission which is a new type of institution. The issue is how the traditional challenges of democracy are reflected in and dealt with in this new institutional setting.

Finn Laurson in Chapter 8, explores what the Commission is supposed to be, what it is and what it may become. To a certain extent, the Commission can be compared with a government in the member states. A distinguishing feature is that it depends less on the European Parliament than most national governments depend on national parliaments, even though the EP's role has been increased in recent years. The SEA and the Maastricht Treaty increased the EP's involvement in legislation but without fundamentally changing the role of the Commission.

The main impetus for creating the Commission was efficiency. Its legitimacy was to follow from its expertise and knowledge. The Commission is appointed by the member states governments. As a result, in a formal sense, the democratic legitimacy of the Commission is still mainly indirect, through the legitimacy of national governments. Its capacity to solve problems can also provide it with some legitimacy.

Finn Laurson discusses the many reform proposals and reports written in relation to the Commission over the years. Comparing the reform proposals of the 1970s with the proposals of the 1980s, there has been a shift towards an increased involvement of the European Parliament in appointing the Commission. Implicitly this suggests a greater concern for the democratic legitimacy of the Commission. The ideal model was clearly that of the federal parliamentary system, even if most reform proposals do not go to that logical extreme. The supernational nature of the EU put limits on what was considered possible, and the reforms eventually introduced by SES had only a marginal effect on the Commission.

Laurson points out that the Maastricht Treaty extended the activities of the Commission more than the SEA, partly by introducing the co-decision procedure and partly by giving the Commission a non-exclusive right of initiative in Common Foreign and Security Policy and Justice and Home Affairs. Although the EP is now involved in appointing the Commission, it cannot itself determine who forms the 'government' of the Union: each member state retains a veto. Those who argue that democratic legitimacy can only exist at the national level will find this natural. Federalists who would like to see more transparency and democracy, as well as efficiency, at the level of the EU will deplore it. There exists no good measures of the actual legitimacy of the Commission but it would seem that the Commission's image is linked to wider developments in the European integration process.

With the enlargement of the Union, it is uncertain how the current EU institutions will cope. The risk of institutional overload is present, while at the same time, the Union must become more open and democratic. However, the dilemma is that too much 'democracy' in the form of too many veto points will decrease the Union's institutional capacity. No matter what form it takes, the Commission will continues to have an important role to play as a 'promotional broker'.

Fiona Hayes-Renshaw, in Chapter 9, shows that the balance sheet of the Council's score in terms of legitimacy and democracy has changed over time and that efforts are currently being made to improve its performance in certain areas.

In terms of legitimacy (i.e. the ability of an institution or system to articulate the interests and provide for the needs of a particular group), the Council does quite well. The two basic concepts underlying the notion of legitimacy are representation and efficiency. Each of the member states is represented at all levels. Efficiency criteria are difficult to apply but criticisms regarding transparency have been taken seriously and measures have been introduced to improve openness, even though it is acknowledged that a completely open system will never be possible.

In terms of democracy, the verdict is less positive. The general perception of the Council is of an undemocratic, unaccountable institution. Efforts have been made to make the Council more accountable to the Parliament but these moves fall short of the wishes of many.

Some regard the increased use of majority voting in Council decision-making as another sign of the demise of national sovereignty, whereas others view the system of majority voting as sign of a mature, healthy and highly democratic system.

The political and institutional system underlying the EU is already straining under the pressure of increased membership. An attempt must be made as soon as possible to reconcile the requirements of democracy with those of efficiency and create a system which can accept new members with a minimum of disruption.

The 1996 Inter-governmental Conference is likely to have such issues high on its agenda, with the possibility that there will be a full-scale political battle between those who want to strengthen the Union and those who would prefer to maintain it as it is or even attempt to shift the balance back towards national sovereignties. The Council, as one of the EU's central and least democratic institutions, is an obvious target for both groups for different reasons.

As the Lane, Maeland and Berg state in Chapter 10, in any collective choice setting, there has to be an identification of the players and the social choice rule aggregating preferences into outcomes. This is true for the European Union and the relevance of institutions to group decision-making cannot be overstated. The two most critical elements are: (1) the assignment of votes to the players, most especially the allocation of votes and seats in relation to country size; and (2) the use of alternative rules for aggregating the votes of the players into a final decision. The amount of power a player has determines its ability to enter winning or blocking coalitions. As a result, this chapter looks at the EU institutions from a voting power perspective and presents one way of looking at democracy in the EU, especially with regard to its two key political institutions, the European Council and the European

Parliament. A key issue is the question of how much influence the players can exercise over joint decision-making in the Council and the Parliament.

The view of the Lane et al. is that the decision rules in the Council of Ministers have to be revised. Following recent enlargements to the EU, the qualified majority rule no longer results in outcomes which are any different from unanimity. The simple majority rule is, therefore, the only one which now makes any sense. The conclusion is that the Council should adopt the simple majority rule in all cases, except where special (such as constitutional reform) matters are at stake which require unanimity.

Moreover, the EU should review the allocation mechanism for relating votes or seats to population sizes. At the moment, the differences in population sizes are reflected better in the Parliament than in the Council. With regard to the Council, the more countries in membership of the Union, the less the voting power of each country, the major nations included. Power will, therefore, become highly diffused in the future. In the Parliament, however, the larger states have more power in relation to the smaller states than they have in the Council. Moreover, the enlargement of the EU has not brought about any substantial reduction in the power of the larger states. The key question is therefore whether the power differentials between the large players and the small players is substantial enough, considering the immense differences in resources and population sizes. This is more immediate issue for the Council than for the Parliament but it applies to both to some extent. It raises the question whether it is possible to uphold the principle of allocating votes proportionately in accordance with the square root principle.

Lane et al. also analysed the power of parties within the Parliament. They found that the set of socialist parties a unique position in the EU Parliament, scoring a high 41 percent power index measure, which makes it easier for them to form coalitions. Over recent years, the voting power of the Left has increased at the expense of the voting power of the Right, which may explain the increased attention paid by the EU to social issues and questions about citizenship rights. With a larger number of players sharing power in the EU power structure, coalition building becomes vital. Lane et al. stress the importance of how coalitions are made in the EU and the need for systematic research into this process. The power structure of the EU will be shaped by stable coalitions based upon the interests in the major policy areas of the member states. Simple majority voting would help to make this process of coalition-building simpler and more transparent.

As Juliet Lodge points out in Chapter 11, democratic legitimacy in the EU has traditionally been regarded in the limited perspective of securing the election of the European Parliament by direct, universal suffrage. The issue is, in fact, much more complex. Legitimacy is contested: it is the subject of dispute regarding the appropriate balance of power and exercise of authority among the key supranational decision-making institutions, and regarding decision-making appropriateness, efficiency, transparency and accountability. The EU's institutions are not visible, tangible and intelligible to voters. The one institution traditionally seen as capable of engendering popular belief in the EU's democratic legitimacy, the European Parliament, suffered from the outset from being a marginal player in the system. The mere fact of it being directly elected was and is not enough to generate the democratic consent needed to give EU authority structures legitimacy.

Originally, the realisation of democratic legitimacy in the EC rested on two key objectives:

1. Expansion of the EP's decision-making powers to enable it to approximate the role traditionally associated with legislatures in Western European democracies.
2. Ensuring that the way in which the EP's members were chosen and exercised their powers conformed to accepted democratic practices. More recently, with the progressive and continuing attainment of earlier goals, the EP has launched into a broader debate about the 'raison d'être' of the EC and its transformation into a European Union.

The European Parliament is still in a position where it has to challenge inter-institutional arrangements. It does so both to justify its own quest for greater legislative power and to check the potential abuse of power by the Council. The European Parliament must continue giving voice to constitutional and policy concerns if it is to be seen as legitimate player and if citizens are to internalise the EU's legitimacy, identify in some way with it and become active rather than passive subjects in the emerging polity. At the moment, the unintentional effect of Euro-elections has perhaps been to indirectly heighten scepticism about the EU's democratic legitimacy, effectiveness and the appropriateness of its institutional arrangements. The EP's dynamic role in advancing a European Union endowed with appropriate, democratic institutions and policy-making and legislative procedures has not been sufficiently visible or appreciated by the public to enable it to justify its claim for greater power with reference to its heightened public esteem. Until this happens, it will be difficult for MEPs to redress the democratic deficit in the way originally foreseen.

THE FUTURE OF EU DEMOCRACY

The point of departure of *Part Four* is that there are challenges to achieving democracy in the EU, and that no simple, one-off solution exists. The challenge of democracy is likely to be a recurring theme at every cross-roads of EU development. The possibilities for future reform are reviewed in two ways. Firstly, the general issues of EU democracy are discussed. Secondly, democracy is discussed in relation to possible EU development, and in the context of those general societal changes which tend to undermine the role of parliamentary institutions.

In Chapter 12, Rolf Gustavsson expresses his view on the future of European Union, with a view to both the Intergovernmental Conference in 1996 and beyond. The basic challenge facing the Intergovernmental Conference (IGC) of 1996 will be to create a new structure for the EU which is compatible with further enlargements. The greatest fear is that further enlargement will prevent the EU institutions from operating effectively. A new balance has to be found. Furthermore, addressing the question of increased efficiency raises opposing arguments about better 'legitimacy', an issue which has become a increasingly important political problem since the Maastricht experience. A solution which balances both these points is necessary but, as Gustavsson says, it seems that only more or less imperfect solutions are available.

One solution would be to invent a new working method for the EU. This would mean abandoning the traditional Monnet–Hallstein method of 'benign conspiracy': the lack of a clear, explicit discussion of long term political objectives because it made it easier to obtain a consensus. However, this method of working is now dangerous when such important issues as national currencies, foreign policy, defence and policing are under discussed.

The government representatives at the IGC will be faced with the choice of voting for either consensus or clarity. If they vote for clarity, they will be voting for radical reforms of the EU institutions. If they vote for consensus, they will be voting for a fine-tuning of the present system, thereby risking postponement of a rapid enlargement of the EU to include the countries of Central and Eastern Europe.

According to Gustavsson, it is possible to distinguish broadly between two different concepts for the future of EU. The first one would be called 'Maastricht Plus'. Its aim would be to pursue the path of European integration and it corresponds to a common idea that enlargement and deepening go hand in hand: more members requires stronger integration. The other concept can be called 'EU Light', a deliberate process of diluting the present EU, with the result that the next enlargement would reduce the EU to a common market, combined with some kind of security regime in connection with NATO. From the point of view of efficiency and legitimacy, there seems to be a clear distinction between the two options.

Andersen and Burns point out in Chapter 13, that although parliamentary institutions are the core of Western political systems, they are undergoing systematic erosion. In everyday policy-making, there is no single centre. Western societies have become highly differentiated and far too complex for a parliament or a government to successfully monitor all the actors in the political process, acquire sufficient knowledge and competence in all relevant policy areas and deliberate on all the issues on the agenda. The situation today is that manifold discourses, negotiations, policy-making and implementation take place in thousands of specialised policy settings or sub-governments. Each specific policy area requires specialised expertise and engages multiple interests and groups with special concerns or interests in the particular, specialised policy area. Such patterns of 'self-representation' contrast sharply with the territorial representation of citizens in parliamentary democracies. As a result, the system of post-parliamentary governance tends increasingly to be one of organisations, by organisations and for organisations. Expert sovereignty tends to prevail over popular sovereignty or parliamentary sovereignty.

Another development which challenges and erodes parliamentary democracy is the expansion of governance to global levels where the logic of 'people's democracy' seems less appropriate or viable. In the case of the EU, the problems to be faced are, for example, who are the 'people' and where is the polity.

Andersen and Burns claim that the development of EU governance lends support to and illustrates their argument that post-parliamentary forms of governance are becoming increasingly prominent. This can be seen very clearly in the EU, most especially in the central role played by interest groups and organisations as well as experts in modern law and policy-making – and the marginality of parliamentary representational forms in many important instances of policy-making. The 'democracy of organisations' tends to replace the democracy of citizens and their territorial representatives, and experts are strategically engaged in policy processes often at the expense of elected officials and government leadership. The current situation gives rise to a frustrating and delegitimising gap between representative democracy's responsibility and its lack of structural capability and control. At the same time, there is a corresponding gap between the actual control exercised by the agents and institutional arrangements of organic governance and their public accountability.

On the level of a normative theory of governance, modern societies are faced with two major challenges, which are also essential to dealing with the democratic deficit such as that existing within the EU. The first is to develop normative principles and guidelines to effectively regulate and hold accountable agents in organic governance. The second is to reconsider and redefine the role of parliamentary bodies. Therefore, Andersen and Burns propose a different constitutional task for the EU than resolving the issue of confederation versus federation. This proposed task would be a reconceptualisation of the role of representative institutions, and especially parliaments, in the context of organic governance.

CONCLUSION

The challenge for the EU today is that is it has to improve both effectiveness and democracy at the same time. The need to improve both makes the task more complex and more vulnerable to setbacks. In national systems the politicians are usually confronted with only one of these two problems at the same time. This permits solutions which make some sacrifices on one dimension to achieve better results on the other, at least for a limited period of time. This is easier as national systems are often both more democratic and more efficient at the outset.

The problems of democracy, legitimacy and effectiveness in the EU can never be solved within the present set of constraints placed upon it by the member states. The 1996 revision of the Treaty must be viewed in this perspective. Even if democratic problems cannot be solved, they should at least be given new prominence in the ongoing process of institutional elaboration in the EU. This debate has taken place in the context increased openness, involving more diverse interests. There exists an increased understanding that further expansion of democracy in the EU is difficult unless federal elements are strengthened. This is not likely to happen in the near future. In the meantime the EU has to live with the shortcomings and contradictions of democracy. Although the EU faces special challenges in this respect, this book has shown that the basic problems it faces are common to all political systems.

About the Contributors

Kjell A. Eliassen is Director of the Centre of the European Studies at the Norwegian School of Management. Professor Eliassen is also professor at the Institut d'Etudes Européennes at the Université Libre de Bruxelles and he has been visiting professor at several American and European universities. His most recent books are *Making Policy in Europe*, with Svein S. Andersen (1993), and *Managing Public Organizations* (1993). He has also published other books and articles on the EU and European Affairs, Public Management and Political Elites. He is a graduate from the University of Bergen.

Svein S. Andersen is professor in organisation theory at the Norwegian School of Management. He has been visiting professor at several American and European universities. His most recent books are *Making Policy in Europe*, with Kjell A. Eliassen (1993), and *The Struggle Over North Sea Oil and Gas* (1993). He has published books and articles on EU and petroleum policy, as well as on organisation theory. He is a graduate from Stanford University.

Mogens N. Pedersen is professor of political science at Odense University, Denmark. He has also taught at Aarhus University and the European University Institute in Florence. His publications and research interests cover legislative studies, elite and recruitment research, electoral research, party systems, municipal politics and politics of higher education and research. He is presently engaged in a major study of Danish local government.

Mogens N. Pedersen has for many years been active in European political science research and its organisations, serving for 14 years as editor of *The European Journal of Political Research*. He is at present chairman of the European Consortium for Political Research.

Professor Dr. **Wolfgang Wessels** is Director of the Institut für Europäische Politik (1973–1993); Director of Administrative and Political Studies at the College of Europe, Bruges (since 1980); Professor at the University of Cologne (Political Science) (since October 1993); Holder of Jean Monnet Chair.

His publications include: *EG-Mitgliedschaft: ein vitales Interesse der Bundesrepublik Deutschland* (co-editor), (1985); *Wege zur Europäischen Integration* (co-editor), (1986); *The European Council. Decision-making in European Politics* (togeteher with S. Bulmer), Houndmills et al. (1987); *Towards a new partnership. The EC and EFTA in the Wider Western Europe* (together with H. Wallace) (1989); Editor of the *Jahrbuch der Europäischen Integration* (together with W. Weidenfeld), annually since 1981.

Christian Lequesne is currently research fellow at the Fondation Nationale des Sciences Politiques (Centre d'Etudes et de Recherches Internationales) and Professor at the Institut d'Etudes Politiques in Paris.

After studying at the Institut d'Etudes Politiques, Strasbourg, and the College of Europe, Bruges, he received in 1992 his Ph.D in political science and his research qualification Habilitation nationale à diriger des recherches from the Institut d'Etudes Politiques, Paris. His present fields of research include the political unification process of Europe with a special emphasis on the process of institutionalisation. He has also published various books, articles and essays in this fields, including: 'Paris–Bruxelles: comment se fait la politique européene de la France', Presses de la FNSP, 1993 and 'L'Union Européene: overture â l'Est?' (with F. de La Serre and J. Rupnik), Paris, Presses Universitaires de France, 1994.

Cecilia Andersen is professor at (UFSIA) Antwerp University where she teaches 'Doing Business in the European Union' as well as 'Business and Society'. She is also associate professor at the Boston University, Brussels, and visiting professor at Helsinki School of Economics and Business Administration. She is Director of the Research Council on Public Affairs of the Conference Board Europe. Her major fields of interest are the development of the public affairs function in European companies and the evolution of the European Union. She has written several books on doing business in the European environment and lectured widely on this subject.

Dr. **Federiga M. Bindi** is researcher at the European University Institute (Florence), where she is mainly working on the European Union decision-making process. She has been visiting researcher at the Norwegian Institute for International Affairs (NUPI) and at the Université Libre de Bruxelles (ULB), and she has previously studied at the Cesare Alfieri in Florence, at the Institut d'Etudes Politiques of Paris and the University of Oslo (Norway).

In addition to many academic articles, Dr. Bindi has contributed to Van Schendelen ed., *National Public and Private EC Lobbying*, Dartmouth, Aldershot, 1993. She is also a member of the ECPR Standing Group on 'European Level Interest Representation Studies'.

Finn Laursen, Ph.D. (Political Science) from the University of Pennsylvania (1980) and cand. scient. pol. from Aarhus University (1974). Currently Professor and Director of the Thorkil Kristensen Institute, South Jutland University Centre, Esbjerg, Denmark, he has also held teaching positions at Odense University, Denmark (1981–86), the London School of Economics (1986–88), and the European Institute of Public Administration, Maastricht, the Netherlands (1988–95). His current research is focused upon various aspects of European integration, especially EU relations with Central and Eastern Europe, the CIS and China. Major books include *Superpower at Sea* (Praeger, 1983), *Small Powers at Sea* (Nijhoff, 1993) and various edited volumes including, *The Inter-governmental Conference on Political Union* (Nijhoff, 1992) and *The Ratification of the Maastricht Treaty* (Nijhoff, 1994), both co-edited with Sophie Vanhoonacker.

Fiona Hayes-Renshaw was awarded a Ph.D. by the London School of Economics in 1990 for her Thesis on the role of COREPER in EC decision-making. She has a BA in European Studies from the College of Europe in Bruges, where she also worked as a teaching assistant for two years. She has taught a course on EC decision-making at the Université Libre de Bruxelles and is currently writing a book on the Council of Ministers with Helen Wallace. Her other publications include articles on the role of COREPER in EEC decision-making, the work of the permanent representations in Brussels and decision-making in the Council in the aftermath of the Single European Act.

Jan-Erik Lane is professor of political science at Oslo University and adjunct professor in public management at the Norwegian School of Management (BI) at Sandvika.

Ph.D. student **Reinert Maeland** and Professor **Sven Berg** are connected with the Department of Statistics at the University of Lund in Sweden

Juliet Lodge (BA, MA, Mphil, Ph.D., Dlitt) is Professor of European Politics, Jean Monnet Professor of European Integration, Director of the Centre for European Union Studies at the University of Hull, England; and director of the Jean Monnet Group Experts on the 1996 IGC on the EU. Visiting Professor at the Vrije Universitet Brussel; lecturer in politics at the Department of Political Studies, University of Auckland, New Zealand; and Visiting Fellow in the Centre for International Studies, Department of International Relations, LSE. She was *European Woman of Europe* 1992. Her research focuses on the European Union, EU institutions, transparency and democratic legitimacy, juridical co-operation and foreign affairs. She has published over 170 papers in professional journals and some 15 books. Among the most recent are: *The EC and the Challenge of the Future* (1993), *The 1994 Euro-Elections* (1995). She is currently working on social policy, citizenship and internal security and the EU.

Rolf Gustavsson was educated at the University of Lund (1967–74). Previous posts include research and lecturing in Economic History in Lund and at the Scandinavian Institute of African Studies, Uppsala in Sweden: Chief Foreign Editor, News department in Swedish Television (1975–77); Correspondent in Rome, Swedish Broadcasting Co-operation (1977–79); Chief Editor, News Department, Swedish Television (1979–84); Correspondent, European Affairs, Brussels, Swedish Television (1984–92); Correspondent, European Affairs, Brussels, Svenska Dagbladet (1992).

Tom R. Burns is professor of sociology at the University of Uppsala, Sweden and a senior research fellow at the Institute of Public Policy at George Mason University, USA. He is the author of numerous books and articles in the areas of social organisations and institutions, the sociology of technology and environment, economic sociology, and theory and methodology. His current research (together with others in the Uppsala theory circle) deals with post-parliamentary governance; bio-technologies, organ transplantation and death; the sociology of ethics and morality; evolutionary institutionalism; and the social theory of games.

Bibliography

Almond, Gabriel A. and Verba, S. (1963) *The civic culture, political attitudes and democracy in five nations*. Boston.

Amato, G. and Bruno, F. (1981) 'La forma di governo italiana. Dalle idee dei partiti all'Assemblea Costituente', *Quaderni Costituzionali*, pp. 33–85.

Amato, G. (1981) 'Il primo centro-sinistra, ovvero l'espansione della forma di Governo', in *Quaderni Costituzionali*, 1981, pp. 293–310.

Amato, G. (1993) 'My experience as Prime Minister', *speech given at the European University Institute* (Florence), in October 1993.

Amato, G. (1994) 'Italy: The Rise and Decline of a System of Government', *Indiana International & Comparative Law Review*, Vol. 4, No. Winter 1994, pp. 225–230.

Andersen, C. (1992) *Infuencing the European Community – Guidelines for a Succesful Business Strategy*. London: Kogan Page.

Andersen, S.S. (1988) 'Bringing culture back in: pluralism and societal corporatism as contexts of strategic adaption', European Journal of Political Research, 16, pp. 513–526.

Andersen, S.S. (1994) *Nærkontakt av tredje grad. Eus lisensdirektiv og norsk påvirkning*. Rapport til Olje-og Samfunns-programmet. Oslo: NFR.

Andersen, S.S. and Burns, T.R. (1992) *Societal Decision-making: Democratic Challenges to State Technocracy*. Hampshire, England: Dartmouth.

Andersen, S.S. and Burns, T.R. (1992a) Societal Decision-Making: Democratic Challenges to State Technocracy. Aldershot: Dartmouth.

Andersen, S.S. and Eliassen, K.A. (1991) 'European Community Lobbying', *European Journal of Political Research*, Vol. 20, pp.173–187.

Andersen, S.S. and Eliassen, K.A. (1992) *Det nye Europa: Den europeiske unions institusjoner og poltitikk*. Oslo: Tano.

Andersen, S.S. and Eliassen, K.A. (1993) *Making policy in Europe: The Europeification of National Policy-making*. London: Sage.

Andersen, S.S. and Eliassen, K.A. (eds.) (1995) *EU How Democratic is it?* London: Sage.

Anderson, C.W. (1976) 'Public Policy and Complex Organization: The Problem of Governance and the Further Evolution of Advanced Industrial Society', in L.N. Lindberg, *Politics and the Future of Industrial Society*. New York: McKay.

Anderson, C.W. (1977) 'Political Design and the Representation of Interests', *Comparative Political Studies*, 10(1), pp. 127–151.

Attiná, Fulvio (1990) 'The voting behaviour of the European Parliament members and the problem of the Europarties', *European Journal of Political Research*, vol. 18, pp. 557–79.

Auken, S., Buksti, J. and Sørensen, C.L. (1974) 'Danmark i EF. Tilpasningsmønstre i danske politiske og administrative beslutningsprosesser', *Nordisk Administrativt Tidsskrift* 1974, pp. 239–286. Revised version, *Journal of Common Market Studies* XIV, pp. 1–36.

Avery, W. (1975) 'Euro-Groups, Clientela, and the European Community', *International Organization* 29, pp. 948–972.

Ball, Alan R. (1979) *Modern Politics and Government*. 2nd edition, London: Macmillan.

Balme, Richard (1995) 'La politique régionale communautaire comme construction institutionelle', in P. Muller, Y. Mény et J.L. Quermonne (eds.), *Les politiques publiques en Europe*. Paris: l'Harmattan.

Balme, Richard and Le Galès, Patrick (1995) 'Stars and black holes: French regions and cities in the European galaxy', to be published in M. Goldsmith and K. Klausen (eds.) *The Europeanization of local government*.

Banzaf, J. (1965) 'Weighted Voting Doesn't Work: a Mathematical Analysis', *Rutgers Law Review*, 19, pp. 317–343.

Bardi, L. (1992) 'Transnational party federations in the European Community', in Richard S. Katz and Peter Mair (eds.) *Party Organizations. A Data Handbook*. London: Sage Publications, pp. 931–73.

Bardi, L. (1994) 'Antipartitismo e mutamento del sistema partitico italiano', *paper delivered at SISP Congress*, 26–28 September, 1994.

Bardi, L. and Bindi, F.M. (1993) 'Italy: the Dominance of Domestic Politics', in M.P.C.M. van Schendelenn(ed)(1993), *National Public and Private EC Lobbying*. Aldershot: Dartmouth.

Barker, Ernest (1959) *The Political Thought of Plato and Aristotle*. New York.

Belgisch Staatsblad, May, 8, 1993.

Bellah, R. (1967) 'Civic Religion in America', *Daedalus*, 96, pp. 1–21.

Bendix, R. (1969) *Nation-Building and Citizenship – Studies of Our changing Social Order*. New York: Anchor Books.

Berg, S., Maeland, R., Stenlund, H. and Lane, J-E (1993) 'Politics, Economics and the Measurement of Power', *Scandinavian Political Studies*, 16, pp. 251–268.

Beyme, Klaus von (1993) *Die politische Klasse im Parteienstaat*. Frankfurt a. M.

Bieber, Roland and Schwarze, Johann (eds.)(1984) *Eine Verfassung fur Europa*. Baden Baden: Nomos.

Bindi, F.M. and Juttner, Schmitd C.(1990) 'L'opinion publique et l'Europe. Deux cas: l'Italie et le Roiyume Unie', *seminar memoires*. Paris: Institut d'Etudes Politiques.

Bindi, F.M. (1992) 'Lobbying the EC: That Unknown power', *NUPI-Notat*, N.454 January 1992, Oslo.

Bindi, F.M. (1994a) 'Italy and the EC', *Arbeidesnotat 1994/4*, Handelshøyskolen BI, Sandvika.

Bindi, F.M. (1994b) 'Eurolobbying: the actors, the stategies, the results', *paper for the E.C.P.R. Joint Workshop*, Madrid, 17–22 April, 1994.

Bindi, F.M. (1994c) *The role of Eurogroups in the EU decision-making process*. European University Institute.

Birenbaum, P. (1985) 'Political Strategies of Regulated Organizations as Functions of Context and Fear', *Strategic Management Journal* (4), pp. 135–150.

Blondel, J. and Muller-Rommel F. (eds.)(1988) *Cabinets in Western Europe*. London: Houndsmills, Basingstoke and Macmillan.

Blondel, J. and Thiebault J.L. (1991) *The profession of Governament Minister in Western Europe*. London: MacMillan.

Bluhm, William T. (1971) *Theories of the Political System*. 2nd ed. Englewood Cliffs.

Budd, S. and Jones, A. (1989) *The European Community, A Guide to the Maze*. London: Kogan Page.

Bueno de Mesquita, B. and Stokman, N. (eds.) (1994) *European Community Decision-Making*. Yale University Press.

Buksti, J.A. and Johansen, L.N. (1979) 'Variations in Organizational Participation in Government: The Case of Denmark', *Scandinavian Political Studies*, pp. 197–220.

Buksti, J.A. and Martens, H. (1984) *Interesseorganisasjoner i EF*. Aarhus: Institut for Statskundskap.

Bundesverfassungsgericht (1993) 'Urteil über die Verfassungsbeschwerden gegen den Vertrag von Maastricht', 12 October , in *Europa-Archiv*, Nr. 22, pp. D. 459–D 476.

Burns, T.R. (1993) 'Post-Parliamentary Democracy: Sacralities,Contradictions, and Transitions of Modernity', in Carlo Mongardini (ed), *Religio and Modern Society*: Proceedings of the European Amalfi Prize Conference, Rome, in press.

Burns, T.R. and Stalker, G.M. (1961) *The Management of Innovation*. New York: Barnes and Noble.

Burns, T.R. and Dietz, T. (1992) 'Cultural Evolution: Social Rule Systems, Selection, and Human Agency', *International Sociology*, 7, pp. 259–283.

Burns, T.R. and Dietz, T. (1995a) 'Social Rule System Theory: Social Action, Institutional Arrangements, and Evolutionary Processes', in R. Hollingsworth (ed), *Social Actors and the Embeddedness of Institutions*. New York: M. E. Sharpe.

Burns, T.R. and Dietz, T. (1995b) 'Human Agency, Institutional Arrangements, and Evolutionary Dynamics', in B. Wittrock (ed), *Agency in Social Theory*. London: Sage Publications.

Burns, T.R. and Flam, H.(1987) *The Shaping of Social Organization: Social Rule System Theory and Its Applications*. London: Sage.

Burns, T.R. and Ueberhorst, R. (1988) *Creative Democracy*. New York: Praeger.

Burns, T.R., DeVille, P. and Flam, H. (1987) 'Inflation and Distributional Struggles in Capitalist Economies', *International J. of Social Science*, pp. 301–320.

Butt Philip, A. (1985) *Pressure Groups in the European Community*. UACES Occasional Paper 2. London: University Association for Contemporary European Studies.

Butt Philip, A. (1987) 'Pressure Groups in the European Community and Informal Institutional Arrangements', in R. Beuter and P. Taskaloyannis (eds.), *Experiences in Regional Co-operation*. Maastricht: EIPA.

Calingaert, M. (1993) 'Government-Business Relations in the European Community', *California Management Review*, Winter, pp. 118–133.

Calussi, C. (1994) 'Il Decreto Biondi: un'analisi', paper delivered at *Giovani Popolari Giuridical Convention*, Firenze, 29 June, 1994.

Calzia, B. (a cura di) (1991) 'L'Europa in mano', *Guida alla Commissione e alle istituzioni CEE*, Sole 24 Ore – Divisione Libri, Milano.

Camera dei Deputati (1993) 'Relazione sulla partecipazione dell'Italia al processo normativo comuntario', *Dossier di Documentazione*, N.28, Roma.

Cameron, David R. (1978) 'The Expansion of Public Economy. A Comparative Analysis', *The American Political Science review*, Vol. 72, pp. 1243–1261.

Camps, Miriam (1966) *European Unification in the Sixties*. London: Oxford University Press.

Carboni, C. and Fara, G.M. (1993) *Il potere in Itali*. Roma: Koinè.

Casini, C., Forte, C. and Preto, A (1994) 'A New Champion for Parliament', *European Briefing*, November, pp. 32–24.

Castles, Francis and Mair, Peter (1984) 'Left–Right Political Scales: Some 'Expert Judgments", *European Journal of Political Research*, vol. 12, 1984, pp. 73–88.

Cawson, A. (1985) *Organized interests and the state: Studies in meso-corporatism*. London: Sage.

CENSIS (1989) *Le pubbliche amministrazioni negli anni '90*. Milan: Franco Angeli.

Ciriolo, A. (1989) 'Les experts nationaux detaches. Decision de la Commission du 26 juillet 1988', in J. Penaud (1989) *La fonction publique des Communautes Europeennes*. La Documentation Francaise, N.617, 13 octobre 1989.

Ciriolo, A. (1989) 'Statut des functionnaires des Communautes europeennes', in J. Penaud (1989), *La fonction publique des Communautes Europeennes*. La Documentation Francaise, N.617, 13.X.1989.

Ciriolo, A. (1991) *Il Dipartimento per il Coordinamento delle Politiche Comunitarie*. Milella: Lecce Commission des Communautes europeens.

Cohen, J.L. (1985) 'Strategy or Identity: New Theoretical Paradigms and Contemporary Social Movements', *Socia Research*, 52, pp. 663–716.

Collins, R. (1986) *Max Weber: A Skeleton Key*. London: Sage Publications.

Collins, R. (1993) *A Complete guide to European Research, Technology and Consultancy Funds: Guidelines for Successful Applications, Lobbying, Acquisitions and Use*. London: Kogan Page.

Commission Europeenne (1994) 'Application du Principe de Subsidiarite (C(94) 1251 fin'.

Confindustria (1990) *L'Industria Italiana e l'Europa*. Roma: Documento della Confindustria per il Semestre di Presidenza Italiana della Comunita' Europea.

Confindustria (1991) *Confindustria*. Chi, cosa, come, dove, Roma: Interstampa.

Consiglio Regionale dell'Emilia Romagna (1992) 'L'Europa degli Spazi Regionali. Le prospettive dopo Maastricht', *Atti del convegno-seminario* (29.5.1992), Bologna: Edizioni del Consiglio Regionale.

Coombes, David (1970) *Politics and Bureaucracy in the European Community: A Portrait of the Commission of the E.E.C.*. London: George Allen and Unwin Ltd.

Corbett, R. and Francis, J.(1992) *The European Parliament*. London: Longman, 2a ed..

Corbett, R (1994) 'The elected European Parliament and its impact on the process of European integration', unpublished PhD thesis, University of Hull.

Corneli, A. (1993) 'E' la Costituzione che fa il partito', *Il Sole 24 Ore*, 6 January.

Corrias, P., Gramellini, M. and Maltese, C. (1994) *Colpo Grosso*. Milano: Baldini & Castoldi.

Cotta, M. (1988) 'Italy', in J. Blondel and F. Muller-Rommel (eds.) *Cabinets in Western Europe*. London: Houndsmills, Basingstoke and Macmillan.

Cotta, M. (1992) 'European integration and the Italian political system', in Francesco Francioni, (ed.) *Italy and EC membership evaluated*. London: Pinter Publishers.

Cotta, M. (1994) 'Ascesa e caduta della partitocrazia', lecture given at *Europa-Kolloquien 1994*, Regensburg 15–17 June.

Cotta, M. and Verzichelli, L. (1994) 'La fine di una élite consolidata e l'ascesa dei nuovi politici', paper delivered at *SISP* Congress, 26–28 September, 1994.

Council Decision of 20 December (1993) on public access to Council Documents (93/731/EC) OJ L 340/43–4.

Council Decision of 6 December (1993) adopting the Council's Rules of Procedure (93/662/EC) OJ L 304/1–8.

Council of the European Union (1993) Declaration on the entry into force of the Treaty on European Union, European Council in Bruxelles , 29 October 1993.

Council Resolution of 8 June (1993) on the quality of drafting of Community legislation (93/C 166/01).

Cox, Andrew and Hayward, Jack (1983) 'The inapplicability of the corporatist model in Britain and France,' *International Political Science Review*, vol.4/2, pp. 217–240.

Criscitiello, A. (1993) 'Majority Summits: Decision-making Inside the Cabinet and Out: Italy 1970–1990', *West European Politics*, N.3/1993, pp. 581–593.

D'Argent, P. (1993) *Le droit de vote et l'éligibilité aux élections municipales et européennes comme attribut de la citoyennetée de l'Union*. Ann.Dr.Lv., pp.221–234, 1993.

Daalder, Hans (1966) 'Parties, Elites, and Political Developments in Western Europe', in LaPalombara, J. and M. Weiner (eds.) *Political Parties and Political Development*. Princeton: Princeton University Press, pp. 43–77.

Dahl, R.A. (1963) *Modern political analysis. Englewood Cliffs*. N.J.: Prentice-Hall.

Dahl, R.A. (1970) 'Democracy and the Chinese Boxe', in H.S. Kariel (ed.), *Frontiers of Democratic Theory*. New York.

Dahl, R.A. (1971) *Polarchy: Participation and opposition*. New Haven: Yale University Press.

Dahl, R.A. (1989) *Democracy and its crisis. New Haven*. Conn.: Yale University Press.

Dahl, Robert O. and Tufte, E.R. (1973) *Size and Democracy*. Stanford.

Dahl-Jacobsen, K. (1964) *Teknisk hjelp og politisk struktur*. Oslo: University Press.

Damgaard, E. and Eliassen, K.A. (1978) 'Corporate Pluralism in Danish Law-Making', *Scandinavian Political Studies*, 1(4), pp. 285–313.

De Gaulle, Charles (1965) 'Conférence de Presse, 29 September', *Discours et Messages*, Vol. 4, Paris 1970.

De Micheli C. (1994) 'Crisi del policentrismo? Alcuni aspetti del funzionamento del Parlamento Italiano dal 1983 al 1992', paper delivered at *SISP* Congress, 26–28 September.

Debates of the European Parliament, Session 1991/92, no. 412, p. 217.

Del Vescovo, P. (1988) 'Il Consiglio di gabinetto. Un tentativo di rafforzamento del Governo', *Rivista Trimestrale di Diritto Pubblico*, n. 4/1988, pp. 900–919.

Delpérée, F. (1990) 'La voie fédérale', *Journal des Tribunaux, Maison Larcier*, Bruxelles.

Delpérée, F. (1993) 'La Belgique est un Etat Fédéral', *Journal des Tribunaux*, 112–nr.5688, pp. 637–646, Bruxelles: Maison Larcier, 16 October.

Delpérée, F. (1994) *La Belgique Fédérale*. Bruxelles: Centre d'Etudes Constitutionnelles et Administratives, Bruylant.

Dewost, Jean-Louis (1992) 'Qui décide a Bruxelles ?, Intérets Nationaux et Communautaire dans les décisions de la Commission et du Conseil' *in Revue Francaise d'Administration Publique*, nr.63, juillet–septembre, pp. 370–399.

DGXIII (1994) 'Europe's Way to the Information Society – an action Plan', *I&T News Review*, Autumn, pp. 1–2.

Dietz, T., Stern, P.C. and Rycroft, R.W. (1989) 'Definitions of Conflict and the Legitimation of Resources: The Case of Environmental Risk', *Sociological Forum* 4, pp. 47–70.

Dinan, Desmond (1994) *Ever Closer Union? An Introduction to the European Community*. London: Macmillan.

Docksey, Christopher and Williams, Karen(1994) 'The Commission and the execution of Community policy', in Geoffrey Edwards and David Spence (eds.) *The European Commission*. Harlow, Essex: Longman, pp. 117–145.

Dubouis, L., and Coret, A. (1989) 'Le critere de nationalite', in J. Penaud, *La fonction publique des Communautes Europeennes*. Paris: La Documentation Francaise, N.617, 13 octobre.

Duverger, Maurice (1951) *Les Parties Politiques*. Paris: Colin.

Easton, D. (1965) *A systems analysis of political life*. New York: Wiley.

EC (1965) 'Traité instituant un Conseil unique et une Commission unique des Communautés européennes et documents annexes', Brussels. [Merger Treaty].

EC (1979) 'Report on European Institutions. Presented by the Committee of Three to the European Council (October 1979)', Luxembourg: *Office for Official Publications of the European Communities* (Three Wise Men's Report).

EC (1985) 'Report of the ad hoc Committee on Institutional Questions to the European Council', *Europe Documents* Nos 1349/1350, 21 March, Dooge Report.

EC (1986) 'Single European Act', *Bulletin of the European Communities*, Supplement 2.

EC (1987) Treaties establishing the European Communities. Treaties amending these Treaties. Single European Act. Luxembourg: Office for Official Publications of the European Communities.

EC (1989) Committee for the Study of Economic and Monetary Union, *Report on economic and monetary union in the European Community*. Luxembourg: Office for Official Publications of the European Communities.

EC (1990) 'One market, one money', *European Economy*, No 44 (October).

EC (1992) Treaty on European Union. Luxembourg: Office for Official Publications of the European Communities (Maastricht Treaty).

Edwards, G. and Wallace, H. (1977) *The Council of Ministers of the European Community and the President-in-office*. London: Federal Trust.

Edwards, G., and Spence, D. (eds.) (1994) *The European Commission*. Harlow, Essex: Longman.

Ehlermann, Claus-Dieter (1990) 'The Institutional Development of the EC Under the Single European Act', *Aussenpolitik* No 2, pp. 135–146.

Einarsdottir, K. (1994) 'The European Union and Member States: Comparative Study of Organisation, Influence and Sovereignty in France and Denmark', MSc. Thesis, Norwegian School of Management.

Eliassen, K.A. (1993) 'Europeiske utfordringer for nordisk forvaltning', *Nordisk Administrativt Tidsskrift*, no. 4, pp. 420–432.

Eliassen, K.A. (1995) 'Legitimacy, Effectiveness and the Europeification of National Policy-Making', in M. Telò, (ed.) (1994) *Démocratie Europeenne*. Brussels: Institut d'Etudes Européennes.

Elklit, Jørgen and Pedersen, M.N. (eds.) (1995) *Kampen om kommunen. Ni fortællinger fra kommunalvalget 1993*. Odense: Odense University Press.

Endo, K. (1994) 'The Principle of Subsidiarity: from Johannes Althusius to Jacques Delors', *The Hokkaido Law Review*, pp. 1966–2064.

Epstein, E. (1969) *The Corporation in American Politics*. Englewood Cliffs, NJ: Prentice Hall.

Etzioni, A. (1968) *The Active Society: A Theory of Societal and Political Processes*. New York: Free Press.

Europe Agence International d'Information pour la Presse (1994) Luxembourg: Bruxelles, July, 29, 1994.

European Constitutional Group (1993) 'A European Constitutional Settlement 1996', *Draft Report*, September.

European Parliament (1984) Draft Treaty establishing the European Union. Luxembourg: Directorate-General for Information and Public Relations, February.

European Parliament working documents (1988) 'Report on the institutional consequences of the costs of non-Europe', rapporteur Sir Fred Catherwood, A2–39/88.

European Parliament working documents (1990) 'G D'Estaing reports on Subsidiarity', A3–0267/90; A3–163/90/Part B.

European Parliament working documents (1987) 'Toussaint report on the democratic deficit', A2–276/87.

Farneti, P. (1974) 'I partiti politici e il sistema di potere', *AA.VV L'Italia Contemporanea, 1945–1975*. Torino: Einaudi.

Feltrin, P. (1991) 'Partitti e sindacati: simbiosi o dominio?', Morlino (ed.), *Costruire la democrazia*. Bologna: Il Mulino.

Feron, F. and Thoraval, A. (1992) *L'Etat de l'Europe*. Paris: Ed. La Decouverte.

Ferraris, L.V. (1992) 'Italian-European foreign policy', in Francesco Francioni, (ed.) *Italy and EC membership evaluated*. London: Pinter Publishers.

Ferraris, L.V. (1994) 'La diplomazia come arte del 'fai da te'', *LiMes*, 4/94, pp. 255–260.

Flam, H. (ed.) (1993) *States and Anti-Nuclear Oppositional Movements*. Edinburgh: University of Edinburgh Press.

Flora, Peter (1986) *Growth to Limits, The Western European States since World War II*. Vol. I. Berlin/New York.

Fondazione, Agnelli (1994) 'Il nostro progetto geopolitico', *LiMes*, 4/94, pp. 147–156.

Fournier, Jacques (1987) *Le travail gouvernemental*. Paris: Presses de la FNSP.

Fowler, C. (1993) *Unnatural Selection: Technology, Law, and Politics in the Rationalization of Plant Life*. Uppsala, Sweden: Department of Sociology Ph.D. Dissertation.

Francioni, F. (ed.) (1992) *Italy and EC membership evaluated*. London: Pinter Publishers.

Friedrich, Carl J. (1969) *Europe: An Emergent Nation?* New York: Harper and Row.

Gable, R.W. (1953) 'NAM: Influential Lobby or Kiss of Death', *Journal of Politics*, pp. 254–273.

Gardner, J.M. (1991) *Effective Lobbying in the European Community*. Deventer: Kluwer Law and Taxation Publishers.

Gerbet, P. (1983) *La Construction de l'Europe*. Paris: Imprimerie nationale.

Gidlund, Gullan (1992) *Partiernas Europa*. Stockhom: Natur och kultur.

Gidlund, Gullan (1993) *Den nya politiska konserten*. Stockholm: Liber-Hermonds.

Gonzales Sanchez, E. (1992) *Manual del negociador en la Comunidad Europea*. Madrid: Officina de Information Diplomatica.

Grant, Charles (1994) *Delors: Inside the House that Jacques Built*. London: Nicholas Brealey Publishing.

Grant, W. (ed.) (1985) *The Political Economy of Corporatism*. London: Macmillan.

Grant, W. (1989) *Pressure Groups, Politics and Democracy in Britain*. London: Philip Allan.

Grant, W. (1990) *Organized Interests and the European Community*. Paper presented at the 6th International Colloquium of the Feltrinelli Foundation, Cortona, Italy.

Greenwood, J. and Grant, J. (1993) 'The United Kingdom: A Changing Kaleidoscope', in M.P.C.M. van Schendelen, *National Public and Private EC Lobbying*. Aldershot: Dartmouth.

Greenwood, J., Grote, J.R. and Ronit, K. (eds) (1992) *Organized Interests and the European Community*. London: Sage.

Grottanelli de Santi, G. (1992) 'The impact of EC integration on the Italian form of government', in F. Francioni, (ed.) (1992) *Italy and EC membership evaluated,*. London: Pinter Publishers.

Haas, Ernst B. (1958) *The Uniting of Europe: Political, Social, and Economic Forces 1950–1957*. Stanford: Stanford University Press.

Haas, Ernst B. (1961) 'International Integration: The European and Universal Process', *International Organization* 15: 4, pp. 366–392.

Hallstein, Walter (1962) *United Europe: Challenge and Opportunity*. Cambridge, MA: Harvard University Press; London: Oxford University Press.

Hallstein, Walter (1965) 'The EEC Commission: A New Factor in International Life', *International and Comparative Law Quaterly* 14 (July), 727–741.

Hallstein, Walter (1972) *Europe in the Making*. London: George Allen & Unwin Ltd.

Hayes, M.T. (1981) *Lobbyists and Legislators*. New Brunswick: Rutgers University Press.

Hayes-Renshaw, F., Lequesne, Ch. and Mayor Lopez, P. (1989) 'The Permanent Representations of the Member States of the European Communities',

Journal of Common Market Studies Vol. XXVIII, No. 2, pp. 119–137.

Heclo, H. (1978) 'Issue Networks and the Executive Establishment', in A. King (ed.), *The New American Political System*. Washington, D.C.: American Enterprise Institute.

Heisler, M.O. (1974) *Politics in Europe*. New York: McKay.

Heisler, M.O. (1979) 'Corporate Pluralism Revisited: Where is Theory?', *Scandinavian Political Studies*, 2(3), pp. 277–298.

Held, David (1987) *Models of Democracy*. Cambridge: Polity Press.

Held, David (1991a) *Political theory today*. Cambridge: Polity Press.

Held, David (1991) 'Democracy, The Nation-State and the Global system', in Ibid.(ed.), *Political Theory Today*, Cambridge.

Helenius, R. (1994). *From Protecting of Rights to Negotiations Reforms?* Paper for workshop: The Logic of Group Membership in the New Europe, Madrid: ECPR.

Hening, S. (1983) 'The European Community's Bicephalous Political Authority: Council of Ministers-Commission Relations', in Juliet Lodge (ed.), *Institutions and Policies of the European Community*. New York: St. Martin's Press, pp. 9–20.

Hening, S. and Pinder, J. (eds) (1969) *European Political Partie*. London: Allen & Unwin.

Herne, K. and Nurmi, H. (1993) 'The distribution of a priori voting power in the EC Council of Ministries and the European Parliament', *Scandinavian Political Studies*, 116, pp. 269–284.

Hernes, G. (1974) 'The open input-output model, collective decisions and policy analysis', *Working Paper*, Bergen.

Hine, D. (1993) *Governing Italy: The politics of bargained pluralism*. Oxford: Clarendon Press.

Hirst, P. (1995) 'The Limits of Representative Democracy', Lecture at the Uppsala Theory Circle Seminar, Department of Sociology, University of Uppsala, February 23, 1995.

Hirst, P. and Thompson, G. (1995) 'Globalization and the Future of the Nation State', *Economy and Society*, Vol 23, #3, in press.

Hollingsworth, J.R. and Lindberg, L.N. (1985) 'The Governance of the American Economy: The Role of Markets, Clans, Hierarchies, Associative Behavior', in W. Streeck and P. C. Schmitter (eds.), *Private Interest Government: Beyond Market and State*. London: Sage.

Huber, John and Inglehart, Ronald (1995) 'Expert Interpretations of Party Space and Party Locations in 42 Societies', *Party Politics*, Vol. 1, pp. 73–111.

Ingelaere, F. (1993) Deputy Chief of Cabinet to the Flemish Minister of Transport, Foreign Trade and State Reform, *The new legislation on the international relations of the Belgian Communities and Regions*.

Inglehart, Ronald, (1971) 'Public Opinion and Regional Integration', in Leon N. Lindberg and Stuart A. Scheingold (eds.), *Regional Integration, Theory and Research*. Mass.: Cambridge, pp. 160–191.

Inglehart, Ronald and Klingemann, H.-D. (1976) 'Party Identification, Ideological Preference and the Left–Right Dimension among Western Mass Publics', in Ian Budge, Ivor Crewe and Dennis Farlie, (eds.) *Party Identification and Beyond*. New York: John Wiley and Sons, Inc., pp. 243–73.

Jaccobsson, K. (1991) 'Sweden and the European Community: The Development of Swedish EC Policy', Dublin: Trinity College Masters Thesis.

Jacque, Jean (1983) 'The European Union Treaty and the Community Treaties', *Crocodile* 11.

Jans, D. (1994) 'La prise en considération de la réalité régionale dans la ommunauté Européenne' *La Belgique Fédérale*. Bruxelles: Centre d'Etudes Constitutionnelles et Administratives, Bruylant, pp.471–483.

Jenkins, Roy (1989) *European Diary 1977–1981*. London: Collins.

Johansen, L.N. and Kristensen, O.P. (1982) 'Corporatist Traits in Denmark 1946–1976', in Lembruch and Schmitter (eds) *Patterns of Corporatism in Policy-Making*. Beverly Hills: Sage.

Jorbert, Bruno and Muller, Pierre, (1987) *L'Etat en action*. Paris: PUF, pp. 171–206.

Kapteyn, P (1991) 'Community Law and the Principle of Subsidiarity', *Revue des Affairees Europeennes*, 2, pp. 35–43.

Katzenstein, P.J. (1985) *Small States in World Markets*. Ithaca and London: Cornell University Press.

Katzenstein, P.J. (1987) *Policy and politics in West Germany: The growth of a semisovereign state*. Philadelphia: Temple University Press.

Kenis, P. and Schneider, V. (1991) 'Policy Networks and Policy Analysis: Scrutinizing a New Analytical Toolbox', in B. Marin and R. Mayntz (eds), *Policy Networks: Empirical Evidence and Theoretical Considerations*. Frankfurt am Main: Campus Verlag.

Keohane, Robert O. and Hoffmann, Stanley (1990) 'Conclusions: Community Politics and Institutional Change', in William Wallace (ed.), *The Dynamics of European Integration*. London, pp. 276–300.

King, Anthony (1969) 'Political Parties in Western Democracies: Some Sceptical Reflections', *Polity*, vol.2 pp.111–141.

Kirchner, E.J. (1981) *The Role of Interest Groups in the European Community*. Aldershot: Gower Publications.

Kirchner, E.J. (1994) 'The European Community: A Transnational Democracy?', in Ian Budge and David McKay (eds.), *Developing Democracy*. London etc., pp. 253–266.

Kohler-Koch, B. (ed.) (1989) *Regime in den internationalen Beziehungen*. Baden-Baden.

Kohler-Koch, B. (1993) 'Germany: Fragmented but Strong Lobbying', in M.P.C.M. van Schendelen, *National Public and Private EC Lobbying*. Aldershot: Dartmouth.

Kohler-Koch, B. (1995) 'The Strength of Weakness: The Transformation of Governance in the European Union', Paper prepared for the Symposium on 'The Future of the Nation-State,' Uppsala University, Uppsala,Sweden, March 22–26, 1995.

Krasner, Stephen D. (1984) *International Regimes*. Ithaca.

La Palombara J. (1964) *Interest Groups in Italian Politics*. Princeton: Princeton University Press.

La Serre, Francoise de and Lequesne, Christian (1993) 'France and the European Union,' in Alan W. Cafruny and Glenda G. Rosenthal (eds.), *The State of the European Community. The Maastricht Treaty and be-yond*. Boulder/London: Lynne Rienner/Longman, pp. 145–157.

Ladrech, Robert (1993) 'Social democratic parties and EC integration: Transnational party responses to Europe 1992', *European Journal of Political Research*, vol. 24, pp. 195–210.

Ladrech, Robert (1994) 'Europeanization of domestic politics and institutions: the case of France' in *Journal of Common Market Studies*, 32/1, march, pp. 69–88.

Lane, J-E, and Maeland, R. (1995) 'Voting power under the EU constituion', *Journal of Theoretical Politics*, 7, 223–330.

Lane, J-E, and Maeland, R. and Berg, S. (1995) 'The EU Parliament: Seats, States and Political Parties', *Journal of Theoretical Politics*, (Fourthcoming).

Lanza, O. (1991) 'L'agricoltura, la Coldiretti e la DC', in Morlino (ed.), *Costruire la democrazia*. Bologna: Il Mulino.

Laponce, J.A. (1981) *Left and Right – The Topography of Political Perceptions*. Toronto: Toronto University Press.

Lasok, D. and Bridge, J.W. (1987) *Law and Institutions of the European Communities*. Fourth edition. London: Butterworths.

Laumann, E.O. and Knoke, D. (1987) *The Organizational State: Social Choice in National Policy*. Madison, Wi.: University of Wisconsin Press.

Laursen, Finn (1990), 'Explaining the EC's New Momentum', in Finn Laursen (ed.), *EFTA and the EC: Implications of 1992*. Maastricht: European Institute of Public Administration, pp. 33–52.

Laursen, Finn (1991) 'Comparative regional economic integration: the European and other processes', *International Review of Administrative Sciences* 57, pp. 515–526.

Laursen, Finn (1992a) 'Explaining the Intergovernmental Conference on Political Union', in Finn Laursen and Sophie Vanhoonacker (eds.), *The Intergovernmental Conference on Political Union*. Dordrecht: Nijhoff, pp. 229–248.

Laursen, Finn (1992b) 'The Maastricht Treaty: A Critical Evaluation', in Finn Laursen and Sophie Vanhoonacker (eds), *The Intergovernmental Conference on Political Union*. Dordrecht: Nijhoff, pp. 249–265.

Laursen, Finn (1994) 'The Not-So-Permissive Consensus: Thoughts on the Maastricht Treaty and the Future of European Integration', in Finn Laursen and Sophie Vanhoonacker (eds.), *The Ratification of the Maastricht Treaty: Issues, Debates and Future Implications*. Dordrecht: Martinus Nijhoff Publishers, 295–317.

Lavaux, P, Uyttendaele, M. (1994) 'La réforme de l'Etat: I. Les Institutions Fédérales: Ruptures, Compromis et Continuités', *Journal des Tribunaux*, 113–nr.5713, Bruxelles: Maison Larcier, 16 Avril 1994, pp. 305–310.

Le Theule, Francois-Gilles and Litvan, David (1993) 'La reforme de la PAC: analyse d'une négociation communautaire,' *Revue Francaise de Science Politique*, vol. 43/5 , pp. 755–787.

Lejeune, M., Charpentier, J. and Engel, Ch. (1992) *Les régions de l'espace comunautaire*. Presses Universitaires de Nancy, pp. 95 et s..

Leonardi, R. e Nanetti, R. (1991) 'L'Emilia Romagna e l'Europa: le trasforazione di una regione in vista del mercato unico europeo and La Regione Emilia Romagna e la Comunita' Europea: valutazioni e prospettive', in Leonardi, Robert e Nanetti, Raffaella *Le regioni e l'integrazione europea: il caso Emilia-Romagna*, Franco Angeli, Milano *LiMes – Rivista Italiana di*

Geopolitica: A cosa serve l'Italia. Perchè siamo una nazione, N. 4/94, Editrice Periodici Cuturali, Roma.

Lequesne, C. (1993) *Paris-Bruxelles. Comment se fait la politique européenne de la France*. Paris: Presses de la FNSP.

Lequesne, C. (1994) *Paris Bruxelles: Comment se fait la politique européenne de la France*. Press de la Fondation Nationale des Sciences Politiques.

Les Avis Legislatifs du Parlement Europeen et leur Impact: Procedures de Consultation, 1: Affaires Etrangeres / Securite (1994) Brussels, May.

Lijphart, A. (1977) *Democracy in plural societies: A comparative exploration*. New haven: Yale University Press.

Lindberg, Leon N. (1963) *The Political Dynamics of European Economic Integration*. Stanford: Stanford University Press; London: Oxford University Press.

Lindberg, Leon N. and Stuart A. Scheingold (1970) *Europe's Would-Be Polity: Patterns of Change in the European Community*. Englewood Cliffs, NJ: Prentice-Hall, Inc.

Lindblom, C.E. (1965) *The intelligence of democracy: Decision making through mutual adjustment*. New York: Free Press.

Lipset, S.M. (1960) *Political Man*. New York: Doubleday.

Lipset, S.M. and Stein Rokkan (eds.) (1967) *Party Systems and Voter Alignments: Cross-National Perspectives*. New York: The Free Press.

Lodge, J. (1982) 'The European Parliament after Direct Elections: Talking Shop or Putative Legislature?', *Journal of European Integration* 5, pp. 259–84.

Lodge, J. (1983) 'Decision-making in the European Community', in Juliet Lodge (ed.), *The European Community: Bibliographical Excursions*. London: Frances Pinter (Publishers).

Lodge, J. (1984) 'European Union and the First Elected European Parliament: the Spinelli Initiative', *Journal of Common Market Studies*, 22, pp. 377–402.

Lodge, J. (1986) 'The Single European Act: Towards a New Euro-Dynamism?' *Journal of Common Market Studies* 24, pp. 47–69.

Lodge, J. (1989) 'The European Parliament – from assembly to co-legislature: changing the Institutional Dynamics' in Lodge, Juliet. (ed.). *The EC and the Challenge of the Future*. London: Pinter.

Lodge, J. (1993a) 'The European Community in the Historical Context of its Parliament', 40 th Anniversary Proceedings of the European Parliament, Strasbourg.

Lodge, J. (1993) 'EC policymaking: institutional dynamics', in Juliet Lodge (ed.), *The European Community and the Challenge of the Future*. Second edition. New York: St. Martin's Press, pp. 1–36.

Lodge, J. (1994) 'Transparency and Democratic Legitimacy', JCMS, 32(1994), pp. 343–368.

Lodge, J. and Herman V. (1977) 'Citizenship, Direct Elections and the European Parliament', *Res Publica* 19, pp. 579–605.

Lodge, J. and Herman, V. (1979) 'Democratic Legitimacy and Direct Elections', *West European Politics*, 2, pp. 226–51.

Lodge, J. and Herman, V. (1982) *Direct Elections to the European Parliament: A Community Perspective*. London: Macmillan.

Lord Mackenzie-Stewart (1992) 'Subsidiarity' – A Busted Flush?' in Curtin D & D O'Keefe (eds.) (1992) *Constitutional Adjudication in European Community* and National Law. Ireland: Butterworth, pp. 19–24.

Louis, Jean-Victor (ed.) (1985). *L'Union Europeenne: Le Projet de traite du Parlement Europeen apres Fontainebleau*. Brussels: Universite Libre de Bruxelles.

Lübbe, Hermann (1994) *Abschied vonm Superstaat, Vereinigte Staaten von Europa wird es nicht geben*. Berlin.

Ludlow, Peter (1991) 'The European Commission', in Robert O. Keohane and Stanley Hoffmann (eds.), *The New European Community: Decisionmaking and Institutional Change*. Boulder: Westview Press.

Ludlow, Peter (1992a) 'Europe's Institutions: Europe's Politics', in Gregory F. Treverton (ed.), The Shape of the New Europe. New York: Council on Foreign Relations Press, pp. 59–91.

Mack, (1989) *Lobbying and Government Relations: A Guide for Executives*. New York: Quorum Books.

Mackie, T.T. (ed.) (1990) *Europe Votes 3. European Elections Results 1989*. Aldershot: Dartmouth.

Macridis, Roy C. (1967) 'Introduction: The History, Functions, and Typology of Parties', pp. 9–23 in Roy C. Macridis (ed.) *Political Parties. Contemporary Trends and Ideas*. New York: Harper and Row Publishers.

Maranini, G. (1958) *Miti e realtà della Democrazia*. Milano: Comunità.

Martin, D. (1991) *Europe: An Ever Closer Union*. Nottingham: Spokesman.

Mattina, L. (1991a) *Gli industriali e la democrazia. La Confindustria nella formazione dell'Italia Repubblicana*. Bologna: Il Mulino.

Mattina, L. (1991b) 'La Confindustira oltre la simbiosi', in Morlino (ed.), *Costruire la democrazia*. Bologna: Il Mulino.

Mazey, S. and Richardson, J. (ed.) (1993) *Lobbying in the European Community*. Oxford: Oxford University Press.

Mazey, S. and Richardson, J. (1994a) *Interest Groups and Representation in the European Union*. Paper for workshop: The Logic of Group Membership in the New Europe. Madrid: ECPR.

Mazey, S. and Richardson, J. (1994) 'The Commission and the lobby', in Geoffrey Edwards and David Spence (eds.), *The European Commission*. Harlow, Essex: Longman, pp. 169–201.

McKinney, D. (1994) *Animal Welfare Groups in the European Union: The Failure of the Philosophy of the Single Market and the Difficulties this presents in the Formation and Execution of a Coherent European Union-wide Campaigning Strategy*. Paper for workshop: The Logic of Group Membership in the New Europe. Madrid: ECPR.

McLaughlin, A. and Jordan, G. (1993) 'The Rationality of Lobbying in Europe: Why are Euro-Groups so Numerous and so Weak? Some Evidence from the Car Industry', in S. Mazey, and J. Richardson (ed.) *Lobbying in the European Community*. Oxford University Press.

Meehan, E. (1993) *Citizenship and the European Community*. London: Pinter.

Menet-Genty, J. (1992) 'Forces et faiblesses de l'Italie a l'echeance de 1993', in J. Menet-Genty (ed) *L'economie italienne. Les paradoxes d'une reussite*. Paris: La Documentation Francaise.

Menet-Genty, J. (ed) (1992) *L'economie italienne. Les paradoxes d'une reussite*. Paris: La Documentation Francaise.

Mény, Yves (1992) *La corruption de la république*. Paris.

Meynaud, J. and Sidjanski, D. (1967) *L'Europe des Affaires. Role et structure des groupes*. Paris: Payot.

Meynaud, J. and Sidjanski, D. (1970) *Les groupes de pression dans la Communauté Européenne*. Bruxelles: ULB.

Millar, D. (1994) 'Why a Weak Ombudsman would mean a weaker European Parliament', *European Briefing*, Nov: 35.

Mondello, F. (1992) 'I Partners sociali di Strasburgo', *Europaforum*, Anno V, N.3 aprile 1992.

Monfort, A.C. (1994) *Plastics: Shaping a Single Vision of Europe*. Paper for workshop: The Logic of Group Membership in the New Europe. Madrid: ECPR.

Monnet, J.(1976) *Memoires*. Paris: Fayard.

Monnet, J. (1978) *Memoirs*. Garden City, NY: Doubleday & Company, Inc.

Moravcsik, A. (1991), 'Negotiating the Single European Act: national Interests and Conventional Statecraft in the European Community', *International Organization* 45: 1, 651–688.

Moravcsik, A. (1993) 'Preferences and power in the European Community: A liberal intergovernmentalist approach', *Journal of Common Market Studies*, (31)4.

Morisi, M. (1991) 'Il Parlamento tra partiti e interessi', in Morlino (ed.), *Costruire la democrazia*. Bologna: Il Mulino.

Morlino, L. (1991a) 'Introduzione', in Morlino (ed.), *Costruire la democrazia*. Bologna: Il Mulino.

Morlino, L. (1991b) 'La Confagricoltura dall'attesa al compromesso', in Morlino (ed.), *Costruire la democrazia*. Bologna. Il Mulino.

Morlino, L. (1991c) 'Le relazioni tra partiti e gruppi. Conclusioni', in Morlino (ed.), *Costruire la democrazia*, Il Mulino, Bologna.

Morlino, L.(ed) (1991) 'Costruire la Democrazia. Gruppi e partiti', *in Italia*. Bologna: Il Mulino.

Mortati, C. (1972) 'Note introduttive ad uno studio sui partiti politici nell'ordinamento italiano', in C. Mortati, *Raccolta di Scritti*. Milano; Giuffrè.

Moulin, H. (1988) *Axioms of Cooerpative Decision Making*. New York: Cambridge University Press.

Nagant de Deuxchaisnes, D. (1994) 'Le renforcement du caractère démocratique de la Communauté Européenne', *La Belgique Fédérale*. Bruxelles: Centre d'Etudes Constitutionnelles et Administratives, Bruylant, pp.440–458.

Nedergaard, Peter (1993) 'EF og det demokratiske spørgsmål: Den danske case', *Politica* 25: 3, pp. 303–322.

Nedergaard, Peter (1994) *Organisering af Den europæiske Union – Bureaukrater og beslutningsprocesser*. Copenhagen: Handelshøjskolens Forlag.

Nicoll, William and Salmon, T.C. (1990) *Understanding the European Communities*. New York: Philip Allan.

Nitzan, S. and Paroush (1982) 'Optima decision rules in uncertain dichotomous choice situations', *International Economic Reveiw*, 23, pp. 289–297.

Noël, Emile (1975) 'The Commission's power of initiative', *Common Market Law Review* 12, 123–135.

Noël, Emile (1988) *Working Together – The Institutions of the European Community*. Luxembourg: Office for Official Publications of the European Communities.

Novelli S. (1994) 'Problemi di scelta di un sistema elettorale', paper delivered at *SISP* Congress, 26–28 September.

Nugent, Neill (1994) *The Government and Politics of the European Community*. Third edition. London: Macmillan.

Nuttall, Simon (1994) 'The Commission and foreign policy-making', in Geoffrey Edwards and David Spence (eds.), *The European Commission*. Harlow, Essex: Longman, pp. 287–302.

Obradovic, D. (1994) *Interest Representation and the Legitimacy of the EC Decision Making Process*. Paper for workshop: The Logic of Group Membership in the New Europe, Madrid: ECPR.

Offe, C. (1972) *Strukturprobleme des kapitalistischen Staates Aufsätze zur Politischen Soziologie*. Frankfurt aM: Suhrkampf.

Official Journal of the European Communities (1994), C241, Bruxelles, August 29.

Olsen, J.P. (1995) 'Europeanization and Nation-State Dynamics', Paper prepared for the Sympoosium on the Future of the Nation-State. Uppsala University, Uppsala, Sweden, March 22–25, 1995.

Paolo, R. (1990) 'The implementation of Community Law in Italy', *College d'Europe (unpublished Working paper)*, Brugge.

Parlament Europeen (1989) Elezioni 1989. Biografie, Direzione generale dell'informazione e delle relazioni pubbliche, Lussemburgo.

Parlament Europeen (1990a) Les organes specialise' dans les Affaires communautaires au sein des Parliaments nationaux, Luxembourg.

Parlament Europeen (1990b) Les deputes du Parlement Europeen 1989/1994, Luxembourg.

Pasquino, G. (1979) 'Gruppi di pressione', in P. Farneti, *Politica e Societa'*. Firenze: Le Monnier.

Pasquino, G. (1988) *Istituzioni, Partiti, Lobbies*. Bari: Saggi Tascabili Laterza.

Pasquino, G. (1988) *Rappresentanza e democrazia*. Bologna: Il Mulino.

Patijn, S. (ed.) (1970), *Landmarks in European Unity*. Leyden: A.W. Sijthoff.

Pedersen, Mogens N. (1987) 'The Danish 'Working Multiparty System', in Hans Daalder (ed.) *Party Systems in Denmark, Austria, Switzerland, Netherlands, and Belgium*. London: Frances Pinter Publishers, pp. 1–60.

Pedersen, Mogens N. (1989)[1994] 'En kortfattet oversigt over det danske partisystems udvikling', *Politica*, vol. 23, pp. 265–278. German translation ('Eine kurzgefasste Übersicht über die Entwicklung des dänischen Parteiensystems') in Pappi, Franz Urban and Herman Schmitt (eds.) *Parteien, Parlamente und Wahlen in Skandinavien*, Frankfurt/New York: Campus Verlag, pp. 91–108.

Percheron, Annick (1973) 'Political Vocabulary and Ideological Proximity in French Children', in J. Dennis (ed.) *Socialization to Politics: A Reader*. New York: John Wiley and Sons, Inc., pp. 211–30.

Perrow, C. (1986) *Complex Organizations: A Critical Essay*. (3 rd edition). New York: Random House.

Peters, B. Guy (1992) 'Bureaucratic Politics and the Institutions of the European Community', in Alberta M. Sbragia (ed.), Euro-Politics: Institutions and Policymaking in the 'New' European Community. Washington, D.C.: The Brookings Institution, pp. 75–122.

Pijnenburg, B. (1993) 'Belgium: Federalized EC Lobbying at Home', in Van Schendelen, MPCM, (eds.) *National Public and Private EC Lobbying*. England: Dartmouth Publishing Company, pp.159–186.

Pistone, S. (ed) (1982) *L'Italia e l'Unita' Europea*. Torino: Loescher.

Pitkin, H.F. (1967) *The concept of representation*. Berkley: University of California.

Pizzorno, A. (1971) 'Il sistema politico italiano', *Politica del Diritto* 1972/2, pp. 197–209.

Pizzorno, A. (1980) *I soggetti del pluralismo*. Bologna: Il Mulino.

Pocar, F. (1991) *Diritto delle Comunita' Europee*, Milano: Giuffre'.

PRAGMA (1987) Italia: Trent'anni d'Europa Comunitaria, Anno XXIII, N.93, Roma.

PRAGMA (1989) Europa 1992. Il Mercato Unico. Informazioni per gli operatori, Presidenza del Consiglio dei Ministri – Dipartimento per l'Informazione e l'Editoria, Roma, 1989.

PRAGMA (1992) L'Europa degli Italiani. Risultati della ricerca e contributi interpretativi, Pragma, Roma, Presidenza del Consiglio dei Ministri.

Puchala, Donald J. (1972) 'Of Blind Men, Elephants and International Integration', *Journal of Common Market Studies*, Vol. 1, pp. 267–284.

Quartermaine, L. and Pollard, J. (1987) *Italy today. Patterns of life and politics*. Exeter: University of Exeter.

Quermonne, Jean-Louis (1991) *L'appareil administratif de l'Etat*. Paris: Points/ Seuil.

Reif, Karlheinz and Schmitt, Hermann (1980) 'Nine Second Order National Elections: A Conceptual Framework for the Analysis of European Election Results', *European Journal of Political Research*, vol. 8, pp. 3–44.

Rémond, Rene (1968) *La Droite en France – de la Premiere Restauration à la V*, Republique. Paris: Aubier.

Report of the High Level Group (1994) , Europe and the global information society, *I&T Magazine*, DGXIII, Autumn, pp. 3–5.

Rhodes, R.A.W. (1991) 'Policy Networks and Sub-central Government', in G. Thompson, J. Frances, R. Levacic, J. Mitchell (eds), *Markets, Hierarchies and Networks: The Coordination of Social Life*. Sage: London.

Richardson, S. (1982) *Policy Styles in Western Europe*. London: Georg Allen & Unwin.

Riker, W.H. (1962) *The Theory of Political Coalitions*. New Haven: Yale University Press.

Riker, W.H. (1964) *Federalism: Origin, Operation, Significance*. Boston: Little Brown.

Riker, W.H. and Ordeshook, P.C. (1973) *An Introduction to Positive Political Theory*. New Jersey: Prentice-Hall.

Rokkan, Stein (1966) 'Norway: Numerical Democracy and Corporate Pluralism', in R.A. Dahl (ed.) *Political Oppositions in Western Democracies*. New Haven: Yale University Press.

Rokkan, Stein (1970) *Citizens, Elections, Parties*. Oslo: Universitetsforlaget.

Rometsch, Dietrich and Wessels, Wolfgang (1994) 'The Commission and the Council of Ministers', in Geoffrey Edwards and David Spence (eds.), *The European Commission*. Harlow, Essex: Longman, pp. 202–224.

Rueschemeyer, D., Stephens, E.H. and Stephens, J.D. (1992) *Capitalist Development and Democracy*. Cambridge: Polity Press.

Sabine, George (1973) *A History of Political Theory*. 4th ed., rev. by Thomas Landon Thorson, Hindsdale, Ill.

Santoro, C.M. (1959) *La politica estera di una media potenza. L'Italia dall'Unita' ad oggi*. Bologna: Il Mulino.

Sapienza, R. (1991) *Il Mezzogiorno e la Comunità Europea*. Firenze: C.T.D.P.

Sargent, J. (1987) 'The Organization of Business Interests for European Community Representation', in Grant and Sargent (1987) *Business and Politics in Britain*. London: Macmillian Educational.

Sartori, G. (1987) *The theory of democracy revisited*. Chatham, N.J.:Chatham House.

Sassen, W.E. (1992) 'Getting through to Brussels (Business Lobbying at the European Commission)', *International Management* 47(2), p. 62.

Sbert, J.M. (1992) 'Progress', in W. Sachs(ed.), *The Development Dictionary: A Guide to Knowledge and Power*. London: Zev Books.

Sbragia, A.M. (1992) 'Thinking About the European Future: The Uses of Comparison', in A.M Sbragia (ed.) *Europolitics: Institutions and Policy making in the 'New' European Community*, pp. 257–292. Washington DC: Brookings.

Scandinavian Political Studies (1979) Special Issue, no. 3.

Schmitter, P.C. and Streeck, W. (1990) 'Organized Interests and the Europe of 1992', in N.J. Ornstein & M. Perlman (eds.) *Political Power and Social Change. The United States Faces a United Europe*. Washington: American Enterprise Institute.

Schmitter, P.C. (1974) 'Still the Century of Corporatism?', in F.B. Pike and T. Stricht (eds.): *The New Corporatism: Social-Political Structures in the Iberian World*. Notre Dame: University of Notre Dame Press, pp. 85–131.

Schmitter, P.C. (1977) 'Modes of Interest Intermediation and Modes of Societal Change in Western Europe', *Comparative Political Studies*, 10, pp. 7–38.

Schmitter, P.C. (1982) 'Reflections On Where the Theory of Neo-Corporatism is Going and Where the Praxis of Neo-Corporatism is Going', in G. Lembruch and P.C. Schmitter (eds.): *Patterns of Corporatist Policy-Making*. London: Sage.

Schmitter, P.C. (1990) 'Sectors in Modern Capitalism: Modes of Governance and Variations in Performance', in R. Brunetta and C. Dell'Aringa (eds) (1990) *Labour Relations and Economic Performance*. London: Macmillian.

Schmitter, P.C. (1995a) 'If the Nation-State were to wither away in Europe, What might replace it?' Paper prepared at the Colloguium on 'The Future of the Nation-State,' Uppsala University, Uppsala, Sweden, March 22–25, 1995.

Schmitter, P.C. (1995b) 'Democracy in the emerging Euro-polity: Temporary or Permanent Deficit?' ms. Stanford, Calif.: Center for European Studies, Stanford University.

Schmitter, P.C. and G. Lehmbruch (eds) (1979) *Trends Towards Corporatist Intermediation*. Beverly Hills and London: Sage.

Schneider, Heinrich and Wessels, Wolfgang (1994) 'Föderales Europa im Widerstreit – Einführung und Übersicht', in: Ibid. (eds.), *Föderale Union – Europas Zukunft* ? München, pp. 7–20.

Schofield, N. (1984) 'Political Fragmentation and the Stabiity of Coalition Governments in Western Europe'. In M.J. Holler (ed.) *Coalitions and Collective*. Wrzburg, Wien: Action Physica-Verlag, pp. 297–319.

Scholten, I. (1987) *Political Stability and Neo-Corporatism: Corporatist Integration and Societal Cleavages in Western Europe*. London: Sage.

Schumpeter, J.A. (1942) *Capitalism, socialism, and democracy*. New York: Harper & Brothera Publishers.

Scoppola, P. (1991) *La repubblica dei partiti*. Bologna: Il Mulino.

Scoppola, P. (1992) 'LEuropa degli Italiani. Risultati della ricerca e contributi interpretativi', in *PRAGMA*. Roma: Pragma.

Seligman, A.B. (1992) *The Idea of Civil Society*. New York: The Free Press.

Senato della Repubblica – Giunta per gli affari delle Comunita' Europee (1991), Indagine conoscitiva sulla partecipazione dell'Italia alle fasi formativa ed applicativa del Diritto Comunitario, Roma.

Shapley, L.S. and Schubik, M. (1954) 'A method for Evaluating the Distribution of Power in a Commitee System', *American Political Science Review*, 48, pp. 787–792.

Shively, W. Phillips (1993) *Power and Choice – An Introduction to Political Science*. New York: McGraw-Hill, Inc. 3rd edition.

Sidenius, N.C. (1994) *The Logic of Business Political Organization in Western Europe*. Paper for workshop: The Logic of Group Membership in the New Europe. Madrid: ECPR.

Sidjanski, D. (1989) 'Communautée Européenne 1992: Gouvernement de Comités?', *Pouvoirs* 48, pp. 71–80.

Sidjanski, D. and Ayberk, U. (1974) Bilan des groupes et du processus des decisions de la Communaute des Six, *Res Publica* XVI:33 e segg.

Sidjanski, D. and Ayberk, U. (eds) (1990) *LEurope du Sud dans la CE*. Paris: P.U.F.

Sjöblom, Gunnar (1968) *Party Strategies in a Multiparty System*. Lund: Studentlitteratur.

Sloot, T. and Verschuren, P. (1990) 'Decision-making Speed in the European Community', *Journal of Common Market Studies* Vol. XXIX, No. 1, pp. 75–85.

Smith, Michael (1994) 'The Commission and external relations', in Geoffrey Edwards and David Spence (eds.), *The European Commission*. Harlow, Essex: Longman, pp. 249–286.

Spierenburg, Dirk (1979) 'Proposal for Reform of the Commission of the European Communities and its Services. Report made at the request of the Commission by an Independent Review Body under the chairmanship of Mr Dirk Spierenburg', Brussels, 24 September.

Spinelli, A. (1958) *Manifest der Europäischen Föderalisten*. Frankfurt a.M.

Spinelli, A. (1966) *The Eurocrats: Conflict and Crisis in the European Community*. Baltimore: Johns Hopkins University Press.

Spinelli, A. (1983a) 'Verso LUnione Europea', *Il Federalista* 25, pp. 115–30.

Spinelli, A. (1983) 'Die Parlamentarische Initiative zur Europaischen Union', *Europa Archiv* 38, pp. 739–46.

Spinelli, A. (1991), *Diario Europeo / II*. Bologna: Il Mulino.

Spinelli, A. (1992) *Diario Europeo / III*. Bologna: Il Mulino.

Stein, Eric, Hay, Peter and Waelbroeck, Michel (eds) (1976) *European Community Law and Institutions in Perspective. Text, Cases and Readings*. Charlottesville: The Michie Company.

Stern, J.P (1992) *European Lobbying – How to Keep Abreast and Wield Influence in the EC*. Club de Bruxelles.

Streeck, Wolfgang and Schmitter, Philippe C. (1991) 'From national corporatism to transnational pluralism: organized interests in the Single European Market,' *Politics and Society*, vol. 19/2, pp. 133–164.

Struys, M. (1994) 'La mise en oeuvre des obligations découlant du droit Européen', *La Belgique Fédérale*, Bruxelles: Centre d'Etudes Constitutionnelles et Administratives, Bruylant, pp.483–495.

Suleiman, Ezra (1976) *Les hauts fonctionnaires et la politique*. Paris: Le Seuil, pp. 202–213.

Sørensen, Carsten Lehmann (1984) *Europas Babelstårn. En analyse af Europaparlamentsmedlemmernes baggrund, erfaringer og politiske synspunkter*. Aarhus: Politica.

Taagepera, R. and Shugart, M.S. (1989) *Seats and Votes: The Effects and Determinants of Electoral Systems*. New Haven and London: Yale University Press.

The European, 14th–17th October 1993.

Thewes, M. (1994) 'La collaboration entre l'Etat, les Communautés et les Régions en matière Européenne', *La Belgique Fédérale*, Bruxelles: Centre d'Etudes Constitutionnelles et Administratives, Bruylant, pp.458–471.

Thomas, G.M., Meyer, J.W., Ramirez, F. and Boli, J. (eds) (1987) *Institutional Structure: Constituting State, Society and The Individual*. Beverly Hills, Calif.: Sage.

Tilly, C. (ed.) (1975) *The Formation of National States in Western Europe*. Princeton.

Tilly, C. (1978) *From Mobilization to Revolution*. Reading, Mass.: Addison-Wesley.

Tindemans, Leo (1976) 'European Union: Report by Mr Leo Tindemans, Prime Minister of Belgium, to the European Council', *Bulletin og the European Communities*, Supplement 1.

Toonen, T.A.J. (1990) 'The Unitary State as a System of Co-Governance: The Case of the Netherlands', *Public Administration*. 68, pp. 281–296.

Traite' de Maastricht: mode d'employ (1992) Paris: UGE.

Tucker, E. (1994) 'Flemings, Wallons, Germans, Pluralist Belgium has loosened its unitary ties in favour of federalism', *Financial Times*, June 2, 1994.

Tulkens, F. (1994) 'La réforme de l'Etat: II. Les Entitées Fédérées: Nouveaux Socles de l'Etat Fédéral', *Journal des Tribunaux*. Bruxelles: Maison Larcier, 21 Mai 1994, 113–nr.5718, pp. 409–413.

Turner, B. (1991) *Religion and Social Theory*. 2nd ed. London: Sage Publications.

Usher, John A. (1994) 'The Commission and the law', in Geoffrey Edwards and David Spence (eds.), *The European Commission*. Harlow, Essex: Longman, pp. 146–168.

Vahl, Remco (1992) 'The European Commission on the road to European Union: The consequences of the Treaty on European Union for the Commission's power base', *Acta politica* 27: 3, 297–321.

Van Panhuys, H.F.; L.J. Brinkhorst and H.H. Maas (eds.) (1968) *A Collection of the Texts of Documents relating to the United Nations, its Related Agencies and Regional International Organisations*. Leyden: A.W. Sijthoff.

Van Schendelen, M.C.P.M. (ed.) (1993). *National Public and Private EC Lobbying*. Aldershot: Dartmouth.

Venturino F. (1994) 'Le conseguenze del nuovo sistema elettorale comunale', paper delivered at *SISP* Congress, 26–28 September.

Verhoeven, J. (1993) *Les citoyens de l'Europe*. Ann.Dr.Lv..

Wallace, Helen (1990) 'Making Multilateral Negotiations Work', in William Wallace (ed.*)*, *The Dynamics of European Integration*. London, pp. 213–228.

Werts, J. (1992) *The European Council*. Amsterdam: Elsevier Science Publishers.

Wessels, Wolfgang (1992) 'Staat und (westeuropäische) Integration, Die Fusionsthese', in Michael Kreile (ed.), *Die Integration Europas*. Opladen: PVS-Sonderheft 21, pp. 36–61.

Wessels, Wolfgang (1994) 'Rationalizing Maastricht: the search for an optimal strategy of the new Europe', *International Affairs*, Nr.3, pp. 445–457.

Wester, Robert (1992), 'The European Commission and European Political Union', in Finn Laursen and Sophie Vanhoonacker (eds.), *The Intergovernmental Conference on Political Union*. Maastricht: European Institute of Public Administration, 205–214.

Westlake, Martin (1994) *A Modern Guide to the European Parliament*. London: Pinter Publishers.

Westlake, Martin (1994), 'The Commission and the Parliament', in Geoffrey Edwards and David Spence (eds.), *The European Commission*. Harlow, Essex: Longman, 225–248.

Wiesendahl, E. (1980) *Parteien und Demokratie. Eine soziologische Analyse paradigmatischer Ansätze der Parteienforschung*. Opladen: Leske.

Williamson, P.J. (1989) *Corporatism in Perspective: An Introductory Guide to Corporatist Theory*. London: Sage.

Wistrich, Ernest (1994) *The United States of Europe*. London/New York.

Worre, Torben (1987) 'The Danish Euro-party system', *Scandinavian Political Studies*, vol. 10, pp. 79–95.

Wright, M. (1988) 'Policy Community, Policy Network, and Comparative Industrial Policies', *Political Studies* 36, pp. 593–612.

Index

**UNIVERSITY OF WOLVERHAMPTON
LEARNING RESOURCES**